YOU'RE GOING HOME
IN A F*CKING
AMBULANCE

Cass Pennant is a writer, historian and film producer based in London, and one of the country's leading commentators on football hooliganism. He has written nine football fan-related books, five of which have been UK Top 10 bestsellers, making him one of Britain's leading commentators on the subject. He wrote or co-authored *Cass, Congratulations, You Have Just Met The I.C.F, Want Some AGGRO?, Rolling With the 6.57 Crew, Good Afternoon Gentlemen, The Name is Bill Gardner, Terrace Legends* (later re-released as *Legends of the Firm), Top Boys, 30 Years of Hurt* and *One-Eyed Baz*. His bestselling autobiography, *Cass*, was adapted into the British cult film of the same name, released in 2008 and directed by Jon S. Baird.

YOU'RE GOING HOME IN A F*CKING AMBULANCE

HOOLIGAN WARS – THE INSIDE STORY

CASS PENNANT

First published in the UK by John Blake Publishing
an imprint of Bonnier Books UK
4th Floor, Victoria House
Bloomsbury Square
London WC1B 4DA
England

Owned by Bonnier Books
Sveavägen 56, Stockholm, Sweden

www.facebook.com/johnblakebooks
twitter.com/jblakebooks

First published in hardback and paperback in 2022

Paperback ISBN: 978-1-78946-190-9
Ebook ISBN: 978-1-78946-191-6
Audiobook ISBN: 978-1-78946-283-8

British Library Cataloguing-in-Publication Data:
A CIP catalogue record for this book is available from the British Library.

Design by www.envydesign.co.uk

Printed and bound in Great Britain by Clays Ltd, Elcograf S.p.A

1 3 5 7 9 10 8 6 4 2

John Blake Publishing is an imprint of Bonnier Books UK
www.bonnierbooks.co.uk

After all the time and reflection taken in putting this book together to where we are today, I find myself thinking about the lads I've met and still know, and then the lads I've met and continue to meet, forging our former rivalry into a bond of friendship and respect. Even more so, perhaps, I think of those lads who are no longer with us but who are as much part of us. It is what is, we are who we are and were, those were the times, and each will have their own thoughts and memories, along with any lessons of life they have learned. So with that all-knowing wink, I will simply dedicate this book to 'the boys'.

CONTENTS

ACKNOWLEDGEMENTS

The author wishes to state that some of the views expressed or contributed are not his own and therefore any content provided by contributors is their opinion, and not intended to malign any religious or ethnic group, club, organisation, company, individual or any other person or organisation.

My background as a published author was a new career chapter in my life from the moment my own life story was first published by John Blake in 2000. Before that, my world was one of crazy days, mad times.

Thanks to everyone on the publishing team, especially Toby Buchan for his faith and patience and special mention to both John Blake and Mary Tobin, who have been there since the beginning. Special thanks to those lads who have been a part of my getting there, with their contributions and interviews and sources of information gathered from all over the UK to create the whole picture. Some names and identifying details have been changed at their request or to protect identities.

Books quoted

A Casual Look: A Photodiary of Football Fans, 1980s to 2001 –
Lorne Brown and Nick Harvey, Football Culture UK, 2006

Congratulations You Have Just Met the ICF – Cass Pennant,
John Blake Publishing, 2002

Inside the Forest Executive Crew – Gary Boatsy Clarke and
Martin King, Headhunter. 2005

Khan – Memoirs of an Asian Casual – Riaz Khan, Old Dog
Books, 2015

*NME: From the Bender Squad to the Gremlins: Inside Newcastle's
Football Hooligan Firm* – Mark Mennim, Steve Wraith and
Stuart Wheatman, Futures Publications, 2013

*One-Eyed Baz: The Story of Barrington 'Zulu' Patterson, One
of Britain's Deadliest Men* – Barrington Patterson with Cass
Pennant, John Blake Publishing, 2013

*Rolling with the 6.57 Crew: The True Story of Pompey's Legendary
Football Fans* – Rob Silvester and Cass Pennant, John Blake
Publishing, 2004

*Steel City Rivals: One City, Two Football Clubs, One Mutually
Shared Hatred* – Steve Cowans and Anthony Cronshaw, John
Blake Publishing, 2012

Top Boys: True Stories of Football's Hardest Men – Cass Pennant,
John Blake Publishing, 2005

Villains: The Inside Story of Aston Villa's Hooligan Gangs –
Danny Brown and Paul Brittle, Milo Books, 2006

Want Some Aggro?: The True Story of West Ham's First Guv'nors –
Mickey Smith and Cass Pennant, John Blake Publishing, 2002

Interviews
Old skin Pat/Pompey, Portsmouth

Mickey Smith (RIP)/West Ham United

Colin Blaney (RIP)/Manchester United

Sammy/Tottenham Hotspur

Bob/Millwall

Bill Gardner G (Gardner)/West Ham United

Nick Sarjeant/Brighton

Peter Hooton/Liverpool

Tony Graham/Manchester United

Phil Thornton/Liverpool

Jela/West Ham United

Riaz Khan/Leicester City

Eddie Crispen/Portsmouth

Rob Silvester/Portsmouth

Paul Chandler/Portsmouth

Jake Payne/Portsmouth

Gooner/Arsenal

DD/West Ham United

Martin Sturgess/West Ham United

Wes/Brighton

Mark Mennim/Newcastle United

Stu Wheatman/Newcastle United

Steve Wraith/Newcastle United

Craig/Middlesbrough

Steve Cowens/Sheffield United

Sean Riley/Leeds United

Hotshot/Manchester United

Scouse/Liverpool

Barrington Patterson aka One-Eyed Baz (RIP)/
     Birmingham City

Danny Brown aka Black Danny/Aston Villa

Gilly Shaw/Wolves

Paul Thompson aka Thommo/Derby County

Gary Clarke aka Boatsy/Nottingham Forest

Darren Smith aka Coalville Daz/Leicester City

Les Muranyi aka The General/Cambridge United

Jon Palmer/Mansfield Town

Dennis Edwards/Luton Town

Mr Y/York City

Ian Bailey/Hartlepool

Finally, the author also gratefully acknowledges a small number of interviewees who asked to remain anonymous – they know who they are.

PREFACE: THE WAY FOOTBALL HAS CHANGED

'YOU SUDDENLY REALISE YOU ARE NOT WATCHING THE FOOTBALL VERY MUCH'

Just as the Edwardian yobs in the towns of industrial Britain chose to represent their neighbourhoods by fighting rival gangs from other streets *Peaky Blinders* style, the growth of football during the twentieth century provided these young men with the ideal setting for their pursuits. Football clubs represented towns and cities, and young men could identify with, and attach themselves to these clubs with a liking for standing behind the goal of the home end and with it came the birth of bovver and aggro frequented on the streets and dance halls. It had found a new outlet into the arena of the national game. Pride and fighting prowess were at stake, and crowd trouble has intermittently flourished down the decades since.

To fill you in on those real early years is old skin Pat, who in 1967 moved up to London from Hayling Island to seek work, but still followed his Pompey around the country, bringing his new-found London experiences with him.

OLD SKIN PAT/POMPEY (PORTSMOUTH): 1966, the year England were to win the World Cup, I went to my first game, Manchester City at home. I was a school kid, a typical 14-, 15-year-old. Some of the lads had got me to go. I wasn't particularly interested in Pompey in any way but I was keen on football, keen on playing it and thought Manchester City was a big name. So, I went along to the game and I can remember walking into Fratton Park. I actually remember the moment I walked in there. You know what it's like the first time ... you see the crowd, you see the Fratton End. A lot of the lads I'd been going with, they'd been going to football every Saturday.

We walked in the Fratton End and there's all these Manchester City fans, right, they're all little blokes with leather jackets and scruffy, greasy hair. But we'd been inundated with info that the hard people were Manchester United, Liverpool – because up until that point the only football violence was them smashing trains up. This is when it was first coming in. And I thought, God, they are going to be dead hard, their fans. So anyway, I get to the ground, and I had no thought of seeing violence or fighting at football, but of course, everybody starts chanting and I could feel, you know, you're getting carried away with it. I suddenly cottoned on that Pompey was going to be as hard as, or even do, Manchester. And then the next thing is I turn up and I see one bloke with wild ginger hair, glasses that thick and, to look at him, you wouldn't think for one second he was going to be hard, you never connected people with glasses as hard. And then I saw Ginger in on them and the next feeling I know is this mad feeling of excitement – Manchester City are running. I'm suddenly clocking that – and everybody says this – you suddenly realise you are not watching the football very much. And then in the second half the trouble died, Manchester City had moved, they tried us, no joy, so they moved. This is very small … it's not like the pitch battles you see later on. Basically, Pompey then had a group of fans, people like Dinksy, Dave Dwaine and that, who I could see were older than me. It's obvious, they've got the nice clothes, obviously got girls and when you're young, you think, I'll never do all this, you know how it is, and so you have that sort of lot. Every football crew had older blokes, might have a suit on, looked a bit like Jimmy Tarbuck, a right mixture. We'd even have Teddy Boys, it was like that, but you were Pompey.

After that I started to go to a few of the home games. The next one was Southampton, this was the same year. That was good because I'm standing outside the ground and about 200 or 300 Southampton fans come up. I still didn't know the score and I see this lot and think, blimey, and then they're all giving it gob, but it's still very low key, not how you would have felt in the seventies … frightening. Then they go in the Fratton End and within ten minutes Pompey had them off and they were burning their scarves on the terrace and I said, 'This is wonderful.' I'm fifteen, I'm terrified. Don't get me wrong, I'd been the first to move. You're just little kids and you're on the periphery of it, you're not right in the centre, and then you start recognising faces. I started to recognise an older kid and I used to watch and see how stylish he was … and that was Dinksy.

The big style and the big thing at the time was that you had a scarf, always tied in a knot, and you had the metal badges. We all had those – well, Dinksy had loads, he also had a Levi's white denim jacket that he'd wear, he'd have Levi's on and the most important thing was he tended to cut the bottoms off and have the white rim about half an inch done like that, that was very, very important. We were called Moddy Boys, but this was sort of very low key. You still had all mixtures. You had the guy of twenty-five with a suit, you had all sorts of mixtures. Generally, the music we liked was in the Top 10 and we'd have a chart record as a football song in ten minutes. So, this is all very low-key stuff.

Season 1967/68, we went to see Chelsea play West Ham and I think you ought to hear about this one, because this was an amazing sight. We get outside the ground and we're kids, and we're like, 'Who you going to follow? Chelsea? West Ham?' Next moment, we hear this noise coming like a train and this fucking mob of West Ham coming up, the whole of West Ham came in one go, hundreds of them. There are skinheads, there's men who look like the Kray brothers, there's men who look absolutely evil with scars up and down them and they are IT. They've all got a little badge on: 'North Bank, West Ham'. They came in and I've never seen a mob like it. I remember thinking, How the hell are Chelsea going to do anything about this?

So anyway, gates open, West Ham pile in, the push

surges from top to bottom, you're going flying, it's unbelievable: slowly but surely Chelsea are coming in chanting 'Chelsea, Chelsea'. They're getting more and more together. I look to Chelsea and give them their due, they give as good as they get. The end was shared, the result was shared, although outside it was basically a West Ham rout. I could see these London mobs are scared of nothing. So, you know, they both have huge mobs, West Ham, Chelsea, Spurs are getting established. Of course, Millwall always had the name, the reputation.

The first time Millwall came to Fratton Park in '66, they'd just come up through the divisions. Now Millwall were getting the reputation on the news. In one particular incident, they'd not lost at home for about two years, and they lost to Plymouth Argyle. It was an absolute riot and Millwall were getting a name. So, we had them at Fratton Park for the first time. They all came in one group and it was led by men of about forty years of age. They were massive. They came in the Fratton End. They were massive and for about ten or fifteen minutes there's a gap between the two sets of supporters, and then the fight's going to start. A bloke started sizing up to Ginger. There's Ginger and one other bloke who has a go. Ginger came out of that with his shirt off and his vest hanging by one thread. I can remember he turned to us and said, 'I'm not having any more of that.' Ginger had more guts than the rest of us put together, he'd have a go, and, of course, you're thinking, Well, if he can't do it ... So Millwall routed the end and absolutely took it. We were all gobsmacked – this was taking it to another level.

We're all mainly youngsters, of the same age. But this Millwall thing, I can remember an incident where I saw fourteen-year-old kids laying into a bloke of about twenty, no fear whatsoever. They were coming up to you, they were looking for it. It was murder. It was a complete and utter rout, no two ways about it. There's no use pretending otherwise, they routed us. That was the first time we had Millwall up there. But over the years there were to be plenty more Millwall stories.

DOWN SOUTH, UP NORTH

'THE FOOTBALL THING NOW HAS REALLY TAKEN OFF IN A BIG WAY'

MICKEY SMITH, WEST HAM UNITED: 1967 was a special year for me, one that changed my life forever. I had been with the old man and his brothers to the football many times – I went with them and saw West Ham do the treble in '64, '65, and '66: FA Cup, European Cup Winners' Cup and the World Cup. West Ham was my life, but from the day I went to Upton Park on my own, things took a very different turn. That day Manchester United came to West Ham and if they won, they would have a title.

The famous Busby Babes were in town. A lot of fans of all age groups had some respect for them, for the way they had rebuilt after the Munich '58 air crash, and just ten years later they were going to win the title with great players like Charlton, Best, Stiles and Stepney. West Ham had the famous trio of World Cup winners –

Hurst, Moore and Peters – and it promised to be a big day, one that I never forgot.

As usual, I left from Mile End Tube station about 11am for the short journey to Upton Park, but things were different. Everywhere you looked Manchester United fans were to be seen – mobs of about a dozen or so singing, carrying on. All the way on the Tube to Upton Park, there were Manchester United fans and not many West Ham around. I was alone that day and lost my scarf to a Man U fan who needed a trophy on that trip. I wasn't the only one – many kids had theirs pinched by that mob. Real big men taking a thirteen-year-old's scarf – there were so many of them I could do nothing, and it would have been silly to as I was so young. I was a skinhead and Jack the lad, but nothing prepared me for this mob. They took the piss out of me and the way I was dressed (all the fashion at the time in London). From that moment on I hated Manchester United.

My hate was soon to turn to hatred with vengeance. Arriving at Upton Park, there were many more Man U fans along with George Best rosettes and pictures. It was like a mini-Wembley with all the colour around. Further towards the ground, there was a massive police presence. There were fights all over, mainly isolated ones.

Normally, I went on the old Chicken Run with my old man and his brothers, but today I was told to go on the North Bank, as I would be safe there and amongst my own. The queues into the ground were nearly back to the gates. I met up with some mates, who were also on their own. When we got into the ground the North Bank was full of Manchester United fans singing and the bars were full. We made our way up to the back of the North Bank, climbed up the back wall and hung on to the iron girders. As a youngster it was the best view of the game and we were too young to go behind the goals. Then I saw something that has stuck with me till this day. About five or six hundred West Ham fans came in a run, charging the Man U fans. It was on. West Ham were trying to claim the North Bank back. There were men fighting all around – five hundred-plus of them kicking, punching, shouting. I had never seen anything like it. The Man U fans held their own and I watched as they lashed out with red-and-white walking sticks and banners, only to be meet with a hail of bottles from the West Ham fans. The police, who were trying to establish a dividing line between the fans, were powerless.

The fighting went on for ages. A hail of pennies being thrown by the Manchester United fans at West Ham was like something out of an old war film with English archers all letting go of their arrows at once. Pennies and bottles were thrown back and in front of me I saw one Man U fan with a dart in his shoulder. His mates took it out and threw it back at the West Ham fans. The screaming and singing were something to see. The Man U fans beat back the West Ham fans, mainly because of the sheer weight of numbers they had. More and more bottles came over towards the Man U fans, who were now shoved down behind the goal. I saw one West Ham fan, with a Man U coloured walking stick, hitting into the fans. This walking stick looked to have barbed wire wrapped around it.

West Ham fans were at the side and back and the police were slowly forming a line. Hammers fans were lighting newspapers and chucking them down on the Man United fans; it made an eerie sight to see paper on fire floating down onto them. More and more bottles and pennies were being hurled; the crowd surging back and forth, but as the time for the game got closer, more and more Man United fans came in. There were thousands of them – I have never seen so many at West Ham. More West Ham fans came in, about three hundred from the Chicken Run side, and ran at Man U's fans, but were beaten back by sheer numbers. Some Man U fans our age tried to climb up in the girders with us but we kicked the shit out of them as they climbed up. The whole of the North Bank was full now and some West Ham fans were still jumping in from the Chicken Run to help, only to be turned back by the Old Bill.

The South Bank (which was for away fans) was covered in Man U fans. The North Bank was gone as well. They covered the whole centre of it down to the goals and two-thirds up to where the police were, and then there were West Ham behind. Groups of West Ham were attacking the sides of the main mob, but police moved in quickly and as soon as one fight was stopped, another load of West Ham fans would attack somewhere else. More bottles were thrown, more lighted paper was sent down – I saw fans in pain with blood streaming out of heads, swearing at the Cockney c**ts.

The Man U mob's plan was simple – get in early, in numbers and hold on and take West Ham by surprise. They succeeded.

I don't remember much of the game, except women and girls screaming for George Best, and we got thrashed 6–1. One incident I remember came soon after our full-back John Charles (the first black player I ever saw) smashed in a long-range shot through a ruck of players to score our goal. He was then involved in the most dubious of penalty decisions, which went United's way after it was alleged he pushed Denis Law in the box. The legend Law took and scored it himself for United's fifth. During it all, as the West Ham defence protested, the Man U fans chucked bananas on the pitch at Charles, and this kicked off more fighting, more pennies and more bottles. Man U were chucking back broken glass and anything else they could at West Ham. As much as they threw, twice as much went back. Man U had taken the North Bank, but not without a fight. I saw Man U fans crying, walking about in disbelief. The kids who had a go at us came back with some older lads and tried to get up to us but we kept kicking and spitting on them and some older West Ham lads joined in. We had a result, our first real off with fans, and we were kings of the world. The blood and excitement were rushing to our heads; we wanted more.

I had seen quite a few punch-ups at West Ham, mainly in the Chicken Run with the older fans, mostly with other London supporters, but nothing like this. I didn't know why my old man and his brothers missed this one, but I found out why later.

The game over, Man U were champions and their fans stayed behind to celebrate. The North Bank half emptied. As we got out as well, we went on to Green Street, where a huge West Ham mob was waiting, thousands of them, for Man U to come out. Lots of fans headed off towards the Barking Road to find the lot from the South Bank and the coaches. We stayed with the main mob. The police were lost as who to follow, and tried to set up a line between us and Man U by the club gates. Still no Man U fans. They were still inside. I saw West Ham fans with half bricks, stones, bottles, sticks, you name it. If it could be chucked, they had it.

Some half an hour later and the Man U fans were still inside. A lot of us moved off towards the Tube because we knew they would have to change at Mile End, and there we would wait. As we got halfway up Green Street to the Tube, near Queen's Market, they came out of the ground and it was on. West Ham turned and charged as Man U ran towards them. The police were powerless, with only a few on horseback keeping up, and Black Marias were everywhere, trying to separate the fans. More missiles were thrown from both sides, and fighting went on for ages until the Old Bill got some grip on it.

I saw a couple of coppers being helped away injured. Someone had seen to them, as one had blood streaming from his temple. It calmed down a bit with the Old Bill getting in between the fans, but then the mob that had gone down towards the South Bank came back, so Man U were in the middle. More bottles and bricks were hurled – I saw one front garden fence being pulled down for ammo. If Man U thought they had come down to take the piss out of West Ham, then they weren't going to do it easily. They still had to go back on the Tube yet, and many fans left for the station. We tagged along on the train. It was full of people screaming abuse at Man U. Tempers were up, and wearing red and white was not a good idea. On our carriage, nearly every one of the overhead handles was gone, taken for weapons. People were carrying bottles, sticks, poles, anything that could hurt.

At Mile End, we got off the train to be greeted by many West Ham fans already there, waiting for Man U. One train-load turned up, and as the doors opened, it was on – bottles were being thrown, a chocolate vending machine was lifted by three or four blokes into one carriage. They had no chance. West Ham stormed the train, kicking and punching as we went. I had my first real result – a Man U skin my age picked me out. He had a quart bottle he was going to hit me with but I got in first, so it was him or me. I hit him with a bottle of Tizer I had and laid the boot in as he went down in a heap. A whole lot of others seemed to converge on him like locusts. He was left lying there, battered. Police started coming into the station from outside but never had a hope. I saw a couple of Man U fans jump the centre tracks, trying to get away. How they didn't get killed, I'll never know. That train finally left and the police tried to move us off the platform. Then the next train came in, this time with loads of Old Bill on it. Out came the Man U fans, being a bit brave with the police around.

Missiles started flying again and many were beaten back onto the train.

The police had the numbers now and were moving us off the station. I lived near Mile End so me and my mates called it a day. We walked home and talked all the way about what had just happened. The game? Who cared? The season was nearly over, roll on next season. This was football violence and I was hooked for life. I always went my own way from then on in – looking for other fans was all part of the fun.

That was the last time the North Bank was taken – and the first, I'm told. Chelsea tried later on in 1969 (also, Celtic got on in number for Bobby Moore's Testimonial in 1970 but without any malice shown) and the Yids (a name for Tottenham team and fans, even used by the fans themselves)* in 1976/77, but no one else dared try. Coming to West Ham was always a hard one for away fans. The location of the ground, the Tube and above all the reputation of West Ham made most away fans think twice.

The next day, the Sunday newspapers were full of what happened at Upton Park. Front-cover stuff, splashed all over: THUGS! HOOLIGANS! the headlines read, with pictures of bleeding fans being led away.

My old man and his brothers were at the game, but were mainly in the Boleyn pub drinking until kick-off. I found out much later they had been in the North Bank

---

*'Yid' has become so commonly associated with Tottenham that in January 2020, the *Oxford English Dictionary* extended the definition of 'Yid' to 'a supporter of or player for Tottenham Hotspur Football Club'.

lot. Your ears flap when you're young and some of the things I heard that went on that day, I was surprised – no wonder they didn't want me around. From what I can gather, about forty of them, mostly dockers, were having a day out and it was adults only.

From that day on I learned a few things, some of which were to carry on for years afterwards. Never wear scarves home or away and, later on, about the way we travelled. This was mainly after a trip to Ipswich one year, where the train that brought us back had quite a few carriages destroyed. Stay with your mates and never let them down. Let them know what's happening, where to meet and spread the word. There's strength in numbers, and remember you are West Ham always.

Manchester claimed to have taken the East End. In truth, they got most of the North Bank for a few hours and they had won the title, but at a cost. Something that we never let them forget every time they came to West Ham. Being brought up in Limehouse, West Ham was your team. God help you if you chose Arsenal or Chelsea, and if you were Man U after that game, your life was made miserable.

From that day on the skinhead movement was kicking off really big. I had left school and started as an apprentice bricklayer. Some of my mates faded into the hippie scene of the Beatles and Dylan. The rest stayed on at school to get O- and A-levels. My new friends were West Ham, people who I became friends with, travelled with to away games and knew I could trust in a fight to back me up.

Gangs of skinheads were starting all over. The Mile End Mafia was one in our area. Although I never personally knew any of these, we knew of their reputation and looked up to them as heroes. They were much older lads, and loved to have it off with rival gangs from south London or up the West End. The Man U game at Upton Park that day seemed to be a breakthrough for hooligans – things were different at games from then on. You were a skinhead or greaser or Mod. As the greasers were a dirty lot, most around our way went the skinhead route – the smart clothes, the look.

The National Front tried to get West Ham fans involved, but never succeeded. There were many blacks at West Ham – in fact, we had one playing for us – so it wasn't a race issue. But the Asians, that was a different story. They were not liked. They never mixed; you never saw them at football or in the pub buying a pint. They wouldn't let their kids mix with us and they isolated themselves from the East End community, which is the real working-class community of London.

Dress of the day was Ben Sherman or Brutus shirts (the short-sleeved red check being a favourite), Levi Sta-Prest trousers in white or off-grey, turned up to the top of the high-leg Doctor Martens boots, or American officer dress boots, sleeveless jumpers, thin red or black braces and a decent overcoat or sheepskin coat – or, if you could find it, an American leather flying jacket. On match days, it was boots – either Doctor Martens or steel-capped cherry reds – Levi jeans and a decent sweatshirt, braces and a flying jacket or monkey jacket.

It wasn't cheap being a skinhead, but it was the scene, and I was part of it.

With the new season looming, all talk was on who was going where and wondering what team was bringing the best support to Upton Park. I was planning to go to London away games and get some trips in further afield. Attending every away game wasn't possible with the money I was earning as an apprentice, and there were always clothes to buy. Being dressed like an Eric was not an option. If you were part of West Ham and the skinhead movement the clothes were as important as the team itself and if you didn't have the right gear, it was soon pointed out to you.

OLD SKIN PAT/POMPEY: In season 67/68, we're doing well. I'm thinking I'm it, we're all thinking we're all it, and then came the wake-up call. I start going to my first away games because Pompey are flying that season. So, I go to Crystal Palace away, season '67, Boxing Day game. Now when I get to Crystal Palace, we go up the other end. There still weren't any real fight ethics going on at that time. Not a lot of madness is happening because you still got the World Cup fever and that. Things are still peaceful. But this Palace game is a very important moment. Nothing happened at Crystal Palace. It was an 11 o'clock kick-off, something like that. So, after the game, me and my mate and all the Pompey fans split up. Some sad bastards went to Charlton versus Millwall, something crazy like that. We went to Spurs versus Fulham. Spurs were always a big popular team amongst Portsmouth fans. West Ham were number one, Spurs second. So, we go to that, you know, good game, big crowd and all of that. Here's the funny bit, you see, Pompey had gone to Spurs in the FA Cup the year before and near on 20,000 Pompey fans had taken White Hart Lane with ease. The reason being that Spurs hadn't formed as a mob in '67. Now if you want to clarify that, read the Chelsea book by Martin King, which was his first away game, at that particular time. So, Spurs were getting turned over at the time. Pompey had gone and turned them over without any fighting, with just weight of numbers. So, I went up to Spurs thinking it wasn't a very dangerous, hard place, because I knew Pompey had turned it over the year before.

Coming out the ground, we got on the underground station, basically in Dimlo clothes, I had a combat jacket on with Pompey on the back, absolute Dimlo. I've got a blue-and-white scarf showing, and all of a sudden there's loads of kids around me, aged fourteen to twenty, and it's Spurs and they're around me and they've clocked the blue-and-white scarf. Straight away, they come up to me and said, 'You fucking Chelsea?' Basically, me and my mate thought, 'What's best?' Shall we just go to pieces? They might leave us alone. We're still kids, you know what I mean? I looked at this bloke and he's like, 'Ah, no leave them alone, they're only kids,' and this bloke sat down. We're sitting down with Spurs all around us, and he starts talking to us, one of the nicer sorts of blokes. I started asking him about his clothes. I couldn't get over it, looking at their clothes. They all had black army boots on – that was the first boot, the black army boot. They all had little checked shirts, they weren't the Ben Sherman, you know, the old man's shirt – they had that later. They had either navy or green sleeveless jumpers, they've all got the Levi's rolled up, got scarves down the front, the suede clipper jackets … Things like this are coming in, I'm starting to see; they've all got braces. I'm starting to ask where they've bought their clothes and I'm getting clued-up, I'm learning fast. Eventually the train pulls in somewhere and there's about thirty Norwich fans they spot. So, the whole lot just goes off and starts kicking … and me and my mate sat there thanking our lucky stars we weren't the unfortunate ones. It was more the fact that we were country bumpkins and looked hicks – if we'd been dressed as skinheads, we'd've been beaten to a pulp, but they probably thought, leave them alone.

And this is where Pompey are wising up. Straight away, you start seeing the emergence of the first serious group, the Southsea Boys as they were known, some good people. I'm beginning to grow up and they're all fifteen, sixteen, but they're beginning to know me as coming from Hayling. I'm beginning to get in. I'm meeting people like Pete Harris, Dave Dwaine … Now these to me were style kings. Now all of a sudden, I'm getting to be a bit of a style king, I've moved up London for a job.

Season 68/69, and football hooliganism now is getting into full flow, it's becoming the purpose now of going to football. I don't like the word 'hooliganism'. I mean, just the whole thing of you're young and that's where it's at and that's what you're doing, that's what you did, if you were with the in-crowd. The thrill, the excitement, everything was on the terrace, and every football book I've ever read will say that. It's part of your growing up and becoming what you think is a man, at the time. You start off down the front. Two, three years later, you're standing in the middle. One day, you might even start a song off. It's all a process.

So come this particular season I'm talking about, this is when we're starting to move into the serious business. Because I've moved up London at the time, I'm on the streets and this is when the skinhead fashion is getting immaculate. Now the big clothes of the time, believe it or not, traditional Burberry fly-front mac, the classic one. They weren't cheap and you could have navy blue or you could have cream. V-neck jumpers, you always had maroon or navy blue; cardigans were coming in and then jungle greens. Now to get jungle greens, there was a shop down Southwark I used to go to. Jungle greens suddenly became the in thing; you'd get them, little rim again, and you'd press them and they'd be high up. Then the boots started coming in: you'd had cherry red Commando boots, you'd have Monkey boots, you'd have long brown ones that came up high. Now you're starting to get with the cult skinhead thing. Trilby hats are coming in, sheepskins are starting to make their appearance, which was a big cult thing – to have a sheepskin, you had to have a lot of money as well. Now the whole of London is buzzing on this, nowhere else in the country is; don't get me wrong, this is a London thing. I don't care what

Manchester and the rest of them say, because I went up there and we just laughed at their attempts. So, the London thing's moving fast now and I'm going to Spurs games.

Now I'm wising up fast, and I'm learning the real great days were the thrill of the underground, the thrill of the chase. I went to Spurs versus Man United. They were great moments. The first thing I learned is that London crews at a game like that would tend to attract supporters from other London clubs if they weren't involved with each other. So there were West Ham and other people there, in that sense, because it was north, it was Manchester. So, I'm looking at Man U, who are meant to be it, and I'm looking at them and they are making me physically sick – they've all got moustaches, they've all got this dodgy sort of hair. They're absolute Dimlos with about thirty scarves round them, they're Dimlos. Lesser people think that it was Man U running the show back then, they make me laugh. Anyway, the Spurs crew are getting smart now, they are really geared up and they've got this look that no one else had. I can remember in the game, I'm standing outside the ground with some Spurs lads I know, and a young black kid, about sixteen, comes up, and says, 'I've been in there and I've been thrown out. I'm going back in, it's fucking great.' I got to talk to him and that was Sammy. At that time, it meant nothing, but Sammy later went on to become the big Spurs leader. He was just a little black kid of sixteen. He had no fear, he just ploughed in there, time and time again.

Spurs and Man U, up to half-time I can see Man U are getting the worst of this. Half-time, we go underneath the Tottenham stand and we're picking off Manchester mercilessly, absolutely mercilessly; they're getting murdered. All of a sudden, I see a strange sight. I see about four or five blokes and they're going 'Arsenal', like, and they're going to these Spurs fans. You know, these Spurs fans are dead hard, yet these four or five Arsenal are barging their way through, and I find out later that one of these blokes was Johnny Hoy, who's another big, big name of those times. At the time, 68/69, everybody seemed to think that Arsenal was it, they had a deadly reputation, but the overall cream of the crop, the people that ran it were West Ham. There was no doubt about it, you knew that West Ham were the ones.

So, I'm up London now and the skinhead thing is kicking off big, although the reggae and the music thing hadn't come so much then, and the main music was the soul things of the time. You tended to find skinheads went out in the evening. They'd be extremely smartly dressed, expensive suits, the cropped hair, the Ben Shermans, the shoes – you had tasselled loafers, you had weave wear, you had Royals, that was a very big shoe. It's taking off big, the real smart look's coming in now and obviously the Crombie is coming in. Not only that, the reggae thing's coming in. I started going to all-nighters. And the main thing about all-nighters was East End lads who were skinheads, rock-steady and reggae. I use the generic term 'reggae', it was more rock-steady. This is the music of the streets; this is when you get the big explosion, the Tighten Up albums starting to come out. The music started coming down here and you started getting a whole thing now where you've got a working-class, young people thing, the football fan. There was Motown, reggae, ska, that's where you were. If you weren't there, maybe you were a hippie, or you could be a biker, but you were a no one. So, the football thing now has really taken off in a big way.

As another football season ends, clubs face up to their number-one problem, to ensure greater protection for those who go along to watch, not fight. Plenty of media reporting and coverage asked how serious the clubs were about stamping out scenes like those that ruined the West Ham–Manchester United match.

West Ham Football club chairman Mr Reg Pratt took to holding a special police conference, where plans were outlined to combat the fighting on the North Bank. Mr Pratt felt the mob element at West Ham was very small, about fifty youngsters. He said: 'The idea of closed-circuit TV cameras to be placed at trouble spots was mooted to the police, who would consider it, but the problem was the time factor in finding the trouble-makers and rooting them out.' He went further: 'We want constructive ideas. You see some solutions are all right in theory, but not so good in practice. I think if we stopped the sale of beer, we would get some angry letters from fans. One thing we will be doing for next season is revising our crush barriers to make a bigger division of people and lessen the chances of avalanches.

'The root cause, I think, is the near-hysteria of a certain type of youth today and it's not just in soccer. We hope it's one of those phrases.

'We have taken measures to stamp out the hooliganism. Sticks and banners have been banned. Plain-clothes police are stationed in the crowd. The sale of bottled beer in the ground has stopped. But the overall difficulty was preventing punch-ups. You can't prevent that. There is no power on earth to stop it. One has to get to the root and stop the escalation. We are anxious, concerned and sickened about the mob element. We are going to do everything we can to stop it.'

Human avalanches could not be imagined post-Heysel/Hillsborough, but West Ham fans would sing and chant their song to start a knees-up on the terraces, resulting in the avalanches described by Mr Reg Pratt. This happened whenever the fans sung 'Knees Up, Mother Brown, under the table you must go, Ee-aye, Ee-aye, Ee-aye-oh ...' A wild knees-up on the terraces would begin from the singing group and spread so various fan groups simultaneously mimicked the outrageous tumbling and pushing down of fans from top to bottom of the stand with only the crash barriers breaking your fall, which, to avoid a sure crushing, you ducked under, still stumbling from the momentum of the surge, losing your original standing positions, as other scattered fans rejoined the celebrating wild bunch singing 'Knees Up, Mother Brown'* until either exhausted with it, or they became aware of the reaction from angry fans to the carnage caused.

---

*'Knees Up, Mother Brown' is a song that became popular in English public houses and was particularly associated with Cockney culture.

MAN UNITED RED ARMY

'IT WAS EN MASSE EVERYWHERE'

Manchester United is one of the biggest football clubs in the game, so their fanatical firm, the Red Army, had the largest numbers at the height of Britain's hooligan problem.

COLIN BLANEY: The Red Army started in the late '60s when the skinheads came out in 1968/69 – the Stretford end had all the skinheads, it was en masse everywhere. The actual truth is the football itself was a bag of shite; we won the European Cup in '68 but after that it all went downhill so the tempers of all the groups were like, hang on, we're not getting success here, so hang on, we'll turn this success into mob violence, which was going on everywhere but we just had bigger numbers than anyone.

The scale of it was I suppose you've got the Cockney Reds, you've got Coventry Reds, you've got affiliations with, I suppose, a lot of hooligans or thugs all over Britain who couldn't really latch onto their local team and they'd just follow the Red Army and they just became as much a part of the Red Army as the local lads of Colliers or the Ancolts lads, whether they were from Coventry or Carlisle, you know.

Big games, we've had fifteen, twenty, twenty-five thousand at Sheffield and places like that 'cos we'd take their end, or we'd share their end, which is still usually big, but we'd have the open end, where we'd have ten to fifteen thousand and another five thousand at the away end. Small grounds like in York, we'd bring ten thousand and they'd only have three thousand seats for us but that's the numbers we were taking in the '70s.

You always read the papers saying it's the minority of all these supporters causing all the trouble. I used to look around and I used to think ... unfortunately, the minority are the straight goers. The majority were thugs and that's why we were comfortable in the Red Army. I suppose for us, we'd all just left school and were working on Smithfield Market and we were like porters, working-class lads doing working-class jobs. At the end of the '60s, it had been Flower Power, the 'free love' brigade beloved by students and the trendy classes, but for us, the Mods had been there but now we could just go and get your old man's braces, your grandad's three-button T-shirt, a pair of bovver boots, cheap second-hand ones from the Army & Navy store and off you went, you could make a stamp on society. I think it was the inner-city working-class lads that were able to join in on something that was part of the revolution going into the '70s and as I say, it was en masse. It was all about taking the other people's ends all the way into the '70s, really. Press and media reported us as being bovver boys and hooligans.

Newcastle, Leeds, Liverpool ... Chelsea had serious mobs, but what's funny is Tottenham, who were massive back in them days, in the 1960s. They were the main rival like you think United and Liverpool were in the 1970s and '80s. But in the '60s, it was Tottenham because of Tottenham's double-winning success. First English team to win in Europe and they played attractive football as well when we played Tottenham. They too had the numbers and they were a massive club, Tottenham.

After the relegation to Second Division in '74, we were promoted back in First Division in '75. Any team that went into the Second Division it took them a couple of years to get back up but United actually bounced back up the very next season. And that's when the Red Army name was huge and it carried on a little bit more. It seemed to change around '77 when we went to Europe because around that time, the punk fashion was out but actually we were the Perry Boys as we had a little bit of a fashion thing going there with the Perry flicks (hairstyle), the Fred Perry polo tops, obviously. Also, we used to wear Levi drainpipes with All Stars, thinking we were cool but when we came back from France in 1976/77 after the St Etienne, we'd helped ourselves to Lois jeans, cords, flares, Kickers and then there was a change so from being in the Perry Boys coming into the

'80s, it started to get a bit more organised, and it was the Inter-City Jibbers that became our crew.

It was an exciting period really 'cos it was like you had the home town to yourself, it was a bit like shag your women, drink your beer and we are here. It was like putting a stamp and leaving your mark. Every newspaper on Sundays had all the coverage but you wanted the locals to tremble in fear that the Red Army was here again. As it was, rolling into town come the Thursday, Friday night, United fans from all over would be camping out and parking up. By the time the Red Army special trains rolled into town the police couldn't even cordon it off, we'd burst through the police ranks but they'd try their best to stop us – it was exciting times, to tell you the truth.

Everyone had football special trains for away matches which used to carry five, six hundred fans, absolutely packed. Very cheap, as well. But some of the big teams, we'd take two or three football specials. If the special landed at about one, half past one, within twenty minutes another one was in and by the time they were going out, another one was in. So that was one hell of a mob, three football specials going out en masse down to the ground, and that's what I say when the Red Army were rolling in. 'Cos the Red Army was so big, and it was Cockney Reds and Coventry Reds and Carlisle Reds and whatever. When we become a bit more organised it was quite easy that we all fitted into each other's gloves, you know. It was an advantage having those separate firms 'cos you could go to Coventry, you could go to

London and stay overnight with some of the lads who were in the Inter-City Jibbers.

I must admit I was arrested quite a lot in those times, and all the courts would give you would be a £20, £30 fine. You'd need to go to court five, six, seven times before you'd get detention or borstal, which is where we all ended up anyway, but we ended up in borstal centres for our criminal activities, which we used the Red Army as like a cover. With them numbers, we would use them numbers to our advantage where the Red Army were drinking or socialising. We would turn the lights off when the bars were full and when the lights went off, we'd be diving over, grabbing the cash boxes and the tills. We'd be off leaving the Red Army to face the music with the police. The press, they'd say it was the Red Army doing it, but it wasn't – it was us, the Inter-City Jibbers.

St Etienne was the first time for the Red Army, a bit of a throwback to the '60s days, where you took each other's end or you invaded their end and that's exactly what we done at St Etienne. We invaded their end and then the game got held up and then it was back on and at the end of the game which we won, which was a rare defeat for St Etienne because at home they were a very strong team. Following the trouble, United were banned by UEFA but they reversed the ban and they let us play the next game at neutral Plymouth and we got through and they made us play a friendly with St Etienne in Paris to heal the feelings. We just went over and went on the rob again.

Because we'd been doing tills in England and stuff when we went over there it was a lot easier, you could sneak a wallet out of the back of a café or something like that and you'd find quite a few grand in it, all the money would just be stored in a pencil case or bank slip.

As soon as you arrived there a friend of mine from Salford, he just had the old Head sports bag which everybody carried, emptied it out at the train station, opened it up and everything went in. When we've seen that, it just gave the green light for everyone to go on the rob. We all came back with new fashions and that was a change, that was a start of a different fashion thing then. The look then was we had Lacoste tops and cardigans, the Lois cords, the semi-flares, the Kicker boots, the Kicker shoes and threw away the Dunlop Greens.

Fantastic, you could even go to a club and cop for the women before you had a bit of a rampage on the way home. So, things changed, and people had a lot more money then as well. It was the Maggie Thatcher yuppie years so there was a lot more cash about. It was very cliquish, I suppose, when you look back at it now.

Basically, the Inter-City Jibbers were all ex-borstal boys who had come out of borstal around '76, '77, '78, and it was a perfect time for all these borstal lads, too. Just knowing with the Inter-City Jibbers that you'd be travelling away and into Europe, you knew that if you got into trouble or landed up in court you wouldn't be going to jail, whereas if you stayed on your own patch back here and carried on doing what you was doing, you'd end up doing borstal, more borstal and heavy prison sentences so there was a green light to travel away and rob and it wasn't as dangerous, especially in Europe, Holland, Germany and France. Actually, certain parts of France were as bad as Spain but Luxembourg, there's another one – places like that, you know. If you did get prison, you'd be out within a few weeks whereas it would be a few years over here. It worked perfect for us because we were all criminally minded anyway. We used to do pick-pocketing but that wasn't really our thing, it was the Scousers' thing. We liked the tills, you banging the jacks and the cash boxes and the turnstiles. Back in the '70s, the turnstiles had a hell of a lot of cash, whether it was Man City, they used to get visits off us all the time and we knew if we were having their money off and it ended up in the papers that United had done Villa, or Coventry it would really piss 'em off, just like us taking their end did. Just to get in the papers that you'd robbed them was making your mark. We had a motto which was to pay is to fail and that's what we all lived by.

Travelling with the Inter-City Jibbers, the younger ones who started off on the firm, what we'd do usually at some point on the train journey there'd be not a strip search but a pat down and you'd look in the ticket pocket to see if they had a ticket for the train. If they did, they'd be off the firm 'cos you needed lads who were jibbing all the way and that's why it was to pay was to fail – you'd fail getting in the crew if you weren't trying to jib the ticket.

The peak was, I'd say, '79, '80, '81. After '81, they were still going in '82 and '83, '84, '85, but by that time, truthfully, myself, I'd moved over to Holland, half of them were in Holland prisons or German prisons so the Inter-City Jibbers were either swanning around Europe or they were locked up all round Europe. Some of the main lads like Black Sam, he got locked up behind the Iron Curtain with United. When he got out, apparently, he got a lot of dodgy pills put into him in the prison in Albania or Georgia or wherever he was. Black Sam was never the same again, so really around that time 84/85, the Inter-City Jibbers had shot themselves in the foot, really.

My position was like, the Inter-City Jibbers was split you had Eddy Beef running the east part. You'd have Coco doing Old Trafford and Moss Side and the south and I was running the north part, Collyhurst, and then Black Sam, he'd be running the southern division. The Cockney Reds and Rob from Coventry ran the middle so it had its lieutenants but we all worked together, you see. I think that's why we were so organised and we had Amsterdam, which we called the magnet 'cos you were always there, which was our base besides Manchester. It does sort of bring a smile to your face looking back at the Inter-City Jibbers, the antics we got up to football fighting wise, some of the things on the road that used to happen; we've even got an Inter-City Jibbers song. It starts in Piccadilly when you're getting the overnight rattler on Sunday nights to London, which got in about six in the morning. So, the song started about meeting in Piccadilly, once you're on the train finding your positions 'cos it's a six-hour journey, you've got to get past this inspector five or six times, you know, and so the song is all about the trip getting there and getting to Europe.

I'd say it came to an end in '85, when I moved. We beat Everton, stopped the Scouse treble. I'd say '84, '85, that's when it come to an end. It had run its course.

TOTTENHAM

'WE REALLY STARTED TO BE A FIRM IN THE '70S'

SAMMY, TOTTENHAM HOTSPUR: When I got into it, I was about fifteen and there was no Tottenham firm at the time. It was the mid-sixties and we just had a row with these Sheffield Wednesday fans. Things just kicked off there, really, as in those days you had local gangs who later locked onto a local football team. Then, rather than have it out with each other, they tend to go somewhere else and have it out with another football team. That's how it all started with me. We were the Harrow Road boys from over Paddington, and we would go with the Edgware Road boys and the boys from West Kilburn. At the time we would clash with a firm we all hated up the road, the Kilburn High Road boys, because they were all Chelsea.

Over at Tottenham, there wasn't really a lot of us. It was after the 1966 World Cup and around the start of when the first skinheads started emerging. We were growing; a load of boys from Stepney and Whitechapel came with us and another big lot from up Enfield used to mingle. But at the time Arsenal used to govern us. The only name I used to remember was Johnny Hoy. But come the early '70s, we got the upper hand on them on a regular basis. We'd just go to Highbury with a lot of boys from Walthamstow and clean the place over. We really started to be a firm in the '70s as before that, Portsmouth were allocated the Park Lane in the FA Cup and Chelsea came over in '67 when we weren't as well established as a firm or in any number.

There has always been a serious rivalry with Chelsea and when I was at school it was Chelsea, both team and fans. Later, it was Arsenal, Arsenal. Ever since, it's been Chelsea, Chelsea. It's got one firm that have done this and done that and always, always, they say they have done us. The only time they will half admit that we've done them is when they say that we've had the numbers. But com'on! They're the biggest liars going. The times they did do us was when they had the numbers and we've done them when we've had less numbers – fact. That's the thing with us and Chelsea, but Arsenal team wise, we hate, period. We just hate Arsenal.

Crazy is how I think about Glasgow Rangers. They played Arsenal at Highbury, 1967/68 season, and on the same day, Tottenham played Celtic at Hampden, resulting in a 3–3 draw in an early August pre-season friendly. At half-time, the correct score was Celtic 1:Tottenham 2, but over the tannoy at Highbury, they gave it Celtic 2:Tottenham 1. Now there was 500 Arsenal who held the back of the North Bank with the rest of the North Bank being Glasgow Rangers. Soon as that incorrect score came out, the Arsenal fans started chanting: 'Celtic, Celtic'. Then all hell broke loose. Even the guys right down in the corner took to lobbing whisky bottles into the North Bank and into the Arsenal. All hell broke out and you couldn't see the ceiling for bottles. They were bottling their own supporters because the bottles weren't reaching that far, they were just flung in the air. It was crazy in there.

I've seen knives, I've seen axes, but I remember something that occurred right in front of me out in Amsterdam. We went to play, I dunno whether it was PSV or Ajax, but we are fighting in the streets with these Surinamese – you know, Dutch East Indies, the Dutch colonies. Next thing you know, we're hearing BANG BANG BANG BANG! There's some c**t there firing a pistol off and everybody near is ducking for cover. Then the Old Bill come up to the geezer and put a pistol under his ribcage to stop him. On the home front, one of our boys became bit of a Tottenham legend back in the '70s when he literally walked through Man City's Kippax End and cleared it out. I dunno if he hit anybody but that axe was pretty effective.

There's a memory that involved myself in '74, down at Finsbury Park with the Gooners. There's 200 of us walking up Woodbury Down district going towards Manor House, followed by 400 of them. We kept turning round, they kept bowling away and one guy stood his ground, a guy called Dave Smith. Three times we had 'em and every time he was the only one who stood. The first two times he got a kicking, but the third time we just left him because it's not worth keep doing a guy because he's got some bottle. We left him alone because we respected him.

Then after that, we've gone down onto Manor House station, they've gone down as well and we've got the train going back to Finsbury Park. We've got the last three carriages and they've got all the front carriages. So, me and another mate have gone down to the platform to the front carriages, picked up this sand bucket and threw it in their door. Next minute, I see this Gooner come out with a shovel and he was going to do my mate Neil in front of me and then he was going to do me. So, the only way out of it was to go for him. So, I got in front of my mate and the guy swung the shovel, catching me right across the throat, leaving me gasping, gobbing and all that. Anyway, the Gooner made the mistake of letting go of the shovel and I have to tell you it was the only time my mind went. The impact of that shovel across my throat was still in the mind, and I was gone.

I couldn't stop myself from what I was about to do. I went into the carriage and just went CHOP, CHOP, CHOP, CHOP until there was at least twenty of them done with that shovel. One geezer, I think I severed his arm. Then I'd chucked the shovel away and went back in the fifth carriage and before you know it, this geezer come in and started hitting people with this same shovel, but the back end of it where I had used the side of the shovel to do 'em. So, I just put my hands up, finding two handles to hold onto, flung myself up and a boot in the face and he was out the door, and that was the end of that.

The Old Bill tried to have me, like. They've gone up to these boys who I had never seen in my life, they were Holloway boys, and they asked, 'What's happened?' They've started saying things like, 'This N*****'s done this' and 'This N*****'s done that.' Immediately, I can see five years in front of me and the Old Bill's got me up there, and they now come back with two black geezers and Old Bill said, 'What's this N***** done?' Soon as he said it using those words, these boys now said, 'Oh, he ain't done nothing,' and the Old Bill let me go. Gotta say the Gooners knew me well from then on. As for the following season, I went over Highbury with only twelve of us, a few mates I knew, and we stood up in the North Bank over by the right-hand corner. But as soon as I walked up the stairs, they were going 'Fucking hell, there's that lunatic, there's that lunatic walking in' and cleared a big gap 'cos they thought I was crazy.

Being I am a Tottenham fan we've always had this thing about being the Yids and I say that's a racist term, but people call us Yids. But now over Tottenham we've come to accept it and now say ourselves we are the Yids, and we'll sing Spurs Yid Army, Yid Army and chant, 'We are, we are, we are the Yids' and that ended up taking the sting out of Yid taunts from our rivals. The truth is, it's not so big a problem here at club level, the

Old Bill now stamp on it, but it incenses me that those East European arseholes, every time a black player represents England, they are spitting, booing, jeering and throwing things at them. Those people to me are living in the old fucking Commie days like, and they've got no clue to the outside world.

Going back to this 'We are the Yids business', we've never had any big Jewish support in the ranks. Personally, I can only remember this girl back in the '70s. It all started off to wind us up and at the beginning we were being wound up and if rival fans know you're getting wound up, they will keep winding you up. But once you accept it and say right, I'm a Yid, so what, you're taking it back away from them.

When the NF were around, I think 1978, I was walking down the road with this girl when I received a shove in the back. I turned round and I've got a gang around me, going NF this and NF that. I said, 'So fucking what,' knowing that they were having a go at me because I was black. Then some old boy tried to say, 'Ignore them,' 'Don't worry about it,' and told me he was actually Jewish himself. So I walk off down the road and meet a couple of mates of mine, told 'em and my mate says that's the lot that sometimes go in the British Queen, they were Tottenham fans, too. So the three of us walks in and half the gang were there, about eight. I walks straight up to the guy that dug me out in the street and pulled him. I said to him, 'What's all this?' and he had a mate next to him, staring at me. I do no more and spank him three times without ever looking at him because I'm still talking to this geezer. Now there was only three of us in there but I'll tell you what, they got out of this pub and gone and we've never seen them at Tottenham again.

Today, it's not really a big deal. Ken Bates, the Chelsea chairman, once trying to stick up or cover for his own fans, said that we the Tottenham fans were racist for using the term ourselves. And, yes, we do march down a road chanting 'Yids, Yids,' but that's because we are Tottenham. If Bates got a problem with that, then what about Birmingham fans chanting, 'Zulus, Zulus'? It's just a football thing.

When we were in the Second Division at Cardiff, middle of the '70s, we'd come out of the ground just before full-time. There was about 400 of us and Cardiff fans were trying to get out of the ground and no way would we let 'em out. We had about a forty-minute tear-up. They kept running out and running back in, running out, running back in. Even to this day, I don't know if Cardiff will remember that, but we do.

Those early years I liked the Levi's, Ben Sherman, and all that. The mid-1970s saw me famed for wearing the old donkey jacket. I only wore it 'cos it was cold and I'll go straight from work to the match. Soon a few of us were all wearing donkey jackets. It sort of said who we were. Now if I go, it's pretty much jeans, jumper and a Tottenham top underneath. As for the worst football fashions, it has to be the Northerners back in the middle '70s, when teams like Liverpool and Manchester used to come down wearing things like flares and baggy high waistband trousers that were ten years behind. It was like once something was long out down here, they were just picking up on it up there.

We went to Middlesbrough, May 2003, and 'Boro are a firm we rate highly. They had called it on. So, the plan was to meet at Darlington by whatever travel means everyone made. We had a serious 250 having a drink in Darlington. The Old Bill just thought we was Orient supporters because Orient were up there playing Darlington. But as soon as the firm moved on to Middlesbrough, the 'Boro Old Bill was already waiting for us, video cameras and all that. They would only let you out one at a time and you had to give your name and where you came from. Everybody – female as well. Zero tolerance from the police out in heavy numbers, though they weren't heavy-handed with us until we got into the ground. That's where it all kicked off and seventy of us were ejected from the ground inside thirty minutes for having a row with the Old Bill. I missed what started it all, but one of the Spurs fans was caught in the middle of it and got put out of the ground. The Old Bill today seem to know what's going on before it goes off. The way round it is the mobile phones, something we didn't have in the past 'cos we relied on word of mouth which, looking back, was more successful as arranged meets back then the Old Bill never got word of until after the event.

There's a lot of boys still going from thirty years ago, and all their sons are there as well, so they're still doing it. And it's like a new generation has taken up the mantle, as I've moved on and try to keep out of it all. Where it comes from, we don't know, 'cos the Tottenham lads today are from all over: Essex, Hertfordshire, Middlesex, northeast London. But the one thing if you're going to get involved is to know who you're with. It's important to know who you're with and if they're going to back yer. Because if you see geezers you know and they're not worth backing, they're not going to back you and you wouldn't go with 'em. You'd say, you go your own way, simple as that. You know if you work as a team and there is a weak link there, you get rid of the weak link. I've done it all, so personally I wouldn't do anything different. I personally don't get involved any more, but the buzz of going can get really addictive, so that for some of us it's hard to get out of it.

WEST HAM V MILLWALL

'GOOD OLD-FASHIONED COCKNEY ROW'

If England is the motherland of football hooliganism then a Millwall–West Ham game is the mother of all hooligan derbies. The bad blood has always been there between east and south of the river. You can go back to your forefathers.

When those two teams meet it goes beyond football. The atmosphere is a feeling of genuine hatred and uncertainty; other clubs' rival fans have long said both Millwall and West Ham have the hardest firms in England. Here is the modern history of where it all began, the rivalry and reasoning behind it.

BOB, MILLWALL: We look forward to a good old-fashioned Cockney row, when you got two teams originally from the dock area, proper Cockneys, old-skool Cockneys, all the old-timers, all the new boys, lot of people support Millwall who outside football are villains, not just football fans.

The police love it, they say they don't but they have cut back on all their resources so it's a chance to get some overtime pay. When it's Millwall, they know it's a chance to get more money.

People must remember Millwall came first as a club in London's East End docks when they formed in 1885 on the Isle of Dogs. West Ham came second in 1895 and just few miles separated them. The local rivalry really came to the fore when there was a dock strike during the General Strike of 1926, the Millwall dock broke the strike to the fury of the West Ham dockers.

My mate Little Jon is a West Ham supporter who would never ever support Millwall after his East Ender dad once said to him when he was a young boy, 'Son, you can be whatever you want to be, but what you can't be is a copper or Millwall fan.' Jon then learned from his father that during World War Two, he was wounded so he was given leave, a medal and a ribbon. While home. he'd gone to a war cup game between Millwall and West Ham wearing his khaki uniform. He and a friend were being abused by some louts and he felt a bump but thought nothing of it as there was no mark or blood until he got home when his wife noticed the back of his army uniform had been slashed in several places with a razor. Money was short and he was back at the front within two weeks and having to pay for a new uniform.

Forget what sociologists say about there being recorded incidents of football hooliganism since Victorian times. The modern hooligan world I have lived through started when the national newspapers were full of what happened when West Ham played Man United in 1967, *'Thugs! Hooligans!'* as fans rioted and many required hospital treatment. That same weekend, Rangers v Celtic resulted in another fan riot. Trouble in both England and Scotland on such a serious scale on the same day led to football violence being widely reported as a new phenomenon.

As the skinhead youth culture spread through the streets of Britain so did the violence and on the terraces and you now had a hooligan league to see who was the hardest set of fans. In the north Man United thought they was, in the south so did Millwall but so did West Ham but they rarely played each other. So, when Millwall crowd favourite Harry Cripps had his football testimonial at the Old Den ground against West Ham, that was when the blood was really spilt. Hooligans from both sides treated it as their own Cup Final as both mobs claimed to be the guvnors of London.

An example of the myth and legend of West Ham's first guvnors 'The Mile End Mob' came from this game. They left Mile End, jumped on the train, went to the ground and walked straight into Millwall's Cold Blow Lane end. That's all they had in mind because people kept saying, 'No one can take Millwall's end.' We'd taken Millwall and it's all before kick-off. More Millwall outside the ground came in and the ground swelled up full. The fighting continued from pillar to post as the Millwall hordes tried to take their end back; the West Ham with the Mile End Mob were being forced out to the sides and pushed up to the back, where they were holding their own in this immortal end.

This was nothing to what went on after the game as the legendary Mile End Mob came out the ground early and together with other West Ham lads, they stood at both exit gates and just waited for Millwall to come out. Bill Gardner recalled he'd never seen that level of violence – that it was frightening to watch.

> **BILL GARDNER, WEST HAM UNITED:** West Ham waited at the bottom of the stairs and eleven times the Millwall fans came out and eleven times they got run back in ... You've never seen anything like it, it was really bad that night. The Mile End Mob had raided the workboxes belonging to the railway and took all the tools out, giant spanners, hammers and large bolts. Half that crowd coming out the ground had not taken part in any violence, but those West Ham with the toolbox selection just didn't care, what happened was pure evil.

The infamous night of the Harry Cripps testimonial decided two things: who ruled London and who were the hardest fans. The hatred aroused that night never left the fans of either team and it has set the seal on a lasting vendetta. Like the time when both clubs were based in east London docks, Millwall on the Isle of Dogs and West Ham at Stratford.

The thing with Millwall is that they are good at the fear of the unknown. Both the fans and that Old Den ground are pure intimidation. The next big derby between the two rivals was in 1974, the Bobby Neil testimonial game between the clubs which was not an as violent a scale as the Harry Cripps testimonial, numbers were lower (maybe due to stories and memories of the Harry Cripps one) but it was another night game with that eerie chant of 'MILL...WA...LL! MI...LL...WALL!' echoing all around their ground.

The Mile End Mob this time was not present as key members

were in prison or had swapped the football scene for the underworld scene. I was sixteen years of age and was now fast making a small name for myself and would back up the older lads fronting Millwall's faces in the Cold Blow Lane end. There was an air of revenge we felt was coming due to lack of numbers we took this time but we each knew what we were going for so could not back out now and we held our own over there until half-time then Millwall got all around us. One almighty roar and surge from the Millwall hooligans and we were truly ousted as the police seized the opportunity to get us out of the ground. For my trouble I received a plank of wood over my head, as I was one of the last left at the top of the stairs when the invisible Old Bill made a grab for me.

Anyone who knows the score knows this rivalry goes beyond Millwall Football Club and West Ham United Football Club – it is east London versus south London.

The general football violence of the 1970s and '80s was never as organised as people thought. It was more a case of like-minded souls thinking the same way. Millwall and West Ham saw it differently as neither would concede that the other was the number-one firm in London. This led to a series of organised tit-for-tat clashes and encounters between them when their teams was not even playing each other. This unfortunately led to two fatalities, one on each side. After both clubs played matches on same night in 1976, Millwall fan Ian Pratt died after falling under a train following an incident involving West Ham fans at New Cross train station. As a result of this when the two teams played in the league at Upton Park in 1978, the biggest police operation was put in place with the first use of police helicopters at a football match. And just in case anyone forgot the reason why, Millwall fans put out leaflets billing it as Judgment Day. Years after that, a West Ham fan was murdered by a Millwall fan after being attacked near Embankment Tube station in 1987.

The '80s brought along what were to become two notorious firms in the Millwall Bushwackers and West Ham's Inter-City Firm. Both firms would study the fixture list to see where one another were playing and if a chance meet was on to do battle. The aptly named Bushwackers ambushed a cream firm of 50 ICF boys at Bank underground station. West Ham were travelling to Aston Villa at the time but were now fighting for their lives with an entire Millwall firm who had them trapped while the train was on the Tube station platform. This scene is later depicted in the movie 'Rise of the Foot Soldier', a biopic about former ICF member Carlton Leach. Revenge came later that very same day after enraged West Ham fans left early from their Midlands game to get back to London before Millwall, also playing away, returned to London. This time it was the turn of West Ham to be firm-handed and plan a revenge attack on Millwall at King's Cross station. Those involved in this raging clash said afterwards that the police just seemed to stand back and let it happen. Maybe it was in the hope that both sets of fans would destroy each other and do their job for them.

Another memorable clash occurred in 1984 when a full trainload of West Ham ICF was travelling to a FA Cup game at Crystal Palace. The ICF deliberately diverted to get off at New Cross to go to the Millwall game instead, basically to humiliate their rivals on their own manor. They filled the road and they were running Millwall lookouts and whoever they thought looked suss and it looked like they'd taken them by surprise but they saw the trap too late. Millwall came out of The Rose pub swinging baseball bats and every other weapon they had stashed in anticipation the ICF was coming (they somehow knew). The humiliation was all West Ham's that day.

Revenge was just a short week away this time as the ICF planned the payback by sending one small firm on the train and another in cars and vans to ambush Millwall meeting at London Bridge mid-morning to travel to the game they had, where they were eager for a clash with the Blades Business Crew (BBC) at Sheffield United, another naughty firm. It was bedlam and the turn of Millwall to be surprised, plus this battle would be remembered for the use of petrol bombs that were hurled onto the station concourse and subway, causing noise and commotion that had police there calling on their radios for a suspected terrorist alert. Firms seeking each other out when their teams are not playing each other does not occur on any regular basis, but when they do, it can be very serious and, in some cases, unfortunately fatal.

Final word on these two teams and their supporters is simply that they should NEVER meet, and the only way you can solve that is to ban away fans. Theirs is a fierce rivalry that is beyond the rivalry of most football derbies. Today, the West Ham and Millwall clubs' fan bases are beginning to change, much like the game itself has in recent years, so don't think it will ever be as bad as the past experiences shared with you here when the divide really was just the River Thames, but football can only hope whenever there is another cup draw or promotion/relegation that has them in same league or in a cup competition these two clubs aren't drawn out of the hat together because for some there will always be scores to settle, just as there were for their forefathers.

CASUALS

'A NEW PASSION AND A NEW OUTLOOK'

The need for a country like Britain to have a youth culture which is either led by teenage angst, political anarchy or musical revolution has always been evident. It just so happens that the Football Casual subculture originated on the terraces and their vehicle was football, fighting and fashion.

> **NICK SARJEANT, BRIGHTON:** It's not just about what you were wearing, but also how you wore it. Not just your clothes but your hair and even the manner in how you walked. You had to have that 'attitude', saying like, 'Here I am.'

It wasn't until the '70s Mod revival began to dissipate at the beginning of the new decade that we first noticed the arrival of wedges, ski jumpers, balloon jeans, Pods, plazzy sandals and of course adidas – this didn't have a name but the music was Kraftwerk and Human League, the clothes Bowie/Roxy, the football Liverpool and Everton ... no one went around calling themselves a scally but you knew one when you saw one.

Then, sixty miles down the road, the Mod thing was also now just *too* formal, the suits and ties were a pain in the arse, and they didn't like it. *Quadrophenia* had done the damage, well and truly, or so it seemed. He had a fully matured flick in late 1979, and was wearing burgundy cords with an auburn rinse in his hair – the sign of the Mod killer ... a polo shirt under a burgundy chunky-knit jumper and a pair of black adidas Samba trainers. These new styles were rampant by the New Year of 1980. This is the original Manc Perry Boys' wardrobe and not since the Mod era in the '60s had lads been so bothered about appearance.

In Italy and France, elegance has always been treasured, and when British fans travelled to Europe with their sides participating in Continental cups, they brought designer clothing back home with them, usually after having violently raided clothing stores. Thus, the inherent hooligan violence always associated with football merged with a new interest for fashion, beginning a progression towards the modern-day football casual. But despite the fans' newly acquired designer attire, football colours continued to be worn on English terraces, along with the aggressive look of those mainly Londoners sporting MA flight jackets worn with Lois jeans with the DM boots swapped for Nike Legend trainers. A familiar look of Chelsea and West Ham mobs around the time of the dying punk scene, mixed with Mod revivalists and the random second-generation skin.

In the 1980s, the police in Britain began to close surveillance of fans wearing football colours both on match days and in general. At the same time Prime Minister Margaret Thatcher supported giving police more authority, and consequently hooliganism evolved to become more organised, and the violent supporters left their sides' scarves and shirts at home as match-day gangs became firms. If you were in the firm you didn't need to overstate you was, people knew by the way you talked, looked and moved that you were a football lad, no colours needed. This was the beginning of the modern-day football casual dominating the scene.

Although the police in the mid-'80s and the beginning of the '90s emerged as winners in the war between casuals and the establishment, the culture survived outside the stadiums, and during the last decade it has again grown steadily despite severe consequences for the individual fan, should he be caught running with a firm or committing crimes related to football. Being a football casual was and is, in its simplest form, about one-upmanship. The term 'casual' is one that tends to stick the most, but there were also 'Perrys' from Manchester and 'scallies' from Liverpool and numerous more other regional names for a similar type of football fan, such as 'dressers' or just 'boys' as they would refer to themselves upon recognition: Look, there's their boys, these are their boys.

Where and when did the whole thing start and with what club? There's been much debate on this, but it's universally accepted that the scene originated from Liverpool in the late 1970s. Liverpool were the kings of Europe and a number of fans started to pick things up on their travels. Before too long, expensive sportswear and designer labels found on the continent were soon finding their way onto the terraces. Sergio Tacchini, Fila and Lacoste tennis shirts were quite popular around this time. Footwear was taking off, too, with the adidas Sambas and Diadora Borg's Elites. Before too long, many football firms were even using the pre-season friendlies as cover if their club had not qualified for European football and were going on 'shopping' trips to Europe to loot a number of German, French and Swiss designer sportswear stores as security was far laxer than in the UK. Over the course of a few years, everybody was wearing the staple brands, with individual firms showing preference for particular brands. Suddenly, one-upmanship was all the rage as more and more brands were being discovered, but often varied in popularity from region to region and as the '70s ended and the '80s began, the casual movement took grip across Britain.

IT STARTED IN
THE NORTH?

PETER HOOTON, LIVERPOOL: I was crowd-watching then as much as I was watching the football so I was always interested in the social and cultural side of football as well as the football you know. The first time I ever recognised anything different was when Liverpool played Manchester United in the year 1977 charity shield. Now we'd played them in the Cup Final in '77. On that day, lads were wearing maybe suede boots and a semi-flares type of thing and there was no real look. By August, there was a new look – there was no doubt about that – and it was Fred Perrys, straight jeans, training shoes (usually, the first ones to become popular were adidas Samba). That was the first time I noticed the haircut, the flick with the one eye, and it was a very effeminate haircut so you had these groups of lads who looked very effeminate – if you saw them now, you'd think, that's a boy band.

Liverpool's European success in the May of 1981 had opened many eyes and given many a young teenager the taste for Continental adventure. Trips to Munich, Paris and the pre-season in Switzerland became an escape from the mundanity of unemployment back home. Plus, there was the added bonus of trainers left out in pairs, clothes without security tags and an array of designer sportswear unavailable in Liverpool.

In Manchester, they were developing their own casual identity with a unique name.

TONY GRAHAM, MAN UNITED:

I remember seeing this group of lads at this disco, about eight or nine of them, and they had a real mystique to them. They looked very different to us in not only the dress but also the hair as well and the dress was very slim so we were very big and baggy and flared and they were very slim, they were wearing V-neck jumpers and polo shirts and very skinny jeans and nice trainers and the haircut was very different. They had this haircut that was really sharp and severe and cut right across here at the ears.

I remember looking at these guys and the girls were really interested in them as well, which was something that was fascinating to me, and I said to my sister, who are these guys? She said, oh, they're the Perry Boys. That's what we called them, Perry Boys because they wore Fred Perry and the haircut was also a Perry haircut, that's what you called it. There was an air of aggression to that haircut because it obscured part of your face, yeah, so you had like a toughness to that look even though it was very effeminate. Some people dyed it and things like that – there was a toughness to it because your face was obscured but also, I think the way that lads could carry it, it was a very posey look and a real reaction to the lads we saw at the match at the time who were big grizzlies. We used to call them dinosaurs and all of a sudden this was a real strutting look, very David Bowie, which is where it maybe came from, the cover picture on his *Low* album. That was all part of the thing so it wasn't just the clothes, it was the hair and the way you carried it, your whole attitude. You had to observe people, you observed the elders at the match, you observed other teams that came to you. Liverpool was a big thing for us and also the nature of having an escort at the match, there was a lot of police escorts then. Liverpool had a massive escort: you could come and you could look across, you could posture like you want to have a fight with them – no chance, you're twelve years old or whatever – but you're looking at those kids and you're seeing what they're wearing.

It's funny with Manchester and Liverpool, there's always these dynamics. It's only sixty miles apart and there's a big thing, you know, with the ship canal and through the '80s, Liverpool were dominant and United were never as dominant as Liverpool were but there's a lot of similarities between Manchester and Liverpool and it always follows. And Liverpool. were madly obsessive with the trainers and Manchester were madly obsessive with the trainers and all these lads used to, because they're all working-class kids from Salford or Hyton or wherever they were spending all their summers going across Europe, grafting together and then spending the whole season probably trying to kill each other. But there was that, so there was that uniform thing that the Liverpool and the Manc kids went over to Europe and brought this back so really it was our thing, the trainers. Adidas in particular was a big northwest thing and to me, I don't remember seeing a Nike trainer till maybe 1983 or Diadora with Björn Borg and stuff but for me, it was always adidas that was the casual thing.

In Liverpool or Manchester these pioneers of the casual movement were obsessed with trainers and one brand in particular.

PETER HOOTON:
We call them adidas – some people call them Adidas. I think it's the classic look, they just look fantastic. It's the three stripes: it's recognisable and Liverpool's always had that love affair. It's flirted with other brands but it's always had a love affair with adidas, it's an adidas city in many respects. My favourite even though they haven't got the three stripes are Stan Smiths. I've always said that. They just look great, you can wear them out in the day but you can also wear them in the night-time and they look good as well, you know.

The early casual movement stayed completely underground until the '80s began. This look at the northwest and its influence on the casual subculture should not overlook the soul boy scene which also had that cool style of the jazz-funker, as did its hip-hop scene sporting Reebok, Kangol, Carhartt and Fila during the '80s. By the time Paul Weller broke up his successful band the Jam and formed the Style Council, the look was rampant across the terraces and no longer exclusive to the north.

PETER HOOTON:

When the media picked upon it around '82 and *The Face* started writing about it and Garry Bushell started writing about it in *Sounds* magazine, that's when the nation paid attention and took note of it. It wasn't until Kevin Sampson's article in *The Face* magazine, which is quite famous now, and he wrote that article I know for a fact 'cos he was the Farms manager, he wrote that article two years before that, he wrote it in '80/'81, but *The Face* wouldn't print it because they were writing about Malcolm McLaren or whatever, so they didn't see it as relevant. They only saw it as relevant when teams like West Ham, Arsenal, Chelsea started dressing … we never called it 'casual', that was a southern term.

PHIL THORNTON, LIVERPOOL:

The cockneys were, I'd say, two or three years behind as a look. I'm not saying there weren't elements of that in the soul-boy fraternity, but, as a mass look on the terraces, I don't think the cockneys really got into it until '82-ish.

PETER HOOTON:

Then all of a sudden Liverpool fans are looking at Arsenal fans and they're like looking in the mirror. You know, and it's Lacoste, adidas, Tacchini, training shoes. The Arsenal fans have all got flicks, you know, it was just ... you know, it was just amazing and when the media started picking upon it, it was just called casuals.

Every firm in those days, they nearly all referred the name for a casual to being a dresser or trendies. Other names used were smoothies, Perry Boys, scallies, wedges and flick-heads.

In all corners of England, Wales and Scotland, casual firms took hold in their communities. The name 'casual' was never meant or attributed to being a name for the lads or firm, unlike the Aberdeen Soccer Casuals, who though later on the scene than their English counterparts, led the way as their city became enriched through the drilling of the North Sea oil, while Alex Ferguson's success in taking the club to winning the European Cup Winners' Cup in 1983 made them number one, both on and off the pitch. The ASC had many a rival Scottish firm adopting the name and use of word 'casual' to mean lads and hooligans.

In the UK, the leading firms behind the movement before it was adopted nationwide did indeed come from Liverpool, Manchester and London, and none of their firms gave themselves this name 'casuals'. More the case they did use the name for descriptive terms of what they were about and how they differed from other fans and their firms were central to this identity. These were the lads of every club with a casual firm. In 1985, a TV documentary called *Hooligan* gave viewers a unique insight into West Ham's gang of hooligans, The Inter-City Firm. I can certainly recall the ICF, which was really started by younger members in the late 1970s, who added the words 'we are cool and casual' to one of their chants.

JELA, WEST HAM UNITED:

We was West Ham's original Under-Fives and it was just our life – everything revolved around being West Ham and being the best and having the best gear and taking liberties with people. You could snatch someone's money and it's a really, really serious offence but it's categorised as 'taking someone's jumper off them'. When these people have gone out and they've got their nice Burberry mac on and they walk into Upton Park, you know, they're asking for it! Do you know what I mean? They're football blokes and if they can't look after themselves, they're gonna get their gear nicked off them. Imagine how they feel, you know? – you were gonna hurt 'em, physically and mentally.

This, which admittedly started in the northwest, was picked up and led by the younger element around the rest of the UK. Firms like the Under-Fives, Bushwackers, Gooners, Baby Squad, among others, influenced the older established terrace hooligans by adding criminality into the mix and changing the nature of the violence, even linking it to their fashion. References to taxing, tea-leafing, Stanley knives, squirt were the typical slang that went hand-in-hand with this new fashion breed to emerge on the terraces, where it had not been seen before.

WHAT'S THIS?
THE BABY SQUAD

RIAZ KHAN, LEICESTER CITY:

I was born in Leicester in December 1965. My parents were from the Subcontinent, my father from Badrashi, a village near Nowshera in the North-West Frontier Province (NWFP) of Pakistan. My mother was from Adda, which is in Jalalabad, Afghanistan, but moved to Pakistan due to to an incident involving her grandfather killing a man. He had already killed twenty people and killing for him became second nature. However, his last victim was from a large family, and they wanted to seek revenge, and this included her grandfather's grandchildren. She escaped in the middle of the night along with her grandparents to Peshawar in the NWFP at a very young age in the late 1940s. My parents are Pathans or Pashtuns, a very famous tribe of people who are known for their fighting abilities across the

Subcontinent and further afield. My father became part of the Pakistani Navy and arrived in Britain in 1958. My mother subsequently came over in 1964. Myself being the oldest of five, we all lived in a two-bedroom terraced house in Highfields, Leicester, with our parents.

My parents were traditional in the sense that they brought what they had learnt as kids here to the UK. They expected the same respect that all parents in the Subcontinent received from their offspring. That was the case with most migrant families as it was with ours.

My parents never really bought us expensive clothes as they were working in low-paid jobs. Asian families in those days never spent money on designer clothes (at that time the labels were Fiorucci, Gabicci and Farah); the clothes we received from our parents were always cheap. Maybe that's why my brother and I after leaving school and starting to earn some money would go out and buy expensive clothes. At school we dressed like typical Asians (not trendy at all) and in a school where we were the only Asians, imagine what that was like?

I do not blame my parents for not buying us expensive or trendy clothes as they worked hard to pay for the mortgage and household bills. The last thing on their minds was to dress their five children in trendy clothes. I realise that now as I have four kids of my own and clothing them can be expensive. It was a good thing that we wore school uniform for the first three years, as we could wear the same clothes day in, day out. However, the last two years, that was not the case. All the kids at school either dressed in Mod outfits or as New Romantics or dressed down as Greebos. During this period, I was struggling with my identity at school as there were no Asians and there was also a tide of racism. I found this quite strange as Mods listened to Tamla Motown and Northern Soul, whilst the Skinheads listened to Ska music. Who were the lead singers in most of these groups? Exactly! Racism in those days was fuelled by the then National Front, who claimed that all immigrants were taking the white man's job. (But we were invited by the government as part of the Commonwealth to work here?)

You would think due to this poison that was around a person like myself would be more attached to their ethnicity but that was not the case with me. All I wanted to do was just to fit in. I could not be a skinhead because of the racist ideology. I could not be a Mod because most held the same views, and I was never going to be a Greebo as they were smelly, scruffy and also racist! I liked the New Romantic look but it seemed a little effeminate for me, yet the music was good. So, I ended up being a Soul Boy. Even though I had already adopted black music like 'Rapper's Delight' and 'Rock with You', I was still unsure of who I was. It was only when I used to watch *Soul Train* along with listening to the Top 100 dance chart on Radio Luxembourg on a Saturday night that made it official. I remember the signal was not that good for Radio Luxembourg but the tracks were awesome. I remember dance-floor classics like Arthur Adams's 'You Got the Floor', Freeez's 'Southern Freeez' and Beggar & Co's 'Somebody Help Me Out'. How did I dress at that time? Stretch jeans, white boots from

Ravel and a blue C&A jacket! I thought I was black for a while to the extent I even had an Afro! This did not last long as I was surrounded by my white colleagues and their influence. I still loved the music though.

My character and attitude were changing rapidly, I became more 'white' than Asian. Some would regard me as a 'coconut' because of the way I spoke (I couldn't speak Urdu properly) and our mannerism was not Asian. As far as Yusuf (my brother, known as Suf) and I were concerned, we were born in the UK, we went to a school full of whites and therefore started to adopt their ways and culture. I did not want to have an arranged marriage or go to weddings or religious ceremonies, the community used to shun us for not being ethnic enough. It was embarrassing when we did attend any function as we would be asked questions in Urdu and we found it difficult to respond as our parents spoke to us in English/Pashto. Our mother tongue is Pashto, and I can get by when conversing with another fellow Pashtun but with Urdu, that was not the case. Even when I was at sixth-form college, my fellow students (who were mainly Asian) could not understand me entirely as they were all attached to their own cultures and traditions. They found me odd if I did not understand certain customs associated with being Asian, whether it would be Sikh, Hindu or Muslim. I was not here or there, not until I found a new passion and a new outlook on my life, the life of the casual.

How did the casual phenomenon start for me? A couple of factors come into play here. I remember reading *The Face* magazine* and the article about the Soccer Casual. It was not so much the article but the photos that I saw that got me intrigued. There were these three young men sitting on a train sporting these flick haircuts and wearing clothes that I had never seen before. There was also another article in a newspaper highlighting a new era of soccer thugs in 1982 and it was focused on the Leeds Service Crew. There was this picture with a group of thirty-odd young white lads sporting flicks and designer gear. I also saw a group of lads in town in 1982 walking through the Haymarket Centre in Leicester, wearing tracksuit tops with bleached jeans and flick hairstyles. This friend I was with said that's so and so. He was pointing to the Top Boy SH. SH was not white, but Afro-Caribbean and he looked the part. He was wearing this red Fila raincoat and I thought to myself, I want a jacket like that. So, I went out and bought a blue Patrick raincoat, thinking it was the same make as his jacket!

However, what really got me going, the catalyst for me dressing towards a casual look, was the video to 'I.O.U.' by Freeez. I was into body popping and dance music at that time (i.e. hip-hop, electro and jazz-funk) and the young lads in the video were all dressed in these tracksuit tops, wearing cords or bleached jeans with slits and white Nike trainers. I had recorded this video and played it over and over again, looking at the style

The Face was a British music, fashion and culture monthly magazine started in May 1980 by Nick Logan, and published until 2004. It was relaunched online in 2019, and republished as a quarterly in the same year.

of clothes that they wore. That was it, I loved the look so I started to save my money that I earned working at Walkers Crisps (during the summer holidays) and when I got paid, one of the places I would go to was the Golf Range. The Golf Range was a place where folks would go to play golf, all types of golf including crazy golf. There was a little shop that sold all the golfing gear, from Slazenger to Pringle to Lyle & Scott. This shop was a five-minute walk from where I lived. My brother and I used to cycle down there every few days on our BMX bikes to look at the new range of golfing gear. We tried pilfering some tops but the owner had eagle eyes like the owner of a corner shop. Only once did my brother manage to get a couple of Lyle & Scott roll-necks when the manager was distracted by another customer. This opportunity only arose because we had already bought some garments previously and had gained his trust by it. In no time we were walking the streets on our estates or pedalling around on our BMXs, wearing these pastel-coloured jumpers, bleached jeans, white Nike trainers and roll-necks. The Asians on our estate would ask us why we dressed like that. We responded by saying it looked cool. When we told them the price of each item, they thought we were mad.

One summer afternoon in '83, I was walking past a group of casuals that were sat at the Clock Tower, wearing my designer gear, and recall one of them saying, 'Who the fuck is that?' They just looked at me and I got the impression that they wanted to start an altercation with me. I got a little paranoid as

I was by myself at that time and I avoided that area on my way back to catch the bus home. This same group, a few weeks previously, had assaulted a man. I remember loafing around the Clock Tower with my friend Kez when we saw this man standing near this same bunch of trendies acting in a threatening manner. SH was not there at that time and this tall guy just stood there, taunting these six or so trendies. I looked on, wondering what these youths were going to do. This man was much older than this group and kept at them. This must have lasted for around five minutes to the point where you would think that these youths had had enough and were not going to entertain him. Then without warning this youth with blond wedged hair, wearing a yellow-coloured tank-top and a white Fila T-shirt, ran at this guy. He just waded into him, he was not throwing jabs, hooks or upper cuts but he was pedalling! That man was pinned against the shop window and he could not defend himself, and the other lads also 'steamed' in, one with an umbrella.

I carried on buying clothes with whatever money I had earned from working during the summer period. To me, it seemed hypocritical that I was dressed in designer clothes but not attending any matches. Eventually I attended Filbert Street [the Leicester City ground until 2002] and became like an official casual.

Anyway, going back to the subject of purchasing designer clothes. It was not an easy task trying to buy the clothes and trainers. There were hardly any stores in Leicester at that time that could cater for the demand in designer sportswear. We had to travel to London to shops like Lillywhites and Nik Naks to keep up with the latest trends. For a short period, every two weeks we would catch the train with our government giros and whatever money we scraped together to help us buy the latest gear. Some of the gear I remember I bought was a pair of green adidas Gazelles; everybody in Leicester was wearing either red or blue. Patchwork suedes and Kappa were not even introduced to Leicester until we wore them. Kappa had just come out when we went to the capital, and it was half the price of Fila and Tacchini. I am not blowing my own trumpet here and I am not lying but we were the first to introduce the above. I remember we were wearing Kappa jumpers and everybody was asking me and my brother, 'What's that?' We would sometimes give our oUnitedated clothes to our younger siblings and when they wore them at school, the kids all wanted to wear the same. These were hand-me-downs but they were still fashionable and different. To keep up with the trends, anything that went out of fashion on the terraces that I wore, I would sell to the Asian lads in Highfields. This would help fund my passion for designer gear.

Leicester did have Christopher Scotney's and Coleman & Son menswear, who did stock Burberry, Aquascutum and Giorgio Armani. MC Sports was another shop for trainers and the odd tracksuit or T-shirt. However, the trends would change periodically! One minute you were wearing designer sports gear like Fila, Tacchini, Ellesse, Diadora trainers and Lois cords, the next more formal casualwear like Christian Dior blazers, YSL shirts, Cerruti 1881 T-shirts, Farah slacks and moccasin shoes or Burberry/Aquascutum Harrington-style jackets and shirts, corduroy jackets, Armani jumpers and jeans (with the brown suede eagle) and adidas Gazelle trainers. Then it would evolve again to Paisley shirts, leather jackets, West Street perms, C17 baggy jeans and New Balance/Nike or adidas jogging trainers. Then it changed again to the Paninaro look of Burberry wax jackets, Best Company/Classic Nouveaux sweatshirts, diamond socks, bob haircuts, rolled up El Charro jeans and meat pie shoes, then again to Stone Island, Bonneville and CP Company tops, worn out 501s (the influence from the Beastie Boys) or Chippie jeans and Converse baseball boots (Beastie Boys again). Even the hairstyles changed with each look.

So, it went on and on and on. New looks were coming in and new labels like Timberland and Ralph Lauren Polo were becoming more and more popular. One label has stood the test of time throughout, and that is Lacoste (remember Izod Lacoste?) with its range of sportswear and casualwear. At one point my brother and I went through a flares stage, copying the Manchester look. We would wear suede hooded jackets and these 18-inch or 20-inch Levi's corduroy jeans. That only lasted about two weeks or so as we got a lot of stick from our fellow colleagues. If you look around today you will see that the fashion for the hooligan has not changed much in twenty years. It has somewhat stagnated. You still see the Stone Island, the CP

Company, adidas trainers, Aquascutum and Burberry scarves and Lacoste polo tops.

We could adapt a style and it would look good. For example, the black dressers would wear Tacchini tracksuits with Kangol hats, infusing hip-hop styles with the casual look. Most other subcultures were not as dynamic as us. For example, the Goths have not changed their style since their emergence, or the Skinhead with the Fred Perry tops and Doc Martens. However, these subcultures were based around the music that they followed. It was slightly different for us. I mean, most of the lads listened to the likes of Simple Minds, U2 and The Smiths. While the lads were swinging their arms around to 'This Charming Man' in Mr Kiesa's (myself included), I and a few others were rocking to Fonda Rae 'Touch Me' and Change 'Change of Heart'. Do not get me wrong, I thought The Smiths were one of the best bands of the eighties, especially with classics like 'There Is a Light That Never Goes Out' but I could not get into Indie pop to save my life. The soccer casual was a revolution in fashion. Had the casual not appeared, there would not be the fashions that you see now. We would still be walking around in donkey jackets and monkey boots!

I was seventeen and this was my first football match that I was going to. Birmingham away! The date was the 1 October 1983. Even though I wore the gear, I was not truly a casual unless I attended the terraces. I remember the feelings I had that morning, putting on my clothes. Feelings of excitement, nerves and adrenaline all mixed in one. I remember listening to Man Parrish's 'Hip Hop, Be Bop (Don't Stop)' and trying to body pop in the mirror. I wore my Lyle & Scott polo neck with my red Fila BJ Settanta tracksuit top, bleached jeans slit at the bottom and sporting a pair of white Puma G Villas trainers. My hair was permed at the top with a step at the back and a blade four all-round the sides. I recall standing in front of the mirror with my £1 umbrella from Poundstretcher, doing these karate kicks and thinking how cool I looked. 'An Asian dressed like this going to a football match? Will I be the only one?' I thought (well, I was wrong!). My brother Suf looked on and wanted to come but I said no as I was his older brother and did not want to get into any trouble with our parents. After having visited the toilet a couple of times (nerves), I sat there waiting for my friend Kez to come round. Now Kez was my best friend at that time. We went to school together and kept in contact after finishing. Kez was not the best of dressers in terms of being a casual. His dress sense was more like a pop star, the brown suit styled leather jacket, shirt, stretch jeans with pointy shoes! However, he did have the umbrella!

I cannot recall how we knew what time the lads were catching the service train. Casuals never caught the Special train that was for the normal fans and the service train was used to avoid being detected by the police. When we got to the station it was like being on the catwalk. I looked around and saw about our lads all waiting for the train. White, black and Asian. Most were dressed in the gear. Wedge/flick hairstyles, MA1 jackets, diamond Pringle jumpers, Sergio Tacchini tracksuits, Lyle & Scott jumpers and roll-necks, Fila ski jumpers and anoraks, Ellesse, Lois jeans or cords, Farah slacks, Kickers, adidas, Diadora, etc.

It was fantastic to see the colours and the differing styles of casual outfits that were being worn on that day. Some of the older lads were dressed normally, normal being no labels; it was the younger ones that looked the part. I did notice that apart from the Baby Squad there were other, smaller gangs hanging around. The Troopers were a small outfit from the Highfields area of Leicester. They were dressed casually and sported the flat caps. Most of the members were black and were raised in the ghetto. Another gang whom I recognised were The Wongs. These lads were mainly Asian but had an unusual dress code. They wore MA1 green replica jackets, stretch jeans with kung-fu slippers. They also had ginger streaks in their hair. The one thing I can say about these lads was that they were brawlers! They all did some sort of Martial Art and could stand their ground, albeit the dress sense! The Wongs and the Baby Squad never got on, they were a few altercations, but on match day this was not an issue as they had a united enemy, that being the opposing fans. This was the case for other, smaller groups that had a beef with each other; they would leave their differences aside and stand side, by side protecting the honour of their home city against a foreign force.

I was standing there admiring the gear that the dressers were wearing when I saw a mate of mine approach us from our school days. Kez and I were gobsmacked to see our mate Riz. It was like a school reunion! He was a member of the Baby Squad. As I looked around, everybody was relaxed and I could not feel any kind of anxiety around me. It was surreal to think that everybody was travelling just for a fight yet there was no fear on their faces. We got on the train and some of the firm were larking about, while others played cards, some sat there drinking cans of lager. I got some looks from some members of the Baby Squad as I was a new face. Riz gave us a brief rundown of the Zulus. Apparently, they were the biggest and roughest firm in the Midlands, and they had a large black following. I was surprised to hear this as I associated football hooligans with being white and racist. To think that there was a large group of black dressers.

We arrived at New Street station within an hour. Getting off the train and entering the station was like something out of *Vanity Fair*. I was apprehensive as others were. We were on foreign territory and had to keep our wits about us. Everybody in the station was staring at us and to be honest, it felt good! Imagine a bunch of young men nearly all looking smart from differing backgrounds marching through a busy station on a Saturday afternoon! Brilliant! One song was in my head, 'Walking into Sunshine' by Central Line! I think that summed up how I felt at that precise moment.

Out of the station and walking into Birmingham, the adrenaline started to pump. I was looking around and thinking, 'I don't know these lads', 'What do I do when it kicks off?', 'Will we get battered?' We went past a bridge that was connected to the Bullring and I looked up. All I could see was these black lads with big Afros looking down at us. Within a few minutes I hear this black lad named Derek say, 'Here they are, lads.' I look around and see a small mob of Zulu Warriors run down towards us, the same bunch that were looking down at us. Our position was situated at a roundabout next to a dual carriageway and this Brummie lad with ginger hair and a bad case of acne was bouncing – 'Come on then' he was saying. It just kicked off around me. I really did not know what to do or where to start. I just went for the ginger lad with my umbrella, ready to give him a hammer blow when I was lifted off the ground by the scruff of my neck. I turned around to retaliate while still in the air. It was a copper: 'You're nicked, sunshine,' he said. 'My old man is gonna waste me,' I thought. To think this was supposed to be my first football match.

I was put in the meat wagon, a dark blue Ford Transit van with grilles on the windows. Inside were these rows of seats which allowed two people to be seated. Against the window on the other side were single-seater chairs. I was sat on a two-seater chair next to the window. All of a sudden, this black lad named Paddy was thrown in the van. Paddy was a scruffily dressed lad but he could take a beating! (Paddy used to hang around the Haymarket with another black lad called Spider. He would always approach us and say, 'Gimme 10p.') He was getting a hammering from the Old Bill and guess where he was sitting? 'You black bastard, you think you can come here and have a go at our Blues boys?'.' Apparently, he threw a copper on the ground when it was kicking off and damaged his collar bone.

I froze with fear; I was thinking, any minute now they are going to start on me, because I was Asian. The abuse and the beatings continued even when they had more arrests. 'C**n', 'N*****', 'black b*****d' were the taunts as they were laying into him. They drove us to a cop station (I cannot remember which one). Before we were put into our guest room, we were searched. One plain-clothes officer asked me if I was gay! I responded in the negative. They put six of us in one cell together while Paddy was put in a cell on his own (after being dragged in). You can imagine what had happened to him. I sat there in this cell worried about what my father (who had high expectations for me) would do to me when he found out about this.

I sat there and looked at the lads in our cell. Everybody was solemn and glum. No one was talking as we did not know each other. So, I started the conversation with something like 'How long do you think they will keep us here for?' 'Until this evening' was the reply. One of the members of the Wongs was amongst us. He was the only white member. There was this chap whose nickname was Geek. The firm called him this because he may have known everything about casuals or he tried too hard to be a casual. Even though he looked the bollocks, it was his persona that let him down. I got to know him quite well after this and all I can remember about him was his escapades with the 'ladies of the night'. There was also one of the top boys by the name of Grey. Grey was a good lad, there was no arrogance about him as you tend to get with some of the top boys. The others I cannot seem to remember for the life of me. Eventually we got released around about 8pm. It was like a reconnaissance mission getting to the train station! All we needed was the forward rolls. Ducking and diving, getting to a corner of a street and waiting for the all-clear. Paddy was not with us and I am not sure when they released him.

I got in around 10.30; I tried to sneak in but I heard a voice saying, 'What time do you call this? Where have you been all day?' As an Asian I was not allowed out too late, so I had to come clean. 'What was it for? Stealing?' he asked. 'No, Dad, it was for fighting,' I replied. 'Fighting? Well, that's OK, go and get something to eat. And don't do it again.' I was surprised by my dad's reaction. I forgot that my parents came from a tradition of wars and fighting was commonplace amongst the Pathans (or Pashtuns, as the British called them). It was inherent and ran in our blood. So, my father was OK with it.

'Make sure you go to college on Monday and study hard,' my father said to me as he was turning in. What he did not know was that I was thrown out of college three weeks previously for bringing in my ghetto blaster and playing electro sounds of 'Space Cowboy' and 'Playing at Your Own Risk' quite loud in the common room. A teacher came down and told me to turn it down as he was conducting a lesson. So, I did but as soon as he had left, I raised the volume again. So, I was expelled for being disruptive. My father was giving me around a fiver a week for college, which I saved and my dole money would buy me the clothes and trainers I needed to look the part. Furthermore, my father used to give Suf and me money for karate lessons on a Saturday afternoon but once we got the football fever, we stopped going and that money went towards the entrance to get into the ground. We could have got to black belt as we were only two belts away. (Eventually my dad found out and stopped giving me the money for college and karate.) That night I lay in bed thinking what a day I had but I still had not been to a match yet! I had to tell Kez what happened and needed to find out how his day went. He came round the next day and told me what had happened in the ground.

As I got the taste for soccer violence Kez and I seemed to drift away from each other. We became less involved with each other as I dressed as a casual and he did not. He did not want to go to the matches and I did not want to walk around with a lad who did not have the same ideals or dress sense. I had made new friends who shared the same values and expectations. How vain I was – just because he was not a casual, I threw away our friendship. You don't realise this at the time, but I felt embarrassed walking around with him and my attitude changed towards him. I would avoid him at every opportunity; when he rang or came round to my house I would tell my siblings to say I was not at home.

This was the life of the casual and I felt that I had evolved away from what I was before. If I saw someone from school, college or from my estate, I would either try to avoid eye contact or pretend I never saw them. If they called my name, I just blanked them or nodded at them. I did this because they were not casuals. I did not want to be classed as a divvy because of the people I was associated with so the best thing to do was to blank them. Looking back at it now, you realise how shallow it may have been. It may have been superficial but it was real, that is how it was.

In the early eighties being an Asian and wearing designer clothes was a novelty, not many Asians dressed like that. I do not think that there ever was any casual hooligan splinter group like ours anywhere in the country at that time! We had Asians, Europeans, blacks and whites. The beauty of our little crew was that we all got on. They were all good lads and I do not recall any of us falling out in those years. OK, we had the odd argument but it was soon forgotten and we did not hold any grudges towards each other. We never looked at our skin colour or religious differences as we had one thing in common, that being football violence. Finally at last I found a place where I felt I belonged.

Before a game we would all meet at Sav's Chippy and either walk into town or go straight to the ground as Filbert Street was only around the corner. Walking down to the ground, we would usually meet other chaps on the way. Eventually the numbers would swell when hooking up with the main firm.

Our lives seemed to revolve around match day. This was something we all looked forward to – the crowd, the chanting, the atmosphere is nothing like I had experienced before, looking at the opposing fans getting ideas of what we can wear and of course the battles with other casuals, these were the primary reasons most attended.

I got abuse from opposing fans, sneers and offensive words like 'P***' or 'W*g', but I was used to it at school, I became immune to it in and around the ground. Even some Leicester fans would comment, those who were still skinheads. However, the other lads I was with did not like what they were hearing and would always say something back. I found that there was a loyalty when you attended the matches if you were one of the crew and it would go beyond the boundaries of colour.

Eventually a big game came along; it was Manchester United at home. What a day! They swarmed us like bees around honey with so many lads; I have never seen a firm like that in my life! Suf says that he has, when he went to Tottenham away later in the season; he claimed that they had well over a thousand boys! My first encounter with The Red Army was in the city centre before the game. Now Man United also had followers from London who called themselves the Cockney Reds. Apparently, they were quite a large firm of Cockneys, so in totality you can imagine their firm in terms of numbers. Anyway, I was sitting in Brucciani's, an ice cream parlour, with a couple of friends, Kelly, Suf and another lad, Sleepy, sitting by the window that looked onto Belgrave Gate. We were drinking chocolate milkshakes (the best in town) when all these lads walked by. We saw Derek and another black lad whom we recognised as part of the Leicester firm at the front of this mob. We rushed out and started walking with these dressers; they must have numbered around three hundred. So here we are walking towards this roundabout that was at the bottom of Charles Street when another firm came running towards us. It starts to kick off, we try to get towards the front but there were too many chaps in front of us. It was toe-to-toe but it looked like the other fans had the upper hand. Then the Old Bill came and split us up. That other firm came out of a side street, chanting, 'Oo, oo, oo!' (a bit like a noise a monkey is supposed to make). I said to my mates, 'That's Leicester.' It was only at that moment I realised that we were standing right smack bang in the middle of Man U's firm. I looked around and noticed these lads staring at us as I made that statement. 'Shut up,' Kelly said in a low voice. 'We better go before they do us.' So, we sneaked off before they turned on us. That was a close shave. It was a good thing the Old Bill was there.

We were confused, what was Derek doing at the front with Man U's firm? We could not work it out until someone mentioned that he was a Man United fan and he was taking them round to look for the 'pop' with Leicester. The next game no one spoke to him because of this, everyone felt betrayed by his loyalty to Man United. Eventually it was forgotten about in months to come. Anyway, we got ran near enough all day from before the game and after the game. We tried to stand but were overwhelmed by the numbers.

After the game I was stood at the Clock Tower (after being ran several times) when I saw their mob. I got onto a bench and looked to see how many they were. It stretched all the way back to BHS from the Clock Tower that was the whole of Gallowtree Gate! All I saw were lads, loads of them; I could not believe my eyes. They just rushed us, some tried to stand but to no avail. I thought this was a losing battle and took the coward's option: I retreated to a position where I could see what was happening. Don't forget this was still new to me and with a mob like that, I was not going to do a kamikaze and commit suicide yet.

After watching these lads charge us in all directions, I decided to call it a day. It was no use, there were too many of them. I got scared and retreated further back. Eventually, I grabbed Suf and I just ran. I knew the Old Bill was there but that did not matter, I just kept running until I could not hear the noise, the sounds of stamping feet, shouts and screams from the innocent bystanders. When I got home I just sat there thinking, 'Why didn't I steam in? Why did I get scared?' This kept going through my mind. 'You were protecting your younger brother,' I thought. I was just looking for an excuse. I could not accept the fact that I bottled it. I sat there dying a thousand deaths. I kept rethinking what I could have done. However, I was still buzzing from the day, what mixed emotions! When I met the lads at Sav's a couple of days later all those thoughts and feelings went as we sat there talking about that day. I soon forgot and realised that everybody gets scared, especially with a mob like that. We were just looking forward to the next game. We knew we got ran, it's just one of those things when you follow a club – you can have a good day or have a bad one. It was part and parcel of soccer violence.

After attending more football games, you tended to become more confident with yourself, it was like playing football for the first time and after playing it several times you would get the feel for it. This was just like football violence. The running, the clothes, the shouting, the charging and the fisticuffs became normality. This organised chaos was the ultimate high. It was addictive, more addictive than any drug. If we did not attend a match, you would be on a 'downer' or going through 'cold turkey' until you got your next fix. Your next fix would be to attend a match or buy a new item of clothing.

The casual became associated with violence and fashion, it was not just about the clothes that you wore but also if your crew could stand their ground. Designer gear and violence came hand in hand like husband and wife. Expensive smart clothing was worn in order to evade the police, who would be on the lookout for the traditional supporter who wore the colours of their club. There were numerous crews or firms, each football club had one, and some were formidable while others were virtually non-existent. The most formidable crews being Manchester United's the Red Army, West Ham's ICF, Leeds Service Crew, Portsmouth's 6.57 Crew, Birmingham City's Zulu Warriors and Millwall Bushwackers. These crews and others wreaked havoc up and down the country. The biggest firm in numbers was The Red Army and the most notorious the ICF and the Bushwackers (formerly The Treatment).

The overwhelming majority of casuals were white, some middle class but mainly working-class young men. Within certain crews there was a small ethnic minority division. However, there were the odd crews that had a large ethnic faction, the primary crew would be the Zulu Warriors whose bulk of members consisted of an Afro-Caribbean background. Another crew would be the Tottenham Yids, whose members were supposedly from a Jewish background. Then you had other crews that had a smaller number of ethnics, like the Man City Cool Cats (or Mayne Line Service Crew), Villa Youth (or C Crew), Arsenal Gooners, Derby Lunatic Fringe (DLF) and Section Five (West Brom). It went to the extent where some crews had ethnics as top boys. Birmingham, Arsenal, West Ham, Leicester, Aston Villa and Derby all had black casuals at the forefront of violence. Some were infamous with the likes of Cass Pennant, Danny Brown and the one-eyed Barrington. I have witnessed myself different races on the terraces even to the extent of seeing a Far Eastern Middlesbrough casual.

However, none of the above or anywhere in England had an Asian following like Leicester City had. Birmingham had a very small number (I cannot recall seeing any) as with West Brom (I saw one) and Arsenal had one Asian (or was he an Arab?). We at Leicester had at least twenty-five members who were Asian. Although we may have belonged to smaller outfits or splinter groups, on match day we became part of the Baby Squad. The Baby Squad was allegedly named after a police officer saw a young group of teenagers and he commented, 'What's this? The Baby Face Gang?' The name stuck. I do not know how true this account is but this is what I have heard. The members of the Baby Squad came from various areas in and around Leicester. They mostly came from the Netherhall and Thurnby Lodge areas. Some came from Oadby, Anstey, Braunstone, Saffron Lane, New Parks, St Matthews, St Marks, St Peters, Knighton and Beaumont Leys. Other lads came from Hinckley and areas in Leicester-shire like Earl Shilton. Some groups had names like the YTS, MMA and the BBB. We all came under the umbrella of the Baby Squad. On a good day at Filbert Street we could muster up to six hundred or more lads. Some were from prosperous backgrounds while others came from poor backgrounds. There were all walks of life and we would band as one group on a Saturday afternoon (or the odd Wednesday night) with no boundaries in terms of social status, race, colour or religion.

THE FASHION, LOOK AND LABELS

In the summer of 1980, we had seen probably the greatest Wimbledon final in its history with the Fila of Borg overcoming the Tacchini of McEnroe to capture a fifth consecutive Men's Singles title. In 1981 McEnroe turned the tables and by the following year, Borg had retired. But these two memorable games were to be etched in our minds for ever. It wasn't the tennis but the sportswear that was to be our inspiration.

Taking a lead from Borg's sartorial elegance meant 1981/82 became a season of top European sports brands. It is this period when the London clubs introduced a more sporting feel to the fashion, with brighter colours and tracksuits pressed home the golf look, and by the 'mid-1980s there were brands which were almost essentials and others which varied from crew to crew. Stone Island and CP jackets were essential, as well as vintage Adidas trainers. Fila BJ, Ellesse, Sergio Tacchini and Lacoste track tops also grew in popularity. Tennis chic is the look which has probably defined the casual look more than any other. Before too long, the likes of Armani, Burberry, Aquascutum, Berghaus, Fiorucci and Lois were soon being added to the wardrobe.

A crew or V-neck Pringle draped over a Lacoste Polo or Lyle Scott roll-neck. Ball, Ciao and C17 jeans. Best company sweatshirts, Cerutti and Kickers shoes, Giorgio Armani. Footwear: Trimm Trab, Forest Hills, Samba, Mamba, Hawaii, Gazelle, Stan Smiths, and Diadora.

The reason these fantastic labels weren't available at home was mainly due to there being no agents set up in the UK. Therefore, the independent shops would need to travel to France or Italy to make purchases and with times being so hard and money so tight, it was a gamble not worth taking. Therefore, our football fans became the importers, bringing back designerwear, knowing that back home the demand far outweighed the supply.

The football casual subculture wasn't about being politically led. Many casuals within the same crews had varying left-wing, right-wing and liberal political views. Nor was it driven by one type of musical style. There's a wide spectrum of musical styles that many football casuals enjoy. Varying from original Mod, revivalist Mod, ska, dub, indie rock, rave, nu-rave, Madchester, punk, post-punk – oi, and even more. Football casual culture had the allure for many of these other musical followers of being able to cross over to the casual – side – and many of them did. Was it a fashion thing? Almost – certainly – but not at first. It was a general look thing, which then transformed into a label slave thing. Was it a violence thing? Yes, but it was more of a by-product of the – one-upmanship – a necessity to show that your crew were number one, both in the fashion – and violence stakes. Violence and fashion were the key – battlefields – but under the banner of the team you supported.

If the casual's joy was being from the terraces, then its demise was always going to be when run off it in the authority's inevitable clampdown in the aftermath of Heysel in 1985. Those that believe the movement started with the Scouse need no convincing the tragic events of Heysel and Bradford then later Hillsborough marked out the football casuals as a subversive threat to the establishment. The Popplewell Inquiry was prior to the Taylor Report of 1990 into crowd control and safety at sports grounds and its effect on football so it came as no surprise that in between police conducted high-profile dawn raids on some of Britain's most notorious terrace casuals. A cull was taking place at the time: the original trendsetters felt their movement had become too mainstream and that people had lost the plot with the awful shell suits. It was time to dress down than end it like that. The South muscled in on an emerging rave scene while Manchester became Madchester and let everyone know that not since the Beatles had the Scouse anything over them to be kings of the cool, still smarting at claims the football casual was born on Merseyside.

PORTSMOUTH 6.57 CREW

'YOU COULDN'T GO TO SOME NORTHERN OUTPOST AND LOOK SCRUFFY'

EDDIE CRISPEN, PORTSMOUTH:

I remember back in the late '70s we were in the Mod or ska movement and we had quite a lot of the soul boys back in the day wearing braces to the football. Also travelling around the country and seeing what the other team's lads were wearing. I remember coming out of the skinhead thing and going a bit more Mod-ish, there were people wearing flight jackets, Lonsdale sweaters and then it went into adidas kick trainers.

I'd have been about eighteen at the time in 1980. You'd see someone who had something good on, ask 'em where they got it and they would say London. So, you'd go down there, see something different, get it and come back and someone else would ask you the same question.

Portsmouth's a small place but you'd have all your

little pockets. Someone in another part of the city would have a golf top on and they'd say they got it in the golf shop, you'd all go up there and tax the shop and then everyone would be wearing the golf jumpers. I suppose it was also down to the music scene; there were still some people into the punk scene and they were still wearing that stuff.

ROB SILVESTER, PORTSMOUTH: It sort of evolved from kick trainers into straight jeans, Fred Perry T-shirts and then it evolved from the bottom up. Safari coats, but that was early '80s – we were getting away from the Mod and rude boy scene into what is now known as the casuals. I was lucky my dad lived in London at the time and he had an account with Austin Reed, so happy days! I remember walking around in a Lacoste top, a long-sleeved one a hockey top, I think they called 'em. I thought I was the bollocks. You'd go to another ground and see someone in a different colour and then you'd think, that's what I'll get for my next Christmas present.

EDDIE: I remember I bought a Gabicci top, which was one of the first things I'd ever bought with the gold G on the pocket. It was all about oUnitedoing the next person and having something better on.

PAUL CHANDLER, PORTSMOUTH: For me, I was still a skinhead until 1980 so was still wearing Lonsdale jackets and flight jackets and from there, it evolved into Pringle jumpers and all that.

ROB: Gear that was two a penny now was more exclusive then. Take Fila, you can get it two a penny now but back in those days, the royal family members used to wear Fila skiing at Cloisters.

EDDIE: I think before the Pringles came in everyone was wearing Slazenger jumpers and Patrick jumpers and cagoules.

PAUL: Remember the jeans were quite tight so in a way it was really easy to fray or split 'em at the bottom.

ROB: Even Nike trainers, the proper running shoes were being resold as casual shoes.

PAUL: I bought a pair of Nike Flames, which were a pair of running shoes with the soul moulded down and the spikes taken out. It was just to be a bit different, really.

EDDIE: And then deer stalker hats came in, didn't they?

ROB: Some firms always labelled us with those suede poncho jackets, patchwork of different suedes and leathers. When we were in London, people always said we looked like a London firm. We didn't care as long as we felt the part and looked the part and more importantly, we were the part – the way you look empowers you as a firm.

EDDIE: Back then, it was a big part of it. I remember going to Preston in the early '80s, and I think Bill Routledge, the Preston lad, put it in his book and he said that he'd never seen a firm like it, he said they got off the train and they were like an army. There was no singing or chanting, they looked like they knew what they were there to do. He said they knew from then they would have to get their act together.

ROB: Don't forget in the early '80s we were in the Third Division so we never came across any big teams but everyone knew who we were.

EDDIE: I remember going to a game and we pulled in at Crewe and Liverpool stations and we still had on Pringle and stuff, and they had what you would describe as a geography teacher's jacket on and Paisley shirts and wedge haircuts. That probably caught on down our way about two years later.

ROB: The thing was, we were just a small South Coast team and they were used to going to Europe and seeing what was going on there and some of 'em were grafting (thieving) over there as well.

EDDIE: The thing with going to Europe was a team like Liverpool would come back and another team would see their fans and then think, we'll have to change our look now.

PAUL: We couldn't buy none of the clothes we wanted down here. We'd have to go up to London to get them 'cos it was so poor down here.

EDDIE: We lived in Portsmouth, we were in our late teens and early twenties, so we used to go to Bournemouth, Brighton and sometimes up to London for the shops. I remember one Christmas going to Chesterfield, we got an early train went up to Shepherd's Bush and bought some Björn Borg Diadora trainers, left the old ones in the locker at Euston station and carried on up to Chesterfield!

PAUL: We also used to go down the Walworth Road in south London and if you meet anyone … Well, if you couldn't get into the violence with 'em, they'd just take the piss out of you, saying, what are you lot wearing? That's so last year sort of thing. You'd say to 'em, you've got your mum's jumper on and all that. I suppose it goes back to that one-upmanship sort of thing – if you weren't fighting them then you'd use other ways?

EDDIE: I remember going to Chesterfield one year and one of our lots who won't want to be named as he's got a good job now! One of our lots had a brand-new Armani jumper on and all the Chesterfields were still dressing like punks and skinheads. He was giving it the big one to 'em, saying, look at you lot, I've got Armani on here and this will cost you a month's wages up here! One of them got the hump and produced this bottle of ink and slung it over the fence. It went straight over his jumper and it was ruined!

ROB: If you wanted to be part of the firm and go to the football then you were a football casual, there was no good being a Mod if you didn't wear Mod gear. It didn't make you any harder or braver but you had to do it.

EDDIE: The good thing was if you wanted to, you could swap something or sell something you'd had to someone else and vice versa. You'd be thinking nice one if you got a thirty-quid jumper for twenty-five or twenty quid.

ROB: There was a lot of people going in the golf shops at the time to buy the gear, I don't think they knew anything about golf! A bit how Millwall dressed all the time. When we first saw Millwall in 1981, the original Bushwackers and they all had walking sticks and you remember thinking, Millwall, south London they looked the bollocks, and they were the bollocks and they all had on frayed Lois jeans and walking sticks and it made you wonder if the top five in England were wearing that gear, then we should all be wearing it.

How you look is as important as anything, you wanna look smart and it's not like you're going to oUnitedo each other as in the firm but you want to look good, you're meeting on the 6:57 train and everyone was going what you got on. It wasn't like anyone would say you're not going 'cos it was safety in numbers. You want to walk the walk and if you can't beat the best then you want to look like you can. But dressing it and doing it though are two different things and there was a lot of people coming home gutted with missing buttons and ripped clothes. Loads of stories of people's clothes getting ruined and you're talking about half a week's wages at the time down the drain. It was an expensive day out but you still went again the next week.

It brought people together – you could see someone and know straight away that they lived up north 'cos of what they were wearing and same down south. I mean, at the time pubs weren't open all day like they are now. You stayed round your manor on a Friday, went to a couple of house parties, bumped into all the other mobs. Everyone got on well, as we had football the next day and that was more important. We played football together, cricket, done some fundraisers. I mean, a few of our boys have passed away over the years and we've got together and sorted things out for them, everyone gets on well. On a Friday or Thursday, it would be 'seen you on Saturday, make sure you are on the 6.57, see you there.'

The 6.57 is obviously the three minutes to seven train that will get you to London for half past eight, get your connection by 9 o'clock – you can be any-where by 11 o'clock. At that time, there weren't a lot of firms that had names. One of our lads wrote a letter into *Face* magazine to say who we were and what we had done. Everyone associated with the 6.57 Crew was a football casual and everyone was wearing the clothes, Farah trousers, Burberry and anything that had an exclusive look to it.

You didn't really respect anyone for what they wore, it was what they did on the day. It was still who your mates were and what you did, it didn't matter what you had on. I'd rather have two punk rockers on my side than a couple of casuals who were going to run away. The northern lads had their different fashions – you had the likes of Liverpool but we never came across them as we were in the Second and Third Divisions. In terms of violence and clothes we were as well matched as anyone we came across.

Millwall always looked good, they were scruffy with an elite edge to them – I always thought they looked the part. Any London club and it seemed strange some teams were into it and others took a while to catch on. Millwall were the best to me though.

We got to know some Millwall lads and did our bit in making the film, *The Firm*. A friend introduced me to film director Nick Love: he wanted to use Portsmouth seafront because it still had a Wimpey on it and looked quite '80s. They wanted to use all the 18–25-year-olds to wear this clobber, Nick Love has got a big thing for Fila. The film did what it did, it portrayed it a bit over-the-top. Not everyone had the gear in real terms, it wasn't all dressers – if there was a hundred people there then probably about 60 to 70 per cent had dresser gear on. There were still a lot of punks/Mods involved.

All I did was coordinate some fight scenes. They asked me to come down as I'd had a bit of aggro with Millwall in the past. I was teaching the Portsmouth actors how to bounce up and down – don't forget you're on film and that, they would warn. But they did use real police dogs and a friend of mine put his hand too near the dog and it bit his finger off!

The acid house rave scene quelled the violence for a couple of years. I wrote a chapter in my book, *Rolling With the 6.57 Crew*, about a break for love in the late '80s – 1988/89. We went from rowing with Millwall to being in their club and everyone being loved-up, talking about it rather than come on then, let's have it – it was violence but on a peaceful thing.

It didn't bring an end to it, I don't think – there were still people that didn't want it to end, some people down here didn't want nothing to do with going up there (south London). Some people benefited from it, with DJs coming down from London and playing here. There was money to be earnt and you were talking about 5,000 people at a rave at a tenner a ticket, serious money, and it worked that way for a while but after the break for love, it all started again with the fashion side.

The clothes went to the Stone Island marina stuff as long as it was big and baggy as you were dancing for twelve hours a day. You didn't want skintight Gabicci, but Pringle sports gear – you wanted a bit of extra room. People wanted bigger stuff to wear, all the sporting gear that was out now, Tacchini tracksuits. I mean you were sweating your nuts off at the end of the day and you just wanted something loose.

It was just another period and some of us were hanging out together with Millwall. I think it was an England game connection and we went to see Pink

Floyd at Wembley and talked to some girls who were talking about acid house and also from talking to some geezers who were just there to dance about and get off their nuts. We met the Millwall lads and they invited us to their club in Millwall territory and the rest is history!

You all get on, mainly because there was money to be made, and when they came down here to do their raves, everyone did earn some money.

EDDIE: Portsmouth was the most disorganised organised firm ever. We used to get off the train at Waterloo and you had firms going everywhere. We saw Marilyn one week and we saw Mark Almond and we were rocking him in his van – it was just one of those mad stories and all football fans had these stories.

Once we all went to Cambridge and we said we'll all go on push bikes. We got off at Waterloo and went across to Liverpool Street. West Ham were playing at Norwich, and I always remember Taffy Aldridge saying this will never catch on Pompey! He thought we were trying to get one-upmanship on them! We all went for a drink in Cambridge and threw our bikes in a pile outside the pub and some Japanese tourists started taking photos of them! I said to them it was modern art and they were all going, 'Ooooohhhh!' You always get a good story from an away game.

We were in the Second Division then and we used to get a lot of respect. We went up to Newcastle and they'd never seen a team get straight off the train before we did a couple of their pubs by the station and they were all wearing flares and that! You'd feel brilliant, you'd be on the train with all your mates and you would be winding each other up but when you got there you were like an army. You felt invincible. Good days.

I remember we went to Cardiff and if we didn't go on the train, we'd go in vans. On the way up we had egg fights between the vans. After the game there were three lads in the front and twenty in the back and the lads in the front said, there's fifty Cardiff here. They said they would give us a tap when we got next to them and they opened the shutter and we got out and ran Cardiff. We chased 'em round the corner and ran into some police. We ran back and got back into the van and then there was a knock on the door and it was someone saying, 'Open this door!' We all said there was no one there but next thing, the door opened and there was a copper there. He threw this Alsatian dog into the van, and it was bedlam, he started biting my arm and I was more worried about my Pringle sweater than I was with the state of my arm! We all had to sit cross-legged on the pavement and then someone started singing 'Oops Upside Your Head' and we all did the dance. The copper went mental and said, get back in the van and if you stop before the Severn Bridge, then you are all nicked!

PAUL: One of our friends used to go to different games and he clocked some of the clothes that the other teams were wearing. What I was wearing at the time was coming to the end so I started looking at what was coming in. It was all skinny clothes which suited me as I was like a pipe cleaner. It would be all Lois jeans and pac macs and you would look like a pipe cleaner!

I wanted some nice clothes and was always on the lookout for clothes you couldn't buy in Portsmouth, it was a very poor area and you had to look at different areas. You didn't think about it at the time, I can't think of much taxing. I remember seeing some Millwall getting off a train in these jelly sandals that your mum would get you to take on holiday. We were like what the fuck are you wearing?

Everyone going to the football at the time was about eighteen to twenty and we were moving up the divisions together as we were getting older. It was always evolving but it did start off with this really slim look, tightest jumpers, stuff evolved from golf, tennis. The clothes were so expensive at the time, you'd pay forty pounds for a cardigan in 1980/81. I mean, Lacoste has kept on with the inflation but other brands like Tacchini, I mean you can buy a Tacchini T-shirt for ten to fifteen pounds today, which is less than we used to pay for them then!

Late '70s, I had a wedge when we were into David Bowie and at the time people had just long straggly hair. Our style was changing every two to three months. Some people did have some dodgy haircuts as there were only two or three hairdressers who could do a proper wedge!

As a casual you did really stand out as you couldn't get a lot of the clothes in this area. We were always in large groups so we didn't really get any problems. It wasn't like years before with the punks and the Mods fighting, as a casual you were alright. It was mental, I was earning good money at the time. I'd give my mum a fiver and have ninety quid and then spend a hundred quid on an Armani jumper. The only reason I could afford it was because I was so tight with my mum. I was earning more than my dad at the time, I think, which was quite embarrassing as he was bringing up six of us! I had mates who could acquire stuff for me cheaply. I had three important things I would spend money on: football, clothes and music. I can't even say which order, they were all important to me and there was nothing left of my money at the end of the week. I got smashed a few times but I didn't care as long as my clothes were alright. I mean, my clothes, man!

ROB: It was the '85 season and we came up with this idea. At the time we were getting watched a lot by the police and we were one of the first teams to come up with the idea of having police spotters. It was King and Hiscock, I think. Anyway, we were away at Cardiff, and we had had a lot of bother with them, so we thought there's no way we'll get away from the police in Cardiff. So, we had all these invitations done up for this wedding and we all dressed up smart on the day in Aquascutum blazers and Farah trousers and we got on the train. We got off in Bristol and let the rest of the firm go ahead and we had a drink.

When we finally got there, we headed out of the station and bumped into the police. They asked us where we were going and we said to a wedding in St

Thomas's. They asked us who was getting married and we said Mick and Julie but someone else had already said Simon and Tracey! We were in the ground by 1 o'clock 'cos the police marched us in there! The other lads had it off but our plan had gone tits up. The picture of us in the police federation booklet was us lot in our blazers, we looked smart!

JAKE PAYNE, PORTSMOUTH: I had left home by the time the 6.57 Crew started but I knew all the boys. I had gone away to work in Minehead Butlins 'cos I kept getting into trouble and wanted to stay out of trouble. When I left in 1979, I was a bit of a dresser and was wearing different clothes to what my mates had on. I was wearing pod shoes and Lacoste and they was still into Mod and skinhead stuff. Going to Minehead was like going to the Third World – I couldn't buy any clothes down there. I don't know if they even had any shops, to be honest. When I came back, I went to Pompey against Wolves and I saw loads of the Pompey boys going into the stands wearing blazers and Farah trousers and I couldn't work it out, I was that isolated from the fashion scene.

I was living all over the place at the time. I lived in Somerset and Torquay and there were always firms down there from everywhere. I used to see lots of Scousers in Nike hooded zip-ups, robbing the Pringle gear! It was all about representing your city when you went away, other people might not understand it but that's how we felt. The way you look when you go away gives other firms the chance to look at you and see what you're about. My mates were still Mods when I left Pompey and coming back was a real eye-opener. You really dressed to impress in those days.

We were all about the same age and some of the lads could afford the top gear and the rest of them thieved it so everyone had it! You have to look the part and get off that train looking sharp. You couldn't go to some northern outpost and look scruffy. If you looked the same then you were together.

EDDIE: We was playing Arsenal, first game Charlie Nicholas played for 'em. After the game we had a mate who lived near Fratton Park and we used to go and watch the football results round his. We saw some Arsenal break out the police escort and run up the road. There was fifteen of us and we steamed into Arsenal, who were wearing flight jackets. Now you have to remember this is Portsmouth in the '80s, we hardly ever saw a black person and suddenly we had all these big black geezers bouncing through, wearing braces and tracksuits and it was Denton and his lot. We were like, what the fuck's happening here? We had never seen a black firm at football before but once we finished talking about that we were on about the clothes they had on, going, they did look smart, didn't they?, and it got us thinking.

GOONERS

'SO WE HAVE GOT A LITTLE MOB OVER HERE'

MAN U

GOONER/ARSENAL: The first game I ever went to was with my dad in 1969 and we went to every Arsenal home and away game that entire season. The year we won the Inter-City Fairs Cup, I was nine and had my first drink. All the fans were celebrating out on the streets and as we were walking past the Plimsoll Pub, someone was throwing crates of beer into the street. Anyway, I ended up with a bottle of beer in my hand.

When I was about twelve, I've stood on the North Bank with all the boys. As I got older, I moved to the Clock End, where we would stand next to the opposition's fans and normally it would go off. There's far too many to rows to recall, but one that springs to mind was when we were playing Man United at home. Just for the crack, a group of us in our home end started singing, 'United'. The Old Bill moved in and chucked about 120 of us onto the edge of the pitch and began escorting towards the Clock End, where the main bulk of the Macs were packed. As we got nearer, they began to chant, 'We're proud of you, we're proud of you,' etc., etc. The ones at the front of their lot had a look of fear on their faces as they had cottoned on we weren't Mancs that had just been trying to take the North Bank. The police opened the gates and threw us in with them and an almighty row started. We ran them back up the terraces and the Old Bill jumped in with the right hump because we'd taken the piss. They rounded us up and threw us out of the ground.

QPR

QPR away in the early 1980s. We had a bit of an ongoing thing with some geezers from west London. It all stemmed from Friday nights at the Lyceum. When we played Rangers away, we all met up in a pub over near Highbury; some people puffed, some took Charlie, the same as any other firm in the country. What goes on in the pubs near the ground on the day of a game is just the same as what goes on in anybody's local boozer on any day of the week. Plus, it was always a good excuse to meet up early, about 400 of us got off the Tube at Latimer Road. As we tried to squeeze and push our way out of the exit, the first half a dozen out onto the street were quickly set upon and laid out by the waiting west London herberts. We charged out and fanned out as they backed off twenty yards. Now there was a lot more space in which to fight. Weapons were drawn and being used. The only thing I never saw was a gun, that will give you some idea of the objects of self-defence on display. There were little personal duels going on all over the street. We were pushing them back, slowly at first, and then a roar filled the air as we had them on their toes. We carried on moving at a brisk pace.

Up ahead about 200 yards was a pub, we smashed every window as they came out and regrouped. We again scattered them in every direction. Every now and again small pockets of them would return with a new assortment of weapons and mount another attack and we, in turn, would give in to them. A few local women came out onto the streets and shouted 'Scum!' and other insults at us. The Old Bill turned up and restored some order and herded us off towards the ground. After the game, a few of our boys were caught on the Tube by a mob of Rangers and were gassed.

MILLWALL

The 'bonkers' afternoon when violent fans terrorised Highbury and if you supported Arsenal or had an N5 postcode in 1988, it's almost certain you'll remember the Battle of Highbury. Some 500 specially trained police officers were unable to contain terrifying violence as Arsenal and Millwall fans clashed.

There were 48 arrests, and 60 people thrown out of the ground. A Tube train was smashed up at Arsenal station. Two pubs – the Arsenal Tavern in Blackstock Road and Plimsoll Arms in St Thomas's

Road – were completely wrecked. The Plimsoll Arms was left without a single window. A police officer suffered a broken leg when a fan forced him off balance and then jumped on him. And cops were pelted with so many coins inside the stadium that they later collected £13.59 for their kitty.

An Arsenal fan told the press:

You could feel something in the air. It felt nasty.

The Clock End was properly rammed with 12,000 Millwall fans. In those days, Arsenal would only get about 30,000 people at games, so you would know the familiar faces. But there was this big mob of geezers in the North Bank I'd never seen before.

I don't know if it was before or after kick-off, but there was this massive roar of 'MILLWALL!' It just went bonkers and these blokes in the North Bank kicked off on anyone they could find. And this revved up everyone in the Millwall end, too.

I remember walking back to Finsbury Park after the game, and every window in the Plimsoll Arms in St Thomas's Road had been smashed up. It was pretty crazy.

This was, don't forget, at the height of football hooli-ganism. And it went without saying that Millwall had a 'reputation'. 'Their fans wanted to prove themselves, off the pitch, as a top-level club. No one remembers the actual game on the pitch.' Arsenal won 2–0.

The local *Islington Gazette* spoke to Arsenal Tavern landlady, Jeanette Moynihan:

We'd been warned by police that there might be trouble, [she told the paper in 1988], but we never expected anything like what happened.

Everything erupted about 1.30p.m. We heard shouting and chanting. People suddenly started surging forward. It was the most frightening thing of my life.

They slashed seats and threw glasses at each other. Within seconds, we didn't have one glass left.

One woman climbed onto a pool table and started telling who to hit who. People were diving behind the bar to try and escape and one of the windows was broken by a customer trying to get away from it all.

It was like another world – and yet the whole thing was over in about five to eight minutes

The *Gazette* spoke to another Gooner, who has worked in Islington since 1983, asking if he could recall the violence.

'Yes, I do remember it,' a stern-faced Jeremy Corbyn replied instantly.

'I wasn't at the match but I certainly picked it up the day after. The Plimsoll Arms pub was trashed by Millwall supporters – absolutely shocking. A shocking event in the history of our borough.'

PARIS ST GERMAIN (PSG)

PSG out in France in about '93 was legendary. There must have been about 350 of us that caught the night boat across the Channel and arrived in Paris at 8 o'clock on the morning of the game. Some went off to put their bags away and check into hotels, the rest of us went straight out on the piss. About 11 o'clock we all met up again. After a while groups went off to the stadium to try to buy some tickets. Soon people were coming back saying it was going off between our lot and small mobs of the French and apparently the Frogs were right up for it.

At about 3.30pm, about 400 of us jump on the Metro and get off the stop before the stadium. We march through the streets, a real tight mob, one of the best in years we've put together. Just before the stadium we come to a square. A few Frogs in ones and twos have tried a few suicide attacks and have been well battered, but up in front of us appears a mob, it's about even numbers. They walk towards us and a roar goes up. We charge and the PSG firm scatter in every direction; a few of their older lot that have had the bottle to stand for the fight get hammered. We are now in the middle of the square, the side roads leading in to it soon fill up with bodies all heading our way. It's game on as the two sets of fans steam into one another. There seems now to be thousands of the bastards coming at us from every direction. Blokes are being knocked to the ground, we're being pushed back by the sheer weight of their numbers. Some of our lot are getting hit with bottles and all sorts of weaponry and I can see a few of the boys covered in blood. People are bent over double trying to catch their breath, but there's no time, you have to fight to survive. There's no police intervention, they're too busy filming the action. The row goes on for about 45 minutes with injuries on both sides. Slowly, the fighting fizzles out and about 200 of us find ourselves with no Old Bill walking up a narrow side street next to the ground. We pass a few bars and the occupants spill out onto the pavement. We look at one another, everyone's thinking, here we go again. Most are exhausted from the first marathon row, but it's got to be done.

A few windows go in and the whole street becomes a mass of angry Frenchmen. I think we've disturbed a hornets' nest here and it's soon toe-to-toe combat. We don't budge an inch, aided by the fact the road is narrow and we're fighting in a bit of a bottleneck. A tear gas canister lands in the middle of the warring hoards and the Old Bill come steaming in, batons drawn, lashing out at anyone within striking distance. A few heads are split and cracked open as they herd everyone up, with dogs straining at the leashes. The fun's over as we're all deported back to England.

To me, since Euro '96, the game of football no longer belongs to the real fans, it's now all about families and corporate entertainment. It's all changed now, gone are the days when just the lads went to the away games. It's now the sad face of football, and it's become boring. The players, managers and coaches and chairman are not loyal. All that kissing the badge on their shirts when they score, it's all bollocks. The only loyal people in football are the fans. That's a fact.

No, our days of organised turnouts are now over. Now it's too easy to get nicked. I'm of the mind if the

Old Bill are around, do nothing except for Tottenham the Yids of course, all day long. They're not on our level as a football club but I still like to learn the Yids' result before I hear the Arsenal score. If the Yids lose, I buy everyone a drink.

WEST HAM U5S

'WE WERE FLASH ARROGANT LITTLE BASTARDS'

DD, WEST HAM UNITED: I was born in 1965 in Hackney but my mum left there when I was ten months old and we moved to West Ham and lived near the station there. When I was about four, I remember my old man coming around and he took me older brother down the Bobby Moore shop, which was a right big thing at the time because he was a legend. My older brother came back with a pair of West Ham socks and I was gutted my father never took me. In 1970, we moved to Plaistow and I remember my mum buying me my first West Ham shirt and I can recall getting a bit of chalk and drawing the number 6 on the back, got to say I felt ten feet tall having this shirt on my back.

In the coming years I went to a few home games with my uncles. I remember Sunderland fans getting run through the west side but after we won the cup in 1975, I remember my dad taking me and my brother to Norwich away, 1975/76 season, we lost 1–0, with Ted McDougal scoring the goal. I remember their Carrow Road ground had big sliding doors with the fans wearing flares, long hair and scarves around their wrists, and when West Ham lost, it kicked off everywhere. I remember the Norwich fans spilled onto the pitch and the fighting would not stop. I was quite frightened as a kid in one way being I was only ten, but in another way, I was fascinated by the power of it and felt half-hooked on the buzz. Later, as things went on, I would hear the stories whenever my brother would come home with nicked scarves, fucking Arsenal, Tottenham but his Millwall one was his pride and joy. I would hear him telling my sister's boyfriend about West Ham and the football violence so I always wanted to go.

I remember when I was a kid and I used to play for my school team in Canning Town. I used to stand over West Ham at twelve years of age and I used to think, do I want to play football for this team or do I want to fight for them on the terraces? The fighting was that much of a buzz that each was appealing as the other. It wouldn't have mattered if I played for the team, won cups or anything because the fighting meant that much as well. I was split down the middle, I wasn't bothered which way I went.

I was fourteen coming up fifteen when we won the FA Cup and I can always remember coming home that day and going into Raffles pub for my first drink with my mates and just crying my fucking eyes out with the emotion of it on that day, it was just unbelievable.

And it was the following season, and I don't know now if it was the Charity Shield or the League Cup Final. I was fifteen years of age. For some reason – we were only kids – we got off at the Embankment. And you look around and everyone's got West Ham scarves. All of a sudden, they've gone 'Millwall!'

and just started hitting people, they were hitting kids. Anyway, from what I remember of it from there they've gone down to Trafalgar Square. So, me and me mate said we'll go there because West Ham were coming back on the Tube, and we were on one of the trains behind. So, we've gone mental, on the hunt for Millwall. We come out the station, there's a full-on firm of West Ham and we've gone two different ways. I was with the lot who gone down to this one pub. And the other lot we got split up with, they've come back up, and we found them at this pub and battered them. The Old Bill had to get in and save them. Everyone was just smiley faces. It was the early lot that got back first from Wembley and got tugged by Millwall and it was a big mistake for them to stay around in Trafalgar Square.

When we clinched promotion that 1980/81 season, the Under-Fives was formed. It was Cambridge at home and I had nearly got kicked out for having a fight but managed to slip away. There was five of us including myself, and we were thinking what to call ourselves, Mini Snipers, Mini ICF, all boring ideas, then someone said 'Under-Fives' and it stuck from there. The others who I can't mention, all them came after. It was a buzz and I've always said as years have gone on that you would rather be caught by the ICF, the older firm, because they would give you a clump and kick shit out of yer but that would be it. But if you got caught by the Under-Fives, you would get beat up, cut, money took, clothes took and kicked all over the place. Yeah, humiliated, set alight and fucking gobbed on. We were flash arrogant little bastards, looking back in hindsight.

Going football was a buzz, I was just hooked. I was on a train going to Birmingham New Street but there was something wrong with the rail track, so the train pulled in at some dodgy stop in the middle of nowhere, think it was Tring, where they kicked us all off, and there were three coaches laid on for us all there. I remember the coach drivers says where do we want to go, so someone tells him Luton v Arsenal because we're all Arsenal.

Now I will tell the start of this from my other mate's recollection, which was he was having a piss on the station when he sees one of the coaches pulling out, so he runs alongside and just about gets on by the skin of his teeth when he looks up to see it was me driving it. Now I remember getting on this coach and getting in the empty driver's seat for a laugh, looking around and seeing all the boys egging me on, so I started it up but what I had to do was put my foot on the accelerator and turn the key while it was in gear because it was on a bit of a hill when it started chugging and began to pick up speed. I remember hitting about two cars, seeing a woman with her daughter in a car petrified. I just scraped their car and some parked cars and got down the road, screeched up, jumped out and slipped off.

We ended up going Luton Arsenal, got in the visitors' end, not everyone but enough, waited for the first Arsenal to come in, smashed them everywhere and the Old Bill just come in and escorted us out. I can remember the whole ground singing, 'We Hate Them Bastards in Claret and Blue' even Luton was singing, 'Chim chimney, chim chiminey, chim cher-oo! We hate them bastards in claret and blue.' Brilliant.

One time, I remember the Gooners, they had joined up with Millwall at Euston, King's Cross, and they wanted to cut us all up. There was only a few of us, the Old Bill was trying to kick us out and they came running out after us. I remember a geezer going to cut me, I've ducked and the chiv went above my head. It was on top that day but they had to join up with Millwall to do it.

Season '84, we went away to Crystal Palace in the FA Cup, but everyone said, no, let's go Millwall and it was our mob, we had about 150 boys get out there, but someone had tipped Millwall off as they all had baseball bats when they all came out of this pub near New Cross Gate station, we all got run. No one could look at themselves, arguments broke out amongst some of us, resulting in someone getting cut then the following week, that someone getting revenge and cutting the guy back and this is amongst mates. I remember personally that shame of being run by Millwall to the point nobody could look at themselves. The talk was to get revenge, word was that Millwall had a big game away to Sheffield United the following week on a Saturday.

The night before, the Under-Fives had gone to a party on the Isle of Dogs. We were all speeding out of our nuts and I remember picking up a plant pot and chucking it around the room, we all got kicked out. We then went back to a local scaffold yard and just sat there making petrol bombs. On the day I did discover that someone else we know had done the same as we pulled up in the motors at London Bridge, down the side streets, and we were around thirty-handed, would say 90 per cent Under-Fives and 10 per cent ICF. To be honest, when we started walking up the slope I was thinking we are going to get hammered here, we should have been nearer one hundred, not thirty. Someone goes their there, another shout of their all there, just as Millwall's mob came out, anything between 150, 200 of 'em. My heart was pounding as I looked around at West Ham and all the sudden see machetes and meat cleavers come out of nowhere, the petrol bombs went off and we run them everywhere. They got trapped inside the station, where they managed to find a load of bottles and held us at bay but they got scattered. Old Bill come and started to nick people, so we managed to slip off, got away.

Dundee United, we played them in a pre-season friendly tournament in 1980 and we went back there in '82 for another friendly. Anyway, the first time up there, West Ham took a mob. You could walk all round the ground, and we're going up to jock's end to have a row with them and they've all come out, so there's two mobs just about to go crash. We're about fifty feet away from each other and the Old Bill's just come screeching in the middle of nowhere and the only three people they've kicked out was me, Lee and Gerard.

So, we're outside the ground. I'm thinking, 'What shall we do?' So, we've gone to the town centre. Walking through, all of a sudden, we've seen three jocks, one of them's got a Man City shirt on. I've just picked up a dustbin and put it over his head, they've fucked off. We've come outside and they've got about thirty of their mates on the corner, a big mob of them. And they're going, 'There they are, there they are, the bastards.' There's three of us. So obviously anyone else would have it on their toes, but we're West Ham, mate. They've come over. We've started fighting them, the three of us like that are just fucking – I've never had a row like it in our lives, 100 miles an hour, like windmill punches. And all I remember, I just kept getting knocked down and Lee and Gerard looking up to the two of them just battling like a windmill, going, 'Get up, c'mon, get up.' And I had to keep getting up and just fucking kept getting put on my arse. We held our own, we really did. That was one of my best moments, I must admit, it just says West Ham.

After the match ended, West Ham's come out, we were

in the pub, about twenty-handed, and the pub's full of jocks peacefully drinking. All of a sudden, I've got the urge to be performing again, jumps up saying 'England,' same time I've smashed a glass. All of a sudden, that was it, as I've thrown the glass, the pub has just erupted and it's just piled out onto the street. I remember these scaffold poles going through the window and this was after the gunfight at the O.K. Corral with glasses and bottles in the pub. I remember that one of the brothers got put in hospital. He also got nicked so me and his brother went to the Old Bill shop to try to see him somewhere in the middle of Scotland where he was. When we come out, we got chased by a mob of jocks and got parted, he's on one side of the street and I'm on the other. Now he's one of the well-known brothers but is a bit ... weren't too fast, shall we say? I remember they was about a foot away from him and I'm thinking, fuck, please don't catch him because I'm knackered and if he goes down, I've got to fight with him, we're both going to get battered and cut up because I know they have blades on them as well. But we managed to get away. We got back and everyone had glass cuts and it was like, well done, DD, you started another fucking row. But it was, it was fucking brilliant.

Some of us – Under-Fives – were quite pally with the Scousers, we'd all sort of dress the same way and all be robbing and all that. For me, the Scousers were the best thieves in Britain. I don't know whether they were more slippery, more devious, or more fucking quick, whatever.

What stood out for me was when we beat them in the semi-final in the Cup at Elland Road, when old Latchford got that header and they had the Kop end and it just looked fucking brilliant. It all erupted; they were all jumping the fence. Anyway, I was having a good thieve, I was having so much fun. I'd slip in the back of shops. So, they just started calling me Deggsie and it's a name that stuck. It's like a Scouse affectionate name. I even go to football, they go, 'Hey, hey, Deggsie.' What actually done it for me is my sister used to go out with a towner who was ICF, now him, Tiderman and Bolo, who was one of the Everton's boys. Now, I was still at school then – '78, I think it was – he's come round and he's took me football. I remember thinking, 'What a nice fella' but, after the game, we come through Queen's Market and I ended up having a fight with an older lad in the shop who I knew from my school and he was a bit mad – he had that mad power, you know, when you've got that mad strength. And I'm fighting him, no one's winning, it's just a proper straight up stand-off, and it's going on and on. In the end it wasn't going nowhere, no one was winning. So, Tiderman's come in and the pair of us have battered him. And I remember my sister's boyfriend going afterwards, 'Yeah, you're going to be one of West Ham's top boys, you are.' And I remember the Scouse geezer. I thought he was a nice fella. And when we went to Everton away the first year we come up, I see him, Bolo, at Lime Street. And he just stood there and walked from the train station to the ground talking to me. That's how I got the nickname. I was always thieving and with the wedge, you know, we still had battles with them, our little mob, Liverpool, Everton, but when they used to come to West Ham, I used to stand in the visiting end talking and all that.

But with the Mancs, all that I remember with them was them being slippery, was them being fucking funny or clever, whatever, but they were dirty c***s with it – well, I think so. Even after the Luxemburg thing, the England riot and ransacking the City Centre, where both Chelsea and the Mancs had proper mobs out. I just got off the train somewhere and I'd just a coat and I put my glasses on, went to a mate, 'This is our day.' And the Mancs were spotted waiting at the end of the platform. We only had a little mob and they've come running through, battering people, and people started running. I run up the stairs, fell over, and I'm starting to get battered as well and a Cockney Reds pulled me out. He's going, 'I'm sorry about that, I didn't mean it.' A few of us got banged up in Luxemburg, he was one of them.

THE ICF ON THE
KONINGIN BEATRIX

'IT'S EITHER HIT AN ICEBERG OR THE
WEST HAM FANS ARE ABOARD'

West Ham hooligan gang, the Inter-City Firm, are alleged to leave a 'calling card' on victims. At a defendant's home, police found cards that read: SURPRISE, SURPRISE. YOU'VE SEEN THE PROGRAMME, NOW MEET THE STARS – THE ICF.

The full story of that incredible day in the middle of the English Channel on 7 August 1986 is told here the way it actually happened, rather than how it was told in the media and the courts. The fighting had been so savage that the captain and his crew were unable to control it. At 1am, as the battle raged in one of the busiest stretches of water in the world, Captain Joost Nargel desperately sent out a distress signal and turned his ship around to return to port.

MARTIN STURGESS, WEST HAM UNITED: There was myself, a guy called Harvey, another guy called Steve and I think someone else who planned to meet at Liverpool Street station. Two of us left Harlow Town and when we got to Liverpool Street station all we could see was a sea of Man United supporters. We had a meal around the station and meet up with Steve who lived in London himself. Went on to board the train down to Harwich and there were a few other West Ham, probably about eight or nine, some I recognised and some I didn't. We got on the train that was an old-style train with couple of individual cabins with sliding doors with corridors going all the way down the length of the carriage.

There was about four of us in a carriage and when the rest of the train started boarding, it filled up with Man United fans and they were looking at us a bit strange and when the train was going along, they were walking past our carriage and looking in. We were feeling a bit uneasy and we noticed the blinds in our carriage had, like, an iron bar so we thought they would come in handy if things start getting a bit nasty.

Some of the other lads who were West Ham and in the other carriages came down to us. I'm sure they had some forged tickets you can get the ferry on to Belgium, I think it was we who were playing. In the end we got down to Harwich docks and the other lads said, c'mon, let's all stick together when we get on this ferry.

Some of the lads had got into the bar whatever, but ironically it was called the Inter-City bar for real and was on the top floor. It wasn't a great deal of money, so we all got up to the bar, where we sat around introducing ourselves to the ICF lads we didn't know. The ferry sought of set sail into the night and while we were sitting in the bar, there was lots of Man United fans around the balconies that surrounded the back of the boat, all with their hats and scarves on. They kept looking in through the windows and whatever. Properly an hour into the journey, some of the lads we knew said, shall we go for a wander around and see what's happening?

We went down the stairs and had a wander around in the duty-free bars, talking to some of the United fans. They realised that we were West Ham fans and a few of them came up and started talking to us. There was just four of us and they were talking about an incident that happened the season before at Plaistow station, where a Man United fan got stabbed. It got a bit awkward, the tone had changed from the earlier trivial chatting to now this incident at Plaistow. They were saying things about CS gas being used, tools brandished, etc. More and more United fans were coming out of the bar and making a horseshoe shape as they circled around us. So, before it started kicking off, we decided to nip back upstairs to the bar we occupied. When we got to the top of the stairs a few of the other lads that were the West Ham fans with us were standing around at the entrance to the bar. Next minute, the Man United fans were shouting out, where is your Top Boy, Taffy Harris? as they charged up our stairs to the bar throwing bottles, to which we retaliated. The fighting went on for about an hour or so, we all had to just defend ourselves so we used fire extinguishers and everything. We undone the fire hoses and put the power on and fought with them.

The Man United fans realised they weren't getting

anywhere in this fight, there certainly weren't any serious injuries on our side and the Man United fans got destroyed, really.

The captain and his crew were trying to stop the battle but it never stopped until the fight naturally fizzled out. I went down to the boat medical room with quite a bad cut on my finger. I saw people we were fighting with quite badly injured and in a bit of a state. The boat was too, with water flooding the stairs washed with blood. After such chaos, the boat was turned around. We got back in the morning and all the British police came aboard but we weren't arrested at that stage. It was in fact as long as three weeks later when the police came to my workplace and arrested me there. As much as it was in all the news and papers and made quite political because I think there was MPs on the boat at the time, even Thatcher made a statement about it. But where I was quite young at the time, just twenty-one, I considered it all part of the fun of it.

I wore Lois jeans, adidas trainers, Fred Perry top with Gabicci jumper and I recall my trainers being so covered in blood that I had to throw them overboard when the police came on as it wouldn't look good for me. Though when I did get arrested and questioned and not knowing how the police worked at that time, I considered the odds we were up against in the fighting on the ferry and admitted throwing a fire extinguisher in self-defence because if the Man United fans had got up those stairs, the only place for us to go was overboard. There was a kitchen behind the bar we used to get knifes from which came in handy after the ferry staff cut the water power off from the hoses. We cut these hoses with knives to use as weapons with the weight and coupling at the end of the hose. The fighting was that wild that even the bikers travelling on the boat wouldn't get involved though a couple of mad Dutch guys joined us.

When we got the train back from the ferry port to Liverpool Street station that's when the press was really out. The radio station LBC was there asking questions and everybody was in high spirits that we made it off that ferry.

Even though the friendly tournament fixture was deliberately not publicised as they didn't want any fans travelling for this game we found out about it, so a couple of the lads said, fancy a weekend of fun.

My solicitor thought I could get five to ten years because there had been a series of dawn raids around that time on all known hooligans and the Chelsea Headhunters lot had got ten years (unbelievable at the time).

I felt disappointed when the ferry turned back because it was my first time abroad, and had heard all the stories and fancied a bit of fun. A few of the lads when the ferry docked got off the boat and then jumped back on again. There were a few lads carrying a few injuries. I had a cut hand that needed eight stitches after being cut from glass being thrown. I had, like, a cigarette bin in one hand with a fire extinguisher in the other. I suppose I must have lost about a pint of blood. By the time we had finished the fighting there was all this blood at the bottom of the bin that come out of my hand. When I got back to London it was not until the following morning that I went to hospital and they said I'm going to need stitches to my cut hand.

It was quite funny really because even though I had the prison sentence, it was just another part of my life. Met some new friends which I still see now but at the time I thought, oh, I'm going into prison, from doing just a couple of weeks on remand and then going through all the different London prisons then on to an Open prison. I got sentenced to six years, which my barrister said he was going to appeal against because it was quite a high sentence for that time. I think them paid for the second appeal after the first one got turned down, even though I hadn't spoken to my parents about it because at the time it made my mother quite ill, she took it quite bad. In this second appeal they knocked a year off, then I got a late parole date and was let out on parole because it was my first offence.

I've never been out of work since I left school, I worked for a place that built cars and had a decent boss. When the Met Police arrested me, they wanted quite a lot of bail money for me.

Ferry incident of 1985, it's still remembered, some of the younger people don't quite know about it, my own children now sort of question about it because it's popped up on YouTube or something, or someone would say, 'Oh, you were on the ferry, Mart. What was all that about?' My memories of it are still quite fresh in my mind because it was such a thing in my life that I still remember it quite vivid.

The whole scene was quite good for me really, it was the way I think and the way I acted about things that made me a stronger person from what I was before. Standing up for myself and even the fear factor because even now there are not a lot of things I fear. It made me a stronger-willed guy, in confidence.

After the fighting stopped, people were relaxing in the bar. I'm sure I even went to sleep for a couple of hours. When people came on board to get people off, I wasn't sure if they were even the police or officials, we got on the train and off we all went. I think it was at the trial it came out there was MPs travelling on the boat, which then made it more political, and they said that they had to make examples of the people that were on trial, hence the high sentences.

Because these West Ham matches it was deliberately not advertised, it was a word-of-mouth thing, out of the twelve West Ham fans I only knew maybe eight of them, if that, really. They were just lads I knew over football, even the lads they arrested there was this guy in his fifties or sixties whose son I didn't know or come across over football was also on the boat. There were so few of us we had to stand and perform just to stop them getting up the stairway. There were two lots of stairways with four entry ways coming up to the first-class bar where we all were. There were probably 200 Man United fans on that boat, so there was a heavy flow of fans coming up those stairs, throwing glasses, full bottles of drink just smashing off the ceiling, using tables as shields to get up the stairs. It was in the papers the following day where they reported the walls were running with blood. What it was, there was a lot of water because we had a power hose to sort of keep the fans back, the blood was sort of mixing with the water, making it a lot worse than what it really was.

The press and media widely reported the incident aboard the *Koningin Beatrix* with jaw-dropping headlines such as SOCCER SCUM and RIVER OF BLOOD, all repeated again when it came to trial, with the *Sun*'s cartoonist even doing a cartoon depicting a sinking ferry with the caption IT'S EITHER HIT AN ICEBERG OR THE WEST HAM FANS ARE ABOARD. This likely in response to Judge Brian Watling's words addressed to the court before sentencing eight thugs to fifty-one years, saying that the ferry captain was so terrified he threw a cordon round his bridge – and raced back to port. It was quite beyond the captain to control the fighting. They thought the man wielding an iron bar was going to kill the captain, he said. The battle raged in one of the busiest stretches of water in the world. The captain would have needed a large-scale naval boarding party to quell this riot, said the judge. The captain's attention was diverted from safe navigation of his ship. The lives of every man, woman and child on board were put at risk. It was tantamount to piracy. This sort of mindless violence is often called 'the English Sickness' by the foreign press. It threatens to destroy civilised life in this country. The riot on the *Koningin Beatrix* could have been a worse disaster than the *Titanic*.

BRIGHTON: URBAN NETWORK FIRM

STU WHEATMAN, NEWCASTLE UNITED: The first hooligan firm in Brighton was the Bosun Boys, which was a pub halfway down West Street. They weren't dressers, as it was 1977–1981, but wore donkey jackets and DMs. The West Street Firm was first established in 1981 and died out around 1986 when V-neck Pringle jumpers, Lyle & Scott roll-necks, Farah trousers or Lois cords and Kickers boots were at that time the casual look. Oh, yeah, and the Farah haircut, which was like a mullet with a perm at the back. My firm was the Urban Network Firm, we were too young for the West Street Firm but we was still there, just taking it all in from remaining in the background.

We came of age from the mid-1980s to the mid-1990s, when playing in the lower leagues made it easier to organise things with each other, which also meant less

Old Bill, no cameras meant no nickings – thirty of us and thirty of them meant that the rucks were more exciting, and no one could hide. Oxford, Reading, Chesterfield, Grimsby, Peterborough, Luton and Portsmouth are just some of the fights we've been involved in. So, we've got a little mob over here, about thirty to forty lads, and main man, he's like an old boy, like forty-five or whatever, and he's a big lump and all that, bald head, game as you fucking like, always. All through the 1970s, '80s, '90s, the boy's been there. Top Man, he is. He's had broken hands, broken arms. In an incident with Man City, we went up to the station to meet him at half ten at night and we were about forty-handed. We went up there and they were all outside the station, about 150 lads. And this geezer comes out, he walks over to us, and he goes, is this all you fucking got?, and whistles and they all come out the pubs and all that. They'd got their beer glasses and we were on our toes.

Our main man stays put and he gets battered by them. And as they're doing him you could hear him, is this all you got? They said, fucking leave him alone, leave him alone, because a couple wanted to Stanley knife him. All he got out of it was a broken arm, but if he didn't have that, he would have got fucking stabbed and everything because they had their knives and all that. And because he stood and all of us fucking ran, made him Top Boy. He doesn't go now, but in our eyes he's the Top Man.

It started off localised with the Brighton lads, but now it's all over the region. You've got lads from Littlehampton, Top Boys, they're forty-handed and come to most games as well. They're always there. You get your bods from everywhere, Crowborough, we've got Eastbourne, Worthing. When I was young, people from the other towns, they weren't allowed. They got slapped and they weren't allowed in. And as West Street firm died away, the other towns boys all come in now, it's better now. There's only one team in Sussex and that's us, so that's three million people, it's a big catchment area. You see Brighton fans everywhere, all round Sussex. In the eighties it was all Brighton, we didn't need anyone, it was all West Street. In the nineties there weren't so many people going, it died a little bit, it really did die a little bit.

Our biggest rivals both team and fan wise are Crystal Palace. The good thing about that is that, Palace, we're their fucking rivals as well. They see us as that both team-wise and fanwise. It's Crystal Palace-Brighton. No other club comes close. This goes back to the early seventies. We got our nickname from them. When they used to come down, they were called the Eagles obviously. They used to chant, 'Eagles! Eagles!' And in the seventies, we were called Dolphins as a club nickname. So we went with Seagulls, to wind Palace up and that's it, that's where we got our club nickname from. We're quite up for that and it is the nearest club. It's located just off the old Brighton Road, isn't it? It's just straight down, it's just one straight long fucking road and they're at the end of it, and we're at the other end of it.

MILLWALL

I remember a few years ago, in 2006, there was three of us in this pub, Millwall come down. It was a cup game, Johnstone's Paint Trophy. We had about forty lads, they had about thirty. They were right good boys. So anyway, they went to the game. We met them up the station. We couldn't get nowhere near them, loads of Old Bill so we left it alone.

They went to the game, and we stayed in the pub because a few of us are banned anyway. So about ten minutes before the end of the game we all jumped in the car, like. As we're going along, we see four Millwall lads, and they're big lads, 35–40-year-old geezers. A couple of them were holding Holsten Pils bottles, empty. They were just holding them by their side for protection or something like that. Anyway, we pulled in the next corner. Thought this is it, we've got to fucking do this now. So, we just all jumped out, ran round the corner and went fucking mental. I had one on the ground kicking him in the head and the Holsten Pils bottle drops out of his hand, so I picked it up and his mate was right next to me, and he was holding this Holsten Pils bottle in my face. I was stabbing the geezer's head going, fucking do it then, come on, fucking do it. Anyway, he didn't do it, so I got the Holsten Pils bottle and launched it at him. It just missed his fucking head, and he was on his toes, started legging it. Anyway, I gave this geezer a couple more boots, that's it. We jumped in the car and sped away with a *Way-hay-hee!*

OXFORD

The Brighton Rock, the Boulevard and the William IV are heaving with people because Brighton is playing Oxford Town. Now, Palace are Brighton's main rivals but due to them being in a different division meant the Seagulls only play them in friendlies so in the early '90s, Oxford became Brighton's rivals and the most anticipated game of the season.

Groups of lads from Littlehampton, Peacehaven, Haywards Heath as well as Brighton, Hove, Southwick and Shoreham are catching up on recent shenanigans. Each group will have its main players, the game lads who you know are solid performers. You will also have yer hard nuts and general lunatics otherwise nut jobs. The latter are in most firms up and down the country! They normally only turn up on match day as they were probably at home making Chinese throwing stars or hammering a flick-knife into their bedroom door like James Coburn in *The Magnificent Seven*.

Obviously, the main topic is about tomorrow and where everyone is meeting and at what time. When that is decided amongst the groups, that info is dispersed around the pubs and bars get louder and the excitement runs rife amongst the beer swillers; those that have managed to neck a dove or Mitsubishi or two are experiencing their own euphoria.

As closing time is called, most go home to watch *The Word* ('nudge wink', Amanda de Cadenet) on the box, while others headed for the club scene, Zap or The

Escape, while the ones who have already dropped an E are still trying to find the exit!

The clothing scene and style had some new introductions on the casual scene as the late 1980s and early '90s saw Massimo Osti's CP Company, Bonneville, Stone Island (all ridiculously expensive at the time), Naf Naf Chipie, Class Nouveau as well as the normal classics worn on the terraces. Lads were also sporting long hair and flares, as groups such as Inspiral Carpets, Happy Mondays, Charlatans and Stone Roses, all from the Manchester region, played an influence on the era and culture of what was your football-going days back then.

Late-Saturday morning arrives, and Brighton train station is the new meeting point. The doors of the Nightingale and Queens Head, which are both facing the station, are full up with everyone awaiting Oxford's arrival. The first London trains arrive but no Oxford firm on them. Someone was sent in to the station to keep an eye on arrivals to try and spot their mob when they arrive. We are in the Queens Head and as we head to noon, a loud roar goes up as someone runs in, shouting, 'They're here, they're here!' The pub empties as the first little Oxford firm bowling out of the station. They were not expecting Brighton to be that close to the station as in a firm. The speed and force of Brighton's frontline hit them and caught them off guard. The first lot out of the station folded under the onslaught and ran straight back into the station, confusing the rest of them, who were about to head out, too. Game over already for Oxford as they're wrapped up by the Old Bill. Brighton split up and head for Hove station for another attempt to get into their firm.

At the ground, things didn't go quite to plan as Oxford arrived before most of the Brighton firm had got there and so they were chasing a small group of our lads at the back of the South Stand towards the West Stand and having a minor result. Then like all good firms you have a few real game changers: one solid Brighton lad runs into them alone, which slows up their success until the cavalry arrive and steam in! One and one fighting takes place as Oxford back-up and the Old Bill come between both firms still rowing, back of the stands.

Oxford now get made to go into the ground, come the second half Brighton are 3–0 down, so word goes about to leave early and instead of the usual heading back to Hove station. The firm headed west along old Shoreham Road and hid themselves in some flats nearby, hoping to ambush Oxford by the Cliftonville pub outside Hove station. But Oxford got put in an escort and Brighton got chased off by the Old Bill. Running out of time to do something, Brighton next head for the Caxton and the Duke of Wellington, which are not far from the station to have it again! The alleyways and back streets are a perfect place to set a trap and it's not long before Oxford arrive. They've managed to shrug off the Old Bill, and they are now marching out of the station and heading down by the pubs Brighton had previously been in. When they realise Brighton aren't in there, they get bold and think they are going to bowl around the town and have a result. However, 200 yards further up they fall straight into a trap! Together with momentum and speed of surprise Oxford's frontline folds as Brighton steam in and chase them back up to the station, fighting takes place with splinter groups here and there but Oxford just get backed up into the safety of the station and the Transport Police. The only other action was when a van full of game lads jumped out, had a scuffle then fled like a scene out of *The Sweeney*.

GRIMSBY

The game wasn't till Sunday but a group of us went up on Saturday, got to a pub on the seafront called Smugglers about mid-afternoon, met some more lads there ... about twenty to thirty of us ... got a phone call from our No1 saying that they know we're here (Grimsby) and will be with us in five minutes ... He said, go outside and take a look anyway. Went outside with a couple of others, looked down the street, saw nothing then looked up and saw three big white vans pull up about a hundred yards away, geezer got out of the passenger side door with a bat then opened the sliding doors. Out jumped about eight lads with bats and bottles, and I saw a fucking chain as well ... Same with the other vans, must have been about twenty or so of them. I looked at my mate in disbelief and said, 'Get the others!'

They came running down the hill looking proper game, shouting and that, launching bottles. My lads came out the pub, some with glasses and bottles, and formed a line across the road, Littlehampton boys on my right, us lot in the middle and Preston Park Tavern (PPT) boys on the left, no stand-off or jumping around, beckoning each other just straight in from both sets of lads. Fucking brilliant! Reminded me of some medieval scene from a film or something. Got hit with bat, then got knocked to the ground as did most of us from both sides and just kept on going, kept looking to my right and could see the Littlehampton boys holding their own, on my left PPT boys were backing away, taking casualties, some were being led back into the pub with cuts and that. The fight had been going on for well over ten minutes and still no Old Bill! An even fight for a while but I could tell we were getting done, the hill advantage – more game lads and a few more extra weapons were taking their toll, but we were still hanging in there! Then the line broke. Some of us ran back into the pub. I tried to follow but the big doors slammed shut on me, so I started running down the road. One of the Littlehampton boys was running with me. As I looked at him, I saw that his ear was hanging off, and said, 'You best go and sort that out, lol.' I looked back up the road, some of the same Littlehampton lads were still having it with them!

Very game boys, the Littlehampton firm they muster about forty to fifty on a good day. Anyway, heard the Old Bill sirens and managed to get around the back of the pub to meet with the others. Grimsby lads were so impressed with us that they offered us up to their pub that night. We didn't go but a couple of the Littlehampton boys went, lol, and it kicked off again the next day after the game, but this time we had the numbers! All the way down towards the station (two miles or so), just little bits here and there, and hardly any Old Bill again! A top firm, the Grimsby boys, it must be said.

If you look back, the most important lesson you learned would be to keep it tight, trust in the people that you're with. Because we had one lad who we let in, we're close and that, but we had one lad that we let in from outside the town. And he was the first to steam into the Old Bill, yet he was never getting nicked because suddenly it turns out he was a police informer, so a lot of people had their names put up. He was in court and one of the lads from football was in court on a driving offence and this lad was getting nicked for something, he was getting done for something, and they turned around and said we're gonna take it into consideration that you're a police informer.

The Brighton Old Bill are so fucking on it anyway, they've got an office where they've got our pictures all over the wall. They make a point on a Saturday: if they don't know your fucking face, they will get it on a Saturday. Because they've come up with that fucking Section 60 and they'll search you and they'll take your details and all that.*

They'll take a photo of you, and you'll be on that fucking wall on the Monday. And we're all on the wall, all our boys. They make a point of letting you know you're there.

*Section 60 of the Criminal Justice and Public Order Act 1994 allows a police officer to stop and search a person without suspicion.

Apart from when Cardiff was here we've never really done anything when the Old Bill's been there. I can't remember any occasions. The police presence at a Brighton game is so heavy, there's not gonna be any trouble now. It's so strong. They could handle any Premiership game, that's how massive they are.

They take it too seriously, I swear to God, they take it far too seriously. No swearing, and things like that, it's like being at a fucking remand centre.

They go to me, all right, where's your boys today, or where are you, what are you doing, what you are doing in here? And you think, fuck, do I need this? And it's really put me off football. I ain't been since I last got done at Luton and then it was the last game. It really has put me off fucking football. The Old Bill are so on you. That and my ten-year ban.

Personally, I'd like to be known as fucking somebody who was there when it happened and didn't let no one down. Can I just rephrase an old song that says, whatever you decide to do, make sure what you do makes you happy, and that's exactly how I live.

THE NORTH WAS A HOTBED FOR TROUBLE

BEING A 'NORTHERN MONKEY' WAS ABOUT THE 1970S. FROM THE 1980S ONWARDS, THE NORTH STARTED TO GET DRESSED UP ...

I think most of us as teenagers living in '70s London discovered the North from a football special train. Before that, I had no idea what northern people and their towns were like and *Coronation Street* painted a grimy image – though I thought Ray Langton was a bit of a lad. As for its history, well, the orders went out from London and the armies marched north, didn't they?

Travelling north for support of yer football club was not only an adventure in the '70s, it was bordering on the suicidal. The West Ham firm were so much younger then, as 12–17-year-olds would bulk up the numbers of the main firm. Most of these lads were typically streetwise, like most Cockneys, with heads on their shoulders far older than their actual years – which was useful, frankly, when experiencing the hatred of all things Cockney up North.

All this serious loathing for the South just went with the buzz though, and you quickly fell into the mindset – the North really hated cockneys, excelled at brick-throwing and had this great community spirit that consisted of 'our kid', 'our Brian' and all that. I've had several experiences of this community spirit, when locals that had nothing to do with the football would come out of their houses and join in the ruck against the cockneys in the street. Even their police took this attitude that it was all northerners together, and just about every London club fan says they felt the bias when the northern Old Bill fought us on behalf of their own clubs.

The North v South divide did actually unite even those northern clubs with a fierce rivalry, which I have to say was not always the same situation down south. Our first evidence of this would come with a trip to Anfield in the '70s – which, little did we know, would mean taking on Everton as well as Liverpool. Every Cockney has got stories of having it with one northern team, only to get done by another! The Mancs, too, had a spell of 'all northerners together', until City got into a spat with United as to who was 'proper Manchester'. (It's true though that we never experienced this truce in yer northeast rivalries between the Geordies, Teesiders, Wearsiders, mackems and Tynesiders. Ignorance of the day meant that we regarded them all as being Geordies.)

If any northerner denies this then they were not around in those barmy '70s and early '80s, when northern clubs were more likely to grace the FA Cup and League Cup finals and have their day out at Wembley. That's when we saw proof of this 'all northerners together' attitude, after the word went around that this is the way you played it if the cockneys turned up for a row. The London firms too would join together, depending on the level of rivalry; it was unlikely that West Ham would go with any rival London club, yet it *did* happen on occasions when London firms would hunt around Trafalgar Square for any early arriving northerners on the Friday night, and again en route to Wembley Way next morning. This little war also included Midlands clubs, as anything past Junction 1 of the M1 was classed as 'northern'. Geography wasn't our strong point, but the same applied to northerners who classed teams such as Brighton, Watford and Luton as 'cockneys'.

Listening to London away fans just confirmed the whole stereotype of what we thought 'northern' was: 'Tetley's' was not a name I'd ever seen anywhere in London, but up north it was everywhere; nor did I understand the term 'down Smoke' used in reference to going to London, as our city wasn't full of chimneys and old mills (or mines, come to that). Then there were the donkey jackets that the away fans wore when they showed at Upton Park; everyone of age had a donkey jacket in the '70s, and the Geordies had them well into the '80s – but we wouldn't have a name printed on ours, unless it was Wimpey and we worked in the building industry. But all the northerners had names printed on the back of this pit or that road construction firm – I guess it was all part of their 'we're working class and we're men' attitude. I used to be amused to see the lads around me wearing donkey jackets, when I knew they hadn't done so much as a day's work. I've seen plenty of our own rubbing their DMs into cement and mud to authenticate themselves as 'workers', while I was in no doubt that the other lot came as they were straight from the colliery.

In a world before the package holidays of the '80s and student rail tickets took us on a European tour, travel meant Lacey's coaches, a Ford transit or a football special train. Going 'up north' was usually a Midlands experience for most of us, as that's who packed out the old First Division, while 'far north' was restricted to Burnley, Blackpool and Carlisle. Away games at the bigger northern cities – Manchester, Liverpool, Leeds and Newcastle – were without question payback time from those clubs. Their home ends were never taken by firms like us even though we specialised in it, because big numbers were seriously needed for that. I can still remember the bravado chant that would go up on the North Bank end, 'Clap yer hands if yer going to any of the fore mention clubs away,' and it seemed like half the end joined in. But, come the game, the reality was that no fucker turned up for the morning meet at Euston. The lads that went hid their scarves, and still got sussed and battered.

Considering the police attitude that 'you're on your own if you come up here,' it was unlikely we'd be given any escort, despite the young average age of the firms back then. The other notable difference was that the grounds always seemed to be miles away from the train stations. I have some great memories (and some not so great) of discovering yer football away-day for it started as soon as you entered town, not when you arrived by the ground. (What a mercy the short walk from Upton Park station down Green Street to West Ham's ground would be, if we had a return match.)

Northern away-days to the likes of Carlisle, Burnley and Stoke were adventures, and we took decent numbers, too. Carlisle was unbelievable, a Rocky Mountain-style trip. Everyone travelling up would be getting excited, buzzing, faces pressed to the window simply at the sight of sheep – *loads* of fucking sheep! – on the great big hills we were travelling up and down. The older boys knew where they were, and would simply announce, 'We're nearly here, this is Carlisle now.' I don't know how they knew, when the train journey was so long that the rest of us couldn't remember how long ago we'd left London. It was the sight of the smog that hit your eyes as you looked out from the train windows – this is what London must have looked like once, and it explained to me why northerners referred to it as 'the Smoke', even though we'd never seen London smog since the '50s. But with all yer mills and factories, you still had towns smothered in smog up north.

All the London clubs – not just West Ham – loved going to Burnley. It's remembered as one of those grounds where the Old Bill would let the fans meet on the terraces, even on the home end and at the sides. They gave you scrapping time, before wading in with a little bit extra themselves. They were reluctant to nick you, too – they'd rather throw you out of the ground so you had to pay your way back in and do it all again. It was incredible, but you knew what you went for and you knew the risks. It was as if they felt sorry for the local inhabitants: 'Why not let them let off a bit of steam on the cockneys, get it out of their system? Because there is fuck-all else ever going to happen for them up here!'

Yes, it was crazy days on the terraces of Turf Moor, with the skinhead-meets-Bay City Roller-style dress sense of Burnley fans. I recall, in the '70s, a row going toe-to-toe on the side of the away stand with lads in white bib and braces, bowler hats, sprayed silver DMs, the full *Clockwork Orange* attire. It was a real tear-up, but don't blame us – even though it was happening in our section, it was Blackburn and Burnley who were at it.

When Danny Dyer presented the TV series *Real Football Factories* in 2006, it featured today's Burnley Suicide Squad.

It also showed Burnley today, with the same dust-covered, rundown, shoebox terraced housing on slopping, hilly streets, with corner pubs and flat-capped regulars (now supping what was maybe lager, instead of brown ale). Back in the '70s, so many asked the question on the trip home: 'Do people really live in those streets?' They were taking the piss then, but in 2006 I found this reality sadly shocking.

If Burnley was somewhere that time forgot, then Anfield was scary in those pre-ICF days. On the walk from Lime Street you would encounter derelict houses, wastelands and bomb craters from the war that ended in '45. But there again, if you weren't from Liverpool then the war was still on. The full experience meant getting run on Scottie Road, those long stick truncheons the 'bizzies' up there carried then, and the terrace song they roared out to us that went, 'He's only a poor little Cockney, his face is all tattered and torn … I hit him with a brick, and now he don't sing, any more': pre-empting the London supporters to hit back in reply: 'In your Liverpool slums … you look in the dustbins for something to eat, you find a dead rat and you think it's a treat.'

I admired the way Scousers carry themselves, they have a strong pride in the way they are and their accent is very distinct – like a Cockney accent, everybody recognises it instantly. They have got an attitude that says, 'The world stops at Liverpool, we should be the capital city because we gave the world the Beatles, blah blah.' 'I'm a Scouser.' Oozes independence and bags of confidence in much the same way as 'I'm a Londoner.' Yet the hatred of all Scousers from London clubs in the '70s was on a par with the Liverpool-Manchester rivalry thing of today. The clashes mellowed somewhat in the '80s, when casual Cockneys and Scousers found a lot in common with each other whenever they met on designer store shopping trips right the way across Europe.

The standalone memories for me of the 1970s are of how a pal that took a kicking said, 'I ain't running from no northern c**t wearing a star jumper!' and of how the northerners influenced the top boys from the South Bank crew into having six-button high-waist trousers, specially made by East End tailors. You couldn't buy such strides anywhere in London, and we started seeing bottle-green three-button baggies first in the Midlands, then the waistband appeared to get higher the further north we travelled. They actually caught on down here, which I think was down to those big pockets on the outside thighs – just the perfect fit for the match programme, can of booze, or whatever the weapon of the day happened to be.

The north-south divide was just as evident on the club and music scene, which for me at that time meant soul and funk: Norman Whitfield, Creative Source, Brass Construction, Fatback, Kool, etc. Then we learnt about the all-dayers advertised in *Blues and Soul* and another magazine called *Black Music*. It would take us to meet our fellow soul music clubbers from the North, who were doing the same as us in checking out all the good clubs in the South. I got told by friendly northerners who spotted the Motown Gold pendant worn around my neck that if I was into Tamla, I should check out the northern soul scene. They would talk it up like it was something else, not to be missed out on. So, with my close pals I often went clubbing with, we headed north in either my mate Mick's Morris Minor car or Bob's Hillman Imp. This particular Easter weekend, the targets were the all-nighters and all-dayers of Wigan Casino, Blackpool

Mecca and Tiffany's in Coalville, via the ripped-out club-advert pages from *Blues and Soul*.

I'm not going to bore you with the whole venture or go into detail about the music, because we knew nothing about northern soul as we wanted to check out the scene with an open mind. If it was something we were missing out on down south, then we would be going back to let everyone know. Anyway, we had a cracking weekend – even though we fucked up with Wigan Casino, as it was shut or it was the wrong fucking day. It meant driving on to Manchester, the nearest place that could save our night. I knew of the Ritzy but we ended up in a couple of clubs, watching people doing spins and shit; then the music would change and you had these electro sounds that just didn't sound anything like soul to me. Neither could we get used to all this unheard music-being-played-in-different-rooms bollocks, with clubbers congregating in and blocking the passageways. The bouncers were putting us on edge, too, and people were too fucking strange to talk to us. I guess we'd come from a totally different club scene, nothing like the one we were encountering in Manchester.

So, we did the cheap B&B thing and, next day, drove to Blackpool to check out the Mecca. There, we found a real northern soul set-up; outside, coach after coach pulled up to join the queues forming to get in. (You never got coaches arriving at London clubs.) We went in thinking, 'It's going to be kicking off in here in no time,' as we noticed the coaches had brought people in from rival areas. We were wrong there, even though the dance floor was like going into a kung fu school, with loads of spins and back flips. OK, we weren't ones for dancing as we were there for the sounds and the birds to chat up, who we'd normally start checking out on the dance floor. But the floor was full of lads wearing bowling shirts, whizzing; it was all about their moves; some were tricky, but lacking the rhythm that the guys who could dance down south would show yer. We'd clocked that the birds remained around the edge of the dance floor and the bars, thinking, 'Hey, we're in here, chaps!' It was our football away-day experiences that had taught us how northern birds would come up and start showing interest from the moment they heard the London accent, while the local geezers wanted to smash yer. But, because of the way the lads were fighting for space to do their speed dancing, we were getting the freedom to move from one group of birds to another without attracting unwanted attention.

I recall how that first trip to the khazi was another new experience. I was greeted by the sight of a banged-out toilet and all these northern lads making what I can only describe as costume changes. There were holdalls containing fresh clothes all laid out on the polished floor tiles and on the sink tops. Then, in a new dry bowling shirt, back out they went, past all the birds they totally ignored, to the dance floor for more spins and back flips to impress their mates. It was what they appeared to care about above everything.

So, you can imagine what we were thinking: the lads that went to the football and the lads that went to the clubs were two different sets of people. It was obviously a pretty serious music scene, but me and the others couldn't get our heads around it, as hard as we tried. They were all getting off on old Tamla Motown B-sides they thought were great, because some DJ said it was rare and they paid big for it. (You dozy northern monkeys! It's rare for a reason, and the reason is that it's shit. Not 'shite'.) As for the birds, we thought we'd pulled on the strength of just opening our mouths and where we'd come from. Then we had to think again. When the last orders were called, and those sweat-stained lads in bowling shirts all headed for the gents for one last costume change before getting back on the coaches, the birds we were with, whose drinks we'd paid for all night, just walked off and followed. Worse still, to our surprise they all kissed and hugged as the boyfriends and girlfriends they must have been all along. We stood open-mouthed as to how these girls, now waving us off from the departing coaches, had played second fiddle to their fellas' love of northern soul, to the point where we were convinced every bird was single and fancied a Cockney.

I don't think anything will ever come close to the North v South divide of the '70s and all of its basic differences. It was all so simple to define: you northerners preferred the pint jug of ale, we took to the cans and then the bottles of lager, all in a smooth half-glass; you worked the pits, we were on the building sites; you had the factories, we the offices; off the pitch, your crews were 'armies' while ours were 'firms'; on the pitch, you had the League titles, the FA Cups and the League Cup – but for all of that we won the World Cup, the one that really matters. So, we understand why you hate the Cockneys, la-la, la-la, la-la ...

NME: FROM THE BENDER SQUAD TO THE GREMLINS

MARK MENNIM, NEWCASTLE UNITED: Make no bones about it, we hate these Sunderland with a passion. Scum of the earth and always in our shadows. Come to think of it, they aren't very fond of us either. It's not just a football thing with us. We are brought up to hate these c***s. I've been abroad on a holiday with my ex and I've spat in their faces. I've kicked a toilet door in to get at one of them whilst he was having a shite, knocking him out in the process, and I've even set one inbreeds red and white top alight at the races … and yes, he was wearing it. I used to ban them from the pubs I ran 'cos I didn't want them in. I remember my first days at the Queens pub in Sherriff Hill and a ackem came in and started talking to me. I stopped him in mid-sentence and took him to the front door of the pub and asked him why the hell he supported that shite when you could see St James Park from his local pub doorway. He couldn't answer me, so I told him not to come back and I put up a sign barring all mackems.

My first real glimpse of football violence was on a trip to Sunderland for a testimonial match on a Wednesday night in the 1970s. Me and a few mates decided to go on the train with the 'Bender Squad'. We were all dressed in jeans, donkey jackets and steel-capped boots as we got to Central station. It was packed and full of older lads, who had all had a good drink. They were singing songs and banging on the windows and luggage racks, some of them had scarves tied around their arms. There was piss trickling along the floor as we arrived at Seaburn station and got off the train.

I started to get a buzz in my stomach. It's hard to explain, but it felt like all my Christmases had come at once. I wasn't scared, far from it, I was looking forward to what might happen. As we walked through the streets heading towards Roker Park, anyone in our way got it. It didn't matter who they were, if they weren't with us then they were against us. We made it down to a couple of their bars just off the Wearmouth Bridge and their boys were waiting for us and it went off big style. I stood back in amazement as I saw our lads go to work. I didn't throw a punch, but I remember chasing a few younger kids my age through the streets and the buzz I got from it. The following year, we did the same again and I ended up getting bottled by one of our own fans. I was at the front baiting the inbreds when I felt something hit me on the top of my head. I put my hand up to feel what it was and when I looked at my hand it was covered in blood and it wouldn't stop. I had no option but to go to hospital. Game over for me that day.

I don't think they ever got over the humiliation of us taking their end in '85 and since then the policing of the games has seen days like that confined to the history books but we have had some notable incidents with them over the years. Sunderland is a rough tough place and people have it hard down there. As a casual firm I've never really rated them if I'm honest till the '90s. You mainly got it with the Vaux boys and that has nothing to do with my obvious bias. They just aren't up there with the likes of Manchester United and 'Boro over the years. The Seaburn Casuals got their act together in the mid-nineties and made a few waves up and down the country and abroad with England, but they never come here to see us in NE1 proper mob-handed and organised without an escort or ever infiltrated our ends although they claim to have on more than one occasion. In '79, at home, the Battle of Bath Lane, they only brought a pathetic 3,500 fans – many of their stay away fans feared for their own safety. And in Bath Lane when they got escorted, they fought back when they were ambushed and attacked by us after the game 'cos, they had no choice but were glad to hear the whistle of their departing train as they came under attack from the word go.

Their tales of trips to Monument and Haymarket Metro stations and not being able to find us are far-fetched. In 1980, at Roker Park, the Bender Squad and the boot boys and every nutter from Tyneside was there that day as we piled off the train at Seaburn station as the battle cry went up. The Old Bill struggled badly with our numbers as we broke through their lines and battled and chased every mackem in sight all the way to the ground – no CCTV in them days gone by. My favourite act was when we played them at home, we used to travel to Sunderland, get on their train to come to Newcastle with a few numbers, mingle in and then when the train was coming over the River Tyne, we used to introduce ourselves to them, boosh! They came through in 1998 ticketless but again escorted. There was a little incident in the Strawberry pub, which I'll touch on in a bit. I speak to a lot of their older lads today and they admit that they have never really been that organised in Newcastle. Having said that, if you travel down to them you can always get a fight – I believe they hate us more than we hate them. I am not gonna blurt on about us having a proper city status airport, mainline train station, etc., but even most Sunderland players live in Newcastle so I'll leave it at that. The phrases 'mack 'em', 'tack 'em' is actually an insult originated from the shipyards of times gone by. We'll mack'em (make them) = Tyneside slang ye tack 'em (take them) = Wearside slang that's why every man and his dog from Wearside are out to greet you and it's certainly not a warm one.

If you were a Newcastle Fan in the late 1970s and early '80s, you were raised on crap football played in front of probably the most passionate, and possibly the most violent fans in England. No one ever came to Newcastle then, but away matches were guaranteed mindless violence. It seemed normal to me, the way it had always been. I entered a different world, and became a different person. By the age of 16, I was proud to be a 'Geordie Boot-Boy'. It was the highlight of my week. After what seemed a lifetime, all of a sudden, we were back, and I was just the right age to enjoy it: twenty, well-paid job, loving life and most of all, loving my days out at wherever Newcastle happened to be playing. Through travelling to away games, I had got to know a bunch of lads who I trusted my life with. We had evolved over a few years, from yobbish cider-drinking skinheads into a sharp, well organised and reliable little squad, as we then called it. The casual fashion was king of the terraces, squads became firms or mobs, and we were the N.M.E. (Newcastle Mainline Express).

Officially, we had about eighty members and we each had a number; we paid a quid a week each to cover each other's fines. Getting lifted gave us status. As soon as the fixtures came out, only one mattered: Sunderland away. We were gonna do them, simple as that. It was all we talked about. It had to be special, we were just too good for it not to be. Some very intelligent, and some very evil minds set to work. It just so happened that two weeks before the game in 1985, Sunderland had reached the Milk Cup final, and didn't we fuckin' hear about it?, which made it worse. We had to shut the mackem bastards up properly. All of a sudden it was on, we were going to buy two hundred tickets for the Fulwell End and humiliate them. They would remember this forever.

Amazingly we got the tickets, two and three at a time mostly, but someone actually asked for and received one hundred. It was agreed we would travel to Sunderland by Metro to Shields, then bus, in three groups and keep our heads down, to escape the bizzies. Our plan worked. We were at the turnstiles, adrenaline pumping, stomach churning, knowing nods and glances, nobody spoke. Fifteen minutes into the match was the time. Nervously, excitedly, we began the stairs, fuck the Fullwell end was big, and full. I still wasn't in when I heard the all-too-familiar sound of violence, a growling sort of roar, and loud as fuck in the middle of the mackems beloved sanctuary, 'NME-NME-NME' then 'United' – the poor fuckers didn't know what had hit them.

They ran in all directions, pulling each other out of the way; not one fought back, we were murdering them. It became a free-for-all, they wouldn't fight back, they just tried to get away in sheer panic. I was loving it, picking targets. Everyone was. The bizzies didn't expect it either, most were at the Roker End where our fans were, it took them two to three minutes to move in. The Roker End was going mental, 'Geordie aggro, Geordie aggro' echoed, the mackems were silent. As the bizzies moved in we just all stopped, instead of hitting them we were bouncing up and down, singing, 'We fucked the Fullwell.' The mackems just watched us do it. The bizzies didn't really pull us out, we walked out, business done. Right up the side of the pitch, while the players looked on. I swear some Newcastle players, (won't say who) were laughing and smiling.

The Roker End was still chanting out, 'Geordie aggro', we passed the main stand packed with furious mackems. We just laughed and flashed wanker signs. The odd coin came at us, and to our great amusement, the Fullwell now wanted to fight. We were buzzing, arrogant, smug, you name it. Right there on the pitch at Roker Park, the mackems were humiliated, and they knew it. The bizzies started to get aggressive, probably because we wanted to do a lap of honour. They started pushing us and whacking us towards the Roker end. About halfway up the pitch lots of us broke into a run towards the mags, arms held high, like we had won the cup or something. The mackems swore vengeance, but thirty-five years later, we are still waiting. They never got over it. Today, they try to play it down, saying the Fulwell was the kids' end. But everyone knows that for derby games it most definitely wasn't.

Through Facebook, I have got back in touch with lots of the lads. It all seems like yesterday, and recently for a laugh, I said it's the 35th anniversary of us doing the Fullwell, we should have a reunion, someone suggested we do it again to celebrate. Within two hours, about fifty grandad hooligans were up for it – ha ha ha, who knows? We might just do it one day.

Stanley mags infiltrated the Clock Stand a few years later. There must have been a good three hundred Newcastle lads simply paid on the turnstiles for the match and got themselves into one corner. It didn't take long for somebody to ask one of the lads where he was from so the Newcastle lad punched first and answered questions later and it was off. The Stanley mags made their way onto the dirt track and took the applause of their fellow mags in the Roker End.

There's many a time when Newcastle haven't had a game and they have been at home that I've gone down looking for a fight with them. It led to me being the first person to be banned from two different clubs' fixtures. The day the mackems got relegated to Division Three at home to Gillingham late '80s is a good example. There were hundreds of us who got the train down to Roker Park that day; in fact, there were that many of us, they had to give us our own section in the away end. I was with a lot of the old 'Bender Squad'. We went down to rub their faces in it and they hated it. The Gillingham fans were thankful for the extra support though. There was a little bit of aggro but not as much as we had hoped for but seeing them go down was reward enough for our journey down there and I'm not even bothered about football.

STU: I guess the most publicised incident between the Seaburn Casuals and the Gremlins happened on 18 March 2000 in North Shields. Sunderland has just played 'Boro at home and we never had a game till the next day and we had arranged to meet them after the match. The location was fixed but had to be rearranged a couple of times and it was finally agreed that we would meet at the Ferry landing in North Shields, The mackems finished their drinks in the Alum House, South Shields and then came by ferry from the south side and travelled to the North terminal landing at North Shields. From there, they went to the 'Chain Locker', where they got a round in and started singing anti-Newcastle songs. They then headed to 'The Porthole', where they armed themselves and carved 'SAFC' and 'UVF' into the tables.

Our lads had all met at the 'Whittington' pub and were finishing their drinks and heading down to the rendezvous point at the Quayside. There were about forty of them and they had a few Manchester City tagging along too as they walked into the lion's den with about fifty of us at first then down to twenty-five after all the 'Will it, won't it?' happen, with all of our lads all baying for their blood. It was a show of strength from our boys brigade that day as we went to town on them. Local residents flooded the phone lines to the police, but it was too late to stop this battle royal. The mackems claimed later that we had agreed on no weapons, but this wasn't the case. They must have thought they were coming to play us at pool with the amounts of balls and cues they left lying around, not to mention the CS spray and chair legs. The fighting lasted for about ten minutes and was no-holds-barred and probably the most vicious seen for many years on Tyneside as well as in the UK – the press dubbed it like a scene from the *Braveheart* movie. By the time the police arrived, it was a crime scene with claret staining the quayside and three mackems lying seriously injured and unconscious. Turned out one of them was that badly injured with brain damage that he could not stand trial.

The aftermath saw 39 lads in total arrested and

heavy sentences for our lads who had arranged the ruck. Their downfall was the use of mobile phones to arrange where to meet. The police were using technology to their advantage now and with the signal of a mobile phone you could determine where and when a person was in a particular area. They also had the capability of reading texts sent on a network. With CCTV ever prominent on our street corners, this was the beginning of the end for hooliganism as we knew it. This was the organised fight that almost never really was if it wasn't for a couple of well-known main lads from North Shields who knew a shortcut through to the ferry landing and caught up with the Seaburn Casuals just as they entered the place. Two main lads from each side got four years each not including others but luckily it was not a murder scene for all involved. Whatever is said about this incident over and over again by people who weren't there, this was the night the casuals became casualties.

The one similarity in most of these stories is that we always travelled down to them more so at Roker Park as well as the Stadium of Light proper mob-handed but they never really visited us back in the day when it mattered proper, firmed up, and give it to us. Whether they will admit this is their issue, maybe they might have stories that they got stopped many times. Who knows? There's always the other side of the coin, yes, sometimes we come unstuck on minor offs, that's the way it goes, but the offer has always been there but they have never taken us up on it up here.

'BORO FRONTLINE

'WE ALWAYS LOVED OUR LONDON TRIPS'

CRAIG, MIDDLESBROUGH: Most will agree that the reputation of Middles-brough's firm has been cemented in the off-the-pitch history books, alongside a host of other respected firms from up and down the UK.

Little old Middlesbrough, a small town in the northeast of England, tough working class with a passionate support for their local team has more than held its own through the '70s and '80s, where football violence and the casual scene was prevalent.

Ayresome Park was a pilgrimage for 'Boro fans, the terraced streets and alleyways, the clunk of the old turnstiles, the concrete steps up to the terrace, the red crash barriers, the old towering corner floodlights, the way the floodlights beamed onto the grass, open-air toilets reeking of piss, the smell of Bovril wafting from the old kiosk, the moody atmosphere, pure carnage.

A sea of arms and legs when a goal was scored are all memories held dear and I'm sure will resonate with any grassroots fan with their team, although it was not such a pleasant experience for the away fan.

In 1995 we said goodbye to Ayresome Park as we moved into the Riverside stadium, at the time excitement was brimming through the town as we had just gained promotion as champions of the old First Division with Bryan Robson at the helm. Robson captivated the spirit of Teesside. His name in the football world at the time was golden, he helped catapult the team into the Premier League with a succession of big-money signings and football that had never been seen before at little old 'Boro.

Due to the success the town was booming, pubs were full, the stadium was full. It was an incredible time which saw the town rise with the prospect of the big clubs visiting and us getting to travel to them, everybody was up for it.

My story covers the '90s into 2000s, a rivalry that developed that would see tit-for-tat battles and attempts to confront each other season after season with the Yids (Tottenham).

Since our move to the Riverside we hadn't managed to land Spurs away on a normal Saturday 3pm KO. We always loved our London trips and would always travel in good numbers as it was a full day out for the lads. I was travelling to pretty much every game at the time back then and would even go as far as London on mid-week trips.

We played Spurs on a night game end of the '90s and I used this game as a reconnaissance mission to suss out some routes for future use. We parked up the car and got the overland rail into White Hart Lane station, which saves that massive walk down the High road from Seven Sisters Tube. On the corner near the station was a pub called the Railway Tavern, which I clocked for next time.

The 1999/2000 season, we got Spurs away on a Saturday. We had about seventy make the trip by train into King's Cross on various trains. As planned out on the reconnaissance, we got the overland straight off at White Hart Lane and into the Railway Tavern. We were early as always and the first thirty or so were having a drink when some doormen started to arrive at the pub; they looked very shocked to see an away mob in there.

We were getting ready anticipating a kick-off but the bouncers played it safe and decided to have a chat with us. They were in a no-win situation: either we wrecked the bar if they tried to get us out or the Yids would come and wreck the bar trying to get us out.

More of our lads were arriving and we moved off across the street, ending up in some sort of club called the Irish Centre. We had been there over an hour with no Old Bill which was quite a surprise and our presence was being noticed by some of the locals.

Not long after the OB had been tipped off and started to arrive outside the club and the chance had been missed. Half-hour before kick-off, we were marched up to the ground by the OB. As soon as we got to the

High Road, the Yids started having a go at our escort, bottles flying into us with both sides trying to break the escort. The horses moved in to push the Yids back and form a line across the road while we were moved off down to the away end and into the ground.

During the game there was a small group of theirs sat near the away fans divide giving it a bit of verbal so just before the end we started drifting out the stand and into the concourse; we signalled to them to meet us outside. About twenty of us marched out fast as we could and we met on the corner and went straight into them. We put them on the back foot straight away as the OB scrambled to restore order.

We were put back into the main group and escorted up to Bruce Grove station. The OB had had enough of us for the day, we had made a dent down the Lane and we were looking forward to the return fixture.

2002 season, jackpot! Spurs away Saturday 3pm kick-off. Right, we're all on this one!

The words gone round to everyone making sure we get train tickets as early as possible: it was one of those games, everybody fancied it! The day comes we got about 150 travelling down, a real top turn-out and we're not going for tea and biscuits.

Were in London early, quick breakfast and tell everyone to split up and get taxis to the Ship Inn on Tottenham High Road. We're in the first two taxis that land on the High Road about 11am. There's a pub a few doors down from the Ship and we can see a few Yids in the window playing pool, looking shocked to see us landing on their manor so early. We're just about to walk into the pub and out comes the spotters who were doing the old pub walk around – you couldn't make it up! Fuck sake, we hadn't even got in the door and they were onto us ... disaster! We got the beers in and waited for the rest, it was too late to try to arrange something else as everyone was en route now. By 1pm the pub was rammed, real good turnout from us but we were surrounded by OB and it was a no go.

The pub had an old courtyard outback that had a large shed with a padlocked door. I wander outside and see one of our characters with a spade wedged in the clasp, breaking into the shed. The Silver Shadow who is no longer with us, god bless him, was always on the rob everywhere we went, he was a crazy character known for carrying a blade. The shed was an overspill for the pub cellar and piled high with cans and bottles. We ended up with a free afternoon on the lash, the poor landlord didn't suss until much later, what a laugh.

The OB marched us to the ground about 2.30pm in a huge escort so it was pretty much a non-starter beforehand other than a few verbals by groups of Yids en route.

Back at the pub, there were about fifteen of ours who didn't have tickets and a few on stadium bans. Unbelievably, the OB just left them in there when we were escorted, the Yids from the pub up the road came straight over, windows go in and CS gas is sprayed at the door.

Boom, it's gone right off; the Yids are in the door

and ours are right at it with them in the doorway. There's bottles and chairs going, my mate Gaz is toe-to-toe with one of theirs. He's right at it, pulls a picture off the wall. Smash! That's gone into him as well. It's gone on for five to ten minutes mins when the OB start turning up so the Yids are away before they get a pull. Inside, one of the lads points out to Gaz he looks like he's took a stripe on the back, luckily it hasn't cut the skin but his Armani jumper's had it. The OB has had enough and escort them up out to the Tube and packed off back to King's Cross – they had had their fun for the day now we wanted ours.

After the game we waited till the crowds started moving so we could blend in more because you're easily spotted when you go too early. We walk out and to our surprise, the OB haven't clocked us as we make our way to the High Road. We've got about eighty together at the start and as we start walking up the High Road, you can see the Yids congregating in the alleyway opposite. At that, there's another group of Yids comes up from the street to our left and it goes off. We're in the middle of the road, we're charging left into the first group and they back off down the street as they're well outnumbered. Then the Yids in the alleyway start pouring out onto the road so we're into them, charging across to the right; it's carnage. Everyone seems to be scrapping across the street with only a few OB running. They didn't know where to start, they had lost control. A few OB with dogs come running up to separate us whilst they're trying to move one end of

Left: Football League Division Two – Cardiff City v Manchester United at Ninian Park, August 1974.

(© PA Images/Alamy)

Right: Football violence, 1970s style – a young Manchester United fan with a dart stuck in his face is escorted by a policeman.

(© Bob Thomas Sports Photography via Getty Images)

Left: The title of this book comes from a terrace chant and taunt that echoed around the terraces during the 70s, particularly when Manchester United were playing; indeed, their travelling Red Army may even be its originators. Crowd trouble has intermittently flourished down the decades since.

(© Roger Jackson/Getty Images)

Right: As the 70s ended and the 80s began, the casual movement took grip across Britain around the time of the dying punk scene, mixed with Mod revivalists and the random second-generation skin.
(© Jake Payne)

Below: As we entered the 80s the violence started to move to the more serious business away from the grounds, where if you lived in London you would find the tube stations, like this one, turned into war zones.
(© Jake Payne)

Casuals: the Football Casual subculture originated on the terraces, with its followers expressing themselves through football, fighting and fashion.
(above and below: © Jake Payne; inset: © Cass Pennant)

Above: Trouble breaks out between police and fans in the streets at a Sunderland v Newcastle derby match in April 2015. *(© Steve Drew/PA)*

Below: Birmingham's fans have aways had a bit of history with Man City because that's where the firm's name Zulus originated. *(© Ed Garvey/Manchester City FC via Getty Images)*

Above: Police move in to separate two sets of rival supporters as trouble flares during a Division One match between Leeds United and Manchester United at Elland Road, 20 September 1980. *(© Harry Ormesher/Popperfoto via Getty Images)*

Below: Football violence had reached its nadir in 1985 with the Millwall riot at Luton Town's Kenilworth Road ground – fans versus police. *(© PA/PA Archive/PA Images)*

Above and below: Pitch invasions can be joyous occasions where fans and players can celebrate together, or they can have a tint of sheer darkness about them. The upper photo shows promotion at Brighton's Goldstone Ground; the image below shows a pitch invasion at Fratton Park, home of Portsmouth FC. *(above: © Nick Sarjeant; below: © Jake Payne)*

Above: Millwall fans gesture before the FA Cup quarter-final game between Tottenham Hotspur and Millwall at White Hart Lane in March 2017. *(© Yui Mok/PA Archive/PA Images)*

Below: The police are out in force to prevent a clash between Tottenham and Millwall supporters before the match. Both sets of fans have a serious reputation for football violence. *(© Yui Mok/PA Archive/PA Images)*

Above: The emphasis has shifted: now we are seeing far more hardcore hooliganism at lower-league football matches. Here Queens Park Rangers and Cardiff fans clash outside QPR's Loftus Road ground before kick-off, August 2015. *(© Scott Heavey/EMPICS Sport)*

Below: Top Boys: (*left to right*) Barrington Patterson aka Zulu Baz, Riaz Khan, Carlton Leach, Gary Clarke aka Boatsy, Ian Bailey, Danny Brown aka Black Danny, and (*seated*) author Cass Pennant. *(© Simon Harsent)*

the mob. We've moved up the road a few meters and met the Yids head on. We steamed into them from the middle of the road. Everyone's at it again, fists flying, and they back off ... We've put on a good show here. An OB van drives right into the middle of us, we all have to dive out of the way ... a pretty successful tactic to separate us.

We keep moving up the High Road and the Yids are shadowing us both sides and having another go. Bottles and cans raining into us, but the OB are starting to get control now and are soon rounded up with vans and horses – the fun's over for us. One of our lads was on the Yids' side of the road and he was set upon. He ended up with a broken ankle and a few cuts and bruises. A few of theirs had some belting black eyes. It didn't take long for word to get out around the country of our turnout. It was some day ... fair play to both sides.

The return fixture at the Riverside was eagerly awaited and the Yids said they were travelling. We were out early and back then there were several pubs around 'Boro railway station which we would move around, hoping to clock the opposition. The station at 'Boro was mobbed with OB, we knew it was going to be difficult so we got word to the Yids once they were at Darlington they should get taxis through instead of using the train. The advice wasn't taken and they came in by train about seventy-handed at 1pm. They were rounded up straight away by the OB and taken to the Bridge pub just nearby. They weren't very happy about the situation and one of theirs set fire to the curtains in the pub, The OB took them all out and marched them straight to the ground, which was a waste. The only chance we had was to wait for them on the dockside road after the game in the hope they could slip the escort. Unfortunately, 'Boro OB are sharp, and the Yids slipped up and left early. They were rounded up and escorted back to the station before the game had even ended so a bit of a disappointment.

Another occasion, 2002, saw Birmingham playing at home to the Yids, which the Yids had taken a large firm to. We coincidentally were playing West Brom away so we decided to make a pit stop at Brum to confront the Yids. We took two coaches, about a hundred lads, to the outskirts of Brum and got the train into Snow Hill station, walking out undetected and around to the Bullring Tavern. There was a small group of Blues across the road, about ten-handed, and we scattered them but it was the Yids we were really looking for, who were plotted up in China Town. We were marching across and the OB vans started screeching up around us, we kept moving until the OB numbers were enough to corral us. Amazingly, the OB said, right, lads, we will escort you to the pub, where the rest of your lads are, and started to walk us there – they actually thought we were more of the Yids' contingent that had travelled that day. We got to the corner of where the pub was and a Yids spotter said, they aren't our lot ... ha, ha.

Can you imagine if the OB had walked us into that pub ... think there would have been some disciplinary action dished out, back at the office. The game was up for us there and we were held then escorted back to the station and we moved on to West Brom.

The 2005 fixture at the Riverside, we all knew they would return the favour ... they had to and we knew it was their main game of the season. We had a massive turnout from early doors.

We had surrounded the train station waiting for them to arrive. 'Boro station separates the town and an area known as 'over the border' – if you've been to 'Boro by train, you will know it's a small station with arrivals from Darlington coming in on the border side. The railway bridge is the through road and today the OB have blocked off the road to home supporters – we can't even walk under. Not to be deterred when the Yids' train arrives at 2.30pm, we all pile into the front of the station, which the OB wasn't expecting. Police with their dogs and batons push us back out of the station as the Yids are funnelling out on the opposite side, it's getting lively.

The Yids have brought 150 firm, good show, but for me played it safe again coming in late on the train. We expected more as we showed when we went to theirs, getting taxis in.

They've come out the station and went to have a go at the Bridge pub but they're surrounded and a few get nicked straight away. They get marched up the dockside road and we have gone all the way round and come through the underpass to get in front of them.

The crowds are heavy near the ground and we're shadowing as they get close but the OB are on us, moving the horses into us. They're pretty determined to not allow any action today.

As they get near, they chant, 'Yid Army, Yid Army,' and the roar goes up as lads try to have a pop from all sides as they get to the car park of the ground; it goes off both sides, have a pop, but in reality, the OB are holding firm. After the game the Yids are surrounded and walked down to the station. Again, all we can do is wait in the side streets and around the station. When they near, there's a bit of commotion near the Bridge pub and under the railway bridge but there's just too many OB. A few Yids are on the deck, the OB nicked about three or four near the station, it's over. We clock a few Yids coming up and have a chat with them. They were up for it today but they hadn't expected the OB turnout, which ultimately won that day.

The '90s to mid-2000s, we were very active and in the end victims of our own success. We had travelled to Maine Road [Manchester City] on three occasions and caused havoc. As for Man United, we got the better of them at Deans Gate one game and that started a cycle of tit-for-tat home and away battles that went season after season. Out of all the clubs, United put the best show on at 'Boro. They tried every way they could to come and have a pop, top respect to them.

Rows with Forest, Everton, Cardiff, Chelsea, Sunderland, Newcastle, Hull, Leeds, Derby, Bradford, Birmingham, Villa, Stockport, Stoke, Wigan, Sheffield United, plus Bristol City the night before we played in Cardiff at the Carling Cup final and a European tour that saw it go off at pretty much every trip. In the end the banning orders came thick and fast for everyone too, three for me in total. The risk versus reward was now too great, it was part of the fabric of football; the casual scene was your life. I lived and breathed it and hold the memories dear. Respect to all the lads from our firm. So many great days with top lads and friends for life and in memory of those who are sadly no longer with us. RIP. Respect to all the lads I've met over the years from other teams, I've made some top friends ... Happy days.

BLADES BUSINESS CREW

'TIME FOR A SHIFT IN POWER IN THE STEEL CITY'

STEVE COWENS, SHEFFIELD UNITED: In Sheffield, it's simple: you are either Red or Blue; a middle ground does not exist in our great city. Sheffield's football divide, and the fierce rivalry that goes with it, has led to numerous arrests and jail sentences, countless injuries, near-fatalities and tragically, even the death of an innocent United fan. The hatred between the two clubs has seen the use of weapons in battle, including acid, petrol bombs, knives, bats and distress flares alongside the more common football weaponry taken from pubs, such as glasses, bottles and pool cues. Other cities sharing two football teams don't seem to have the intense problem that Sheffield has; in Liverpool, for instance, the Scousers can share the same pubs and ends on match days, but, in Sheffield, that is simply not possible. The Steel City divide has even been known to split families and ruin friendships.

But why do the Sheffield clubs hate each other with such a passion? Although both clubs' fans share a mutual dislike for their rivals, in the '50s and '60s, some fans from both teams used to go to Hillsborough one week then Bramall Lane the following week. My grandad was one of those fans and, although he definitely went to watch Wednesday lose – well, he hoped they would lose – he really went to watch a game of football. Something changed during the late '60s and early '70s – perhaps it was the explosion of gang culture, when Teddy Boys, skinheads, rockers and Mods made it seem cool to be part of a gang, or maybe it was simply part of the social unrest amongst young men that was so evident at the time. This, coupled with the fact that Maggie Thatcher's policies triggered the collapse of the national coal industry, lead to a reduced population in Sheffield.

Commonly known as the City of Seven Hills, Sheffield is surrounded by stunning countryside and the city itself has more trees per person than any other city in Europe. Sheffield is England's fifth-largest metropolitan area with a population of 1,811,700, most of whom are from a working-class background, which helps make the city's people some of the friendliest, most welcoming people on our shores.

It has also bred football fans that will fight for their clubs' territory and pride. This pride is often channelled into violence and Derby Day is not a place for the faint-hearted. Both sets of fans refer to each other as 'pigs', a derogatory term which originated in the late '70s. Both sides can explain their reasoning for this: Wednesday say they call us pigs because United's red and white shirts actually remind them of streaky bacon, while United fans argue that Hillsborough – Swillsborough – was actually built on a piggery, a fact backed up by local history books.

Sheffield in the '70s was a hotbed for trouble at football. In 1973, United fans topped a football league of shame. The United hooligan element had seen 276 arrests, with Wednesday finishing third in the table with 258 arrests. So, over a season, the two clubs had seen arrests totalling 534. Sheffield was fast becoming the home of football-related violence. The year before the table was published, there was large-scale disorder at United's games throughout the season. In April.

In 1972, Newcastle's visit to Bramall Lane led to 54 fans being arrested, the return game saw a further 83 locked up, then a month later another 30 arrests were made during the game with Manchester United which saw running battles on the Shoreham Kop as Manchester's Red Army battled it out with the SRA. When Chelsea's visit produced another 41 arrests, Sheffield United games had now become a policeman's nightmare. The stark reality of it all was in just four United home games there had been a total of 192 arrests.

Over at Hillsborough, Manchester United's visit in the same season produced 113 arrests, although, of that amount, over 30 were juveniles. What is interesting is that the numbers of police allocated to the games at this time were around 120, although by 1976 the number of police keeping order at football had doubled.

At the Sheffield derbies nowadays or a high-profile game, over 280 police are now on duty, when the violence is nowhere near as bad or as out of control as it used to be.

Wednesday knew they had the upper hand but their arrogance during the late '70s and early '80s was to prove their downfall. It was quite weird at times in our city; both sets of lads would often drink together in the Blue Bell in town. People like Smids from United were good mates with Bender from Wednesday and in certain situations the two groups would drink in the same pub without a hint of trouble.

Leeds United's visit to Hillsborough in September 1982 confirmed this when an 80-strong United firm went in the Blue Bell on the High Street. Inside were over one hundred Wednesday. Both groups didn't really mingle together: our mob was at one end of the pub, the other firm were at the opposite end and the middle ground was for the few people that knew each other, keeping a sort of peaceful barrier between the two mobs, as there was no doubt a few who wanted to knock seven shades out of each other but in the name of Sheffield they bottled their hatred up for once. Even though Sheffield turned out over 200 mixed lads, they would not fight side by side as this day proved.

Leeds actually got into town and Wednesday left the Blue Bell to engage them in combat. United stayed put, which, looking back, was weird really. News came back that Wednesday had been done by Leeds and that Leeds were heading our way via the hole in the road.

We left the Blue Bell via the back doors and in the little alley between the Dove and Rainbow and the Blue Bell, it kicked off with Leeds. Ribina shoe shop was raided and stiletto heels were used by United's lads against Sheffield's most hated city. The stilettos were the last thing Leeds had to worry about as Trimmer had a ratchet screwdriver and he twice plunged it into the back of the neck of some poor Leeds lad.

Leeds backed off and we argued that we had done Wednesday's work for them as they weren't up to it. Later that night, the unlikely peace between Wednesday and United turned into violence as both sides clashed in town. It was probably the last time the two groups tolerated each other. It had been a situation that seems unbelievable nowadays and one that most lads didn't want in the first place but, because a few respected lads knew each other and got on, the others tried to keep the cart on the rails.

The shoots of a new breed of fan at Bramall Lane were beginning to stir around this time. United's plight on the pitch was at an all-time low, and defeat to Walsall in the final game of the 1979/80 season saw the Blades ply their trade for the first time in English football's basement, the Fourth Division. Wednesday fans mockingly call the day United were relegated 'Thank Givens Day', after Don Givens missed a last-minute penalty that would have kept United up.

Perversely, the relegation actually made the club's fans stronger; everywhere we went, we took big numbers and, to 16-year-old lads like me, it was an ideal time for serving an apprenticeship in terms of football violence. The youngsters, of which we had many, surfaced into this new world, a world of tennis, golf and designer wear and fighting at football. The Casual movement had erupted onto the scene and with it, a new breed of football hooligan.

Wednesday, for their part, failed to see this new breed emerging in big numbers across the city. They treated our firm with contempt and that was Wednesday's downfall. Three years later and with numerous battles under our belts, we were ready to take it to Wednesday and take it to Wednesday we did, with bells on.

The older United lads began to realise that these young lads in Fila and Tacchini were well up for the challenge and a new optimism swept the hooligan corridors around Bramall Lane. It was time for a shift in power in the Steel City.

MOLOTOV MADNESS

One Friday evening in late autumn 1985, 30 United lads were drinking in the Pheasant Inn on London Road. Nothing was different really, same lads out, same pub crawl, but this night was to be the start of two months of hostility between United and Wednesday that got seriously out of hand. The rumour mill had been in overdrive, Wednesday were turning up here, there and every-fuckin'-where. That night, we got a tip-off via the pub phone from a Blade in town, who told us Wednesday had up to fifty lads in town and they looked like they were heading our way. Sure enough, Wednesday walked a firm straight up to the Pheasant. It was like they wanted to try to stop this young Blades firm in their tracks and show them who was boss – wrong! When we realised our foe was on our doorstep, the pub emptied, with the snooker cues exiting as well. Hand-to-hand combat broke out in the middle of London Road and Wednesday were backed off before they turned and ran. One of their main men got captured and ragged a bit, as did a lad who had his dreadlocks ripped from his scalp, Red Indian style. They were pinned on the wall of a pub on London Road as some sort of trophy with a little written sign underneath that read, 'Wednesday dreads, ripped from head'! Another Wednesday lad was laid out unconscious and we were concerned about the state of him. Some of ours laid him out in the recovery position and tended to him until the Old Bill showed. Wednesday had regrouped in the Roebuck in town but United had tasted victory and wanted to finish this Owls' firm off, for one night anyhow. We went up and, as Wednesday poured out of the pub, we put them to flight again.

The following weekend, 50 of us went up West Street to search for the snorters. Wednesday were in the Saddle just up from the Limit and the pub was attacked, with Wednesday getting out in the doorway only to be overpowered. A few Wednesday were assaulted later on as they stood in the queue to get in the Limit. It all got a bit silly really; it wasn't safe to be either a Blade or an Owl around this time.

The code of conduct, if ever it has existed between the two groups, was shot to pieces as it became a no-rules affair with reports of both Wednesday and United lads attacked in town while out with either non-hooligan mates or girlfriends. The tit-for-tat attacks carried on weekly, with Wednesday being run off London Road twice more. The third and final time Wednesday were run, they didn't even stand long enough for a punch to be thrown, and I knew at this point that we had got to them mentally.

Then the following Friday we heard through the hoolie-vine that Wednesday were turning a big team out to launch an attack on our London Road territory; they were going to put us in our place once and for all, or so they said. Because there had been plenty of trouble in the previous month or so, the OB had a large presence in the area so we would have to be at our cunning best to get any action from the night. Around a hundred of our firm were plotted up on London Road when I arrived.

I had made elaborate plans and I'd bandaged my leg up and carried a crutch even though I had no injury. We had been told that Wednesday would be well and truly tooled up so it was a case of meeting fire with fire. A few United lads had also taken the threat seriously as three baseball bats were hidden behind the fruit machine in the Pheasant. As always, we had people on patrol in cars. The scouts had clocked Wednesday and they had similar numbers to us. Wednesday's plan was to come on to London Road via the back-walks and avoid coming in through town. The OB were all over London Road like a rash and we knew that we might have to take a few arrests tonight, but business needed to be taken care of. To be honest, Wednesday had been lost off our radar. We had no idea where they had gone from the last sighting and things started to get tetchy. Then news of Wednesday's whereabouts came from an unexpected source, a copper's radio. Bingo, we now knew that the Wednesday firm were heading up St Mary's Gate.

Four of us jumped into Frankie's car to suss out their mob. Two distress flares were loaded as we drove off. Wednesday were clocked on Denby Street entering the Sportsman Inn. A distress flare was shot in their direction. The Wednesday firm cheered as the flare rose above their heads and crashed into the pub wall. Our lot were literally 300–400 yards away tucked up and waiting for news. We headed back and relayed the news. We had to get the OB away from the Pheasant, so, in a cunning plan, we sent 20 lads down London Road towards the Lansdowne.

Sure enough, the OB followed. The rest of us headed off in dribs and drabs to meet up in the Sheldon car park and then walk down towards Wednesday en masse. As we got closer, the snorts sussed us and started screaming at the tops of their voices to their colleagues inside the pub. It was at this point that a few of us started to jog towards them. One of our main actors shouted for everyone to walk and keep quiet. It was a bit weird and didn't get the old adrenaline pumping like normal as we walked casually towards Wednesday, who were by now going crackers in the road.

Once within throwing distance, Wednesday threw the lot at us – it was a case of covering your face as you couldn't see the missiles in the dark. The roar went up and our casual walk was no more as we all hurtled down at them. Later, Wednesday maintained that the OB ran them back into the pub and left us alone; in truth, Wednesday had started to do one before the OB arrived and the Plod actually came from behind us and ran through, clubbing anything in their way. The police came from everywhere and I limped off as the Plod steamed everyone. As I hobbled around the corner, I bumped into Sam. Then, as we made our way back to London Road via another street, 10 of Wednesday's main boys came around the corner; they had missed the battle: 'Run again, you mugs.'

They came at us but I just tucked the crutch under my arm and my limp became a sprint, it's a miracle! Miracle over, as I ran around the building and straight into four Old Bill. Shit, crutch back to the floor and limp back in fashion. Sam copped a clip but I was left and told to clear off.

Later that evening, a Blade was blinded in one eye as he was hit with a glass as we attacked a pub with Wednesday inside. Ten lads had been arrested that night, eight were Blades and two were young OCS lads. The two Wednesday lads had been arrested while carrying four petrol bombs in a rucksack; I knew them both and they were obviously doing other people's dirty work, as they didn't even have it in them to fight at the time, never mind throw a petrol bomb. While the two of them were on remand in Hull Prison, they were attacked by a couple of Blades.

Later, they both received two years in a young offenders' unit. The petrol bomb was a frightening and sinister new development in the war for supremacy between the rival groups. Two days after the tear-up with Wednesday, I popped in the Sportsman during my dinner break. The Shaw family had just taken over the pub and Graham the landlord showed me a bag of sharpened triangles of lead that Wednesday had left under the seats. They would have no doubt blinded someone if they had hit their target.

The trouble and arrests, and even the fact that one Blade lad had permanently lost the sight in one eye, didn't stop the trouble continuing. Two weeks later, a group of 20 Blades attacked around 10 Wednesday in a pub on West Street and chased them into the women's toilets. Things had got seriously out of hand.

WEDNESDAY CENTENARY, 1989

The 1989–90 season was United's centenary year. To celebrate, a pre-season friendly had been arranged with the old foe, Sheffield Wednesday. The game was to be played in August at Bramall Lane and would be a nice warm-up for our now very strong firm.

On the day of the game, we met as usual in the Pheasant on London Road. When I turned up at midday, there were only around forty of our firm gathered in the pub. Wednesday were meeting at the Arbourthorne

Hotel, a pub situated on a tough council estate around three miles from beautiful downtown Bramall Lane. Wednesday had been making big noises that they were turning everyone out and this new Blades firm were going to be put back in their place after taking over proceedings in Sheffield. A few telephone calls were made and I spoke to a top Wednesday lad. He told me that Wednesday had about 150 lads out and that the firm they had was the best they had turned out for many a year. I could tell by the tone in his voice that he fancied their chances but then again so did I. It was agreed that Wednesday would make their way down to the Earl of Arundel and we would head for the Sheaf; hooligan kick-off time was arranged for 2.30.

With more of our lot turning up by the minute, by one o'clock we had well over 100 lads out and, to be fair, they were all our main firm of mid-20-year-olds, who were by now seasoned thugs. Our average age at this time was probably around twenty-four, while our rival firm's average age would have been thirty to thirty-five. To us, it didn't matter about the numbers or quality Wednesday had out, as we knew that we would steam into them and, when you have over 100 lads who are all of the same mind, then Wednesday are going to struggle to cope. In truth, man for man, Wednesday probably had a harder firm than us but this was football violence and it didn't matter how handy individuals were, the firm who wanted it most were the ones who were going to come out on top.

One of our scouts pulled up in the car outside the Pheasant and told us Wednesday were on the move and also confirmed they had a massive team out. Good, no excuses then, I thought. They were keeping their end of the deal by heading to the Arundel, so we supped up and headed for our appointed destination, the Sheaf. We'd split up into twos and threes as the Plod were all over London Road like a rash and we didn't want to attract their attention by walking en masse to our destination and ruining our chances of an off.

Everyone was buzzing and well up for it outside the Sheaf, as lads went around encouraging each other and shaking hands as if to confirm the tightness of our firm. Bang on 2.30, we set off. I walked in front with Tiler. We both knew that neither of us would back off an inch, so we bounced in front of our firm, whose strides were getting quicker and longer with every step.

The Sheaf was only 500 yards from the Earl but not visible until we walked around the corner. We were by now 300 yards from the Earl and Wednesday spilled out of the pub and began running up towards us. We fanned and our quick walk soon became a jog. I looked at Tiler, who was running down parallel with me. 'Don't stop, straight in,' I yelled but Tiler didn't need telling. I was just getting the old adrenaline pumping through my body. Wednesday did indeed have a great mob and, to be honest, I thought we were going to have a big job on our hands to shift them along; the least I expected was a toe-to-toe battle as Wednesday had turned every face out.

'BBC, BBC! was shouted with an aggression I had never heard before.

Wednesday completely filled the road and pavements. Around ten black lads were fronting for Wednesday. I knew most of them and they were respected geezers in our city, but this was football and it wasn't about individuals, it was about who wanted it most, who was the gamest, who had the bottle.

As the two firms got within launching distance of each other, glasses, bricks and bottles filled the air. We didn't slow in our charge. The two front rows tore into each other but Wednesday had committed the cardinal sin of stopping their charge and standing flat. Big mistake – it's the first sign of loss of nerve.

Anyhow, Wednesday had managed to get 100 yards from the pub so perhaps the bog hiders missed the action but Wednesday started to lose nerve and backed off. I ran and hit one just as he was turning to run; he went down but was back on his feet and running in a split second. They were screaming at each other to 'STAND' but we'd got them on the hop and continued our assault on the disappearing Wednesday line. That sight of Wednesday's best firm in total retreat was a buzz and a half. Some game lad called Zack had stood on his own and was copping a beating from around ten of our lot who had captured him. I ran over and pulled a few of our lot off him; fair play to him, he was the only one with the bollocks to stand his ground, and kicking him into the middle of next week was the last thing he deserved.

I escorted him to the sanctuary of the surrounding roadside trees. He shook my hand, muttering that Wednesday were shit. I ran to join up with the rest of our firm, who had totally written off Wednesday's firm. In that one 45-second brawl, we had proved we were still the top firm in Sheffield. They had turned out every face and every big gun they had but our young casual firm were too strong and too game. A lot of their older heads seemed to disappear from their ranks after that day.

The OB got the bedraggled OCS firm together and marched them slowly to the ground. Quite a few of us waited near the top of Bramall Lane, as we wanted to mock their firm and rub the result in as much as possible. The OCS made a token effort to break from the escort as a few of us were shouting 'runners' and 'shit Wednesday'. The half-hearted attempt at breaking free was greeted with a cheer from our lot; they had had the chance to dance but failed. We went in the ground but a lot of United's lads didn't bother. Wednesday for their part sloped off into town under the OB escort.

BLADE V OWL / BBC V OCS

I knew that the BBC (Blades Business Crew) would turn out big numbers for this game in March 1992; there was a much better chance of a dance for the evening game at Hillsborough than there had been at Bramall Lane. The fact that United had sold their 7,200 allocation in hours meant that a lot of Blades bought tickets for

Wednesday's Kop and seats, so trouble was guaranteed. At teatime, 300 BBC and other Blades had gathered in two pubs in town.

The plan was to drink our way to Hillsborough and hit the back of their Kop around kick-off time. The OB were all over us like a rash. Ten riot vans backed up by Plod on horseback and foot monitored our movements. Then the march to Hillsborough was on. United's mob looked impressive as it stretched out along Penistone Road for over 200 yards. I knew that when we hit the crowds at the ground, the Plod would have to be on top form to stop us breaking from the escort. Sure enough, around forty of us broke out and, in trying to get us rounded back up, the escort fell to pieces. We were now all over the place, on enemy territory and up for a ruck.

Bang outside the Wednesday Kop, it went off. Hundreds of Wednesday fans were in massive queues at the turnstiles.

'BBC, BBC,' rang out and to be fair, a lot of Wednesday were prepared to fight against this intrusion. The BBC went about their work and battles raged right along the back of their Kop as the United firm had split into smaller groups. I ended up with 20 others towards the top end of Penistone Road. A lot of Wednesday who were walking down from various pubs like the Gate and the Travellers ran up to join in the battling. We ran into them football-style and they had a good go. Another surge in from us and we ran them. One stood his ground and was beaten to the floor.

At this point, I thought we were going to get done as Wednesday had regrouped and, as more and more numbers swelled their ranks, they came charging back at us. There seemed to be hundreds of them but we stood firm and traded. I copped someone's size nines in the bollocks, and I nearly spewed up as the pain of my nads being rattled had me bent double. The OB managed to get control by forcing United's firm across the road. I sat on a wall, cupping my bollocks.

Seven United lads were nicked; one was Shammy, whose face was all over the front page of the *Sheffield Star* when he went to court. They were all banned from attending for a period of one year.

I was in a bit of a dilemma at Hillsborough, as the OB tried to force us to the away end, as I'd got a ticket for Wednesday's stand. Around twenty-five good lads had obtained seats towards the Kop end of Wednesday's North Stand. When I got inside, I met up with the rest, who had sensibly ignored their seat numbers and sat right at the back so, when or if it came on top, we had the high ground.

We had a great view of the fighting as it broke out on Wednesday's Kop. Hundreds of United fans had infiltrated it and it was kicking off all along the front as fans battled it out. The police took ages to sort out the situation and, just as they had removed one lot of Blades, it would kick off again.

It just shows the depth of feeling in our city when two really young lads, who were dressed in United tracksuits, gave Wednesday fans, along with their dad, the wanker signs as they were escorted around the perimeter track after being ejected from the Kop.

United came out and I stood in proud admiration of our fans. It was like a scene from the San Siro as a dozen red distress flares lit up the Leppings Lane End. Thousands of balloons bounced around and two massive flags were passed along the end. I was proud of my fellow supporters and the atmosphere they created was second to none. The team rewarded such great support with a fine 3–1 victory, with Sheffield lad and staunch Blade Dane Whitehouse notching again along with two from on-loan Bobby Davison. Each United goal had been greeted with sporadic fighting all around the ground.

At the final whistle, we stood on the seats clapping the team off and generally going shitpot-crazy.

As the crowds vacated the ground, we could see trouble at mill in the shape of a load of Wednesday lads coming up towards us. We just waited patiently for them to get within reach of us. Wayne then roundhouse-kicked one in the side of his face and he was sent crashing over the seats. That was it; we all surged over the seats at them and they in turn surged over the seats in panic to get away. They were falling all over each other and pulling each other back in their haste. Outside, we mobbed back up at the petrol station as planned and the two hundred or so of us walked the three miles back into town. In town, clubs were packed with Blades celebrating a famous Sheffield double.

Forty-two fans were arrested during the night: 37 Blades and five Wednesday.

Fighting between the two rival mobs was at its height around this time, and the early to mid-1990s saw trouble involving the BBC and the OCS escalate into weekly encounters. Both groups started to concentrate more on each other than on the teams they were playing. We could have a game with great potential with, say, Barnsley away but the Beeb were more interested in staying in Sheffield because Wednesday had Grimsby at home and they would be turning a firm out. It got ridiculous.

Even Friday nights had started to see regular trouble. The police started to get sick of it, so arrests became more commonplace as the OB sought to stop these marauding mobs of football thugs. Charges got more serious, and the police adopted a new tactic of getting lads on a higher charge with the view that they might accept a lesser charge later in court. An offence which would usually carry a charge of threatening behaviour was upped to a charge of affray, which would be today's equivalent of violent disorder. When they hit the courts, the lads were offered the choice of having the charge dropped to threatening behaviour. A lot of lads accepted this and the police started to see a few results in court rather than the 'Not Guilty all the way' attitude that football lads had previously adopted.

We Blades will enjoy being number one in Sheffield while it lasts. We are realists and know that fortunes can change. As always, we will continue to follow and support our team with the pride and passion that we have in our club. Bramall Lane is a special place with an atmosphere that is rarely mirrored and Sheffield United are indeed a very special club.

You fill up my senses, like a gallon of Magnet.

Like a packet of woodbines, like a good pinch of snuff Like a night out in Sheffield, like a greasy chip butty. Like Sheffield United, come fill me again.

Up the Blades.

LEEDS SERVICE CREW

A LOINER'S LALE

SEAN RILEY, LEEDS UNITED: Born and bred in a tough but good working-class background in Leeds, Grandad who had survived Gallipoli and the Somme in World War I, took Dad, who was also a tough Normandy veteran, to his War of the Roses game [against Man United] in 1930. My brother and brother-in-law took myself in 1969, to see one of the greatest and most hated footballing teams on earth. The atmosphere was addictive and we won. I knew nothing else though then and expected it. I in turn took my own son in 1997 when he was four years old to Elland Road. It's just how it is – you're from Leeds, you support them.

We've laughed, cried, drank, fought together or even fought each other on mad occasions. We've berated each other, jumped trains together, robbed together, slept rough together, blagged it together, got nicked together, been chinned together but when it came down to it (what matters the most) stood together as one unit. The Harehills and the Old Lot, Service Crew (our little bunch becoming a big bunch; VYT, the lads from all over Yorkshire, afterwards and recent times, all know what it's is like to stand together with one cause, being Leeds).

It didn't matter if some couldn't fight or some were seriously hard lads, most enjoyed it and it became an addiction, you all did it together because we just did. 'We are Leeds' and there's a certain duty that goes with that, a lot of baggage, too, but I wouldn't swap it. A duty that you look the next man at the side of you in the eye and think, 'Let's do it.'

Everyone who follows Leeds United has their reasons for doing so and I'm certain that they will all lead to the same outcome – one love for our club, the one-team city that is Leeds!

THE RIVALRIES

Where do you start? There's many teams I can say we have rivalry with, probably everyone because it feels like everyone hates us.

I say that with a wry smile now in my older age, I've never really got wound up about it but more so enjoyed it. Our lot know it's a You against Them survival attitude; we've certainly taken that onboard and embraced it, we've had to. I'd be lying if I said we didn't enjoy going to many of the grounds, underdogs on the day but overturning it off the field. Like most firms holding their own, sometimes taking a loss and definitely winning more than our fair share when we should not have done.

There's going to be firms out there disappointed they haven't got a full mention. I respect you no less than any other and some more than others. The Millwalls Chelsea, West Ham (great place to go, the old Upton Park and good firm), 'Boro, Scousers (both but more so Liverpool because of the Shankly–Revie thing), Man City, the Yorkies (more so for them than us), Birmingham, Wolves, Derby, Forest (steady outfit), Cardiff, Bristol Rovers, none are less than anyone mentioned. We have taken some cracking firms to all of them; we've done it with little firms, too, and enjoyed every minute of it, whatever the outcome. There's one team that we in Leeds have a very tough, special rivalry with and it will surprise many– Tottenham!

I know now there's a few raised eyebrows up and down the country. I personally have many experiences with them home and away but more so away. It's just that ground we have to go to and do so; if you are of a certain age you will know why and also what it means to our Firm.

That is the one we have struggled with more so at times. From 1979 onwards it was always mayhem and very bad to travel to, whether you were on the coach or train. Other firms have had more aggro with Arsenal, we've had fun there, too, in the past but it was and is always Tottenham for us. A lot of my pals and old Leeds will tell you this, too, it's not as widely broadcast in the media but it is well known around the hooligan world. Personal injuries, nickings and some fantastic victories spring to mind on many occasions with Spurs and there's a book alone from Leeds' experiences on their N17 rivals, I'll say it from us all.

Everybody around the country hears that name Leeds and they associate it with aggro, a big day out for their team whether that's home or away. Some of these fans have never faced Leeds before but have seen/heard the hatred from their dads, grandads, uncles or anyone who says, 'I hate Leeds.' They want to see what it's like against Leeds, feel it, taste it and quench their curiosity or restore old rivalries. I'm the same with many other clubs we look forward to facing throughout the season or in the cups. Some of them obvious rivalries, some that are rivalries obtained over the years that are not so obvious to the majority of firms but are to those clubs and also our own lads. Maybe more so with our lads.

TOTTENHAM

The Tottenham thing had gone on in the '70s with Leeds, and I guess it's that personal experience every firm has with a surprising one: in 1980, we took 14 on the Service Train down to Tottenham and it was absolutely mental outside. Couldn't get out of the ground, every time those big gates opened it went bang. Until we decided to walk back with the coaches then go from there.

We walked out of the ground with the coach lot and

left into an estate, they came straight into us through the Old Bill. There were even women throwing stuff off the flats at us. Ha ha, we held our own until we had to walk to the overground. We had a go outside but then they came in, onto the platform and into us. We ended up getting legged down the lines, stood out like sore thumbs, in our northern scally gear and wedge haircuts.

Year after was fantastic though, known as the building site year '81. We had a good firm to be fair, a couple of hundred on the Service Train. Been boozing in Piccadilly and met some of our old lot, who were working and grafting in the Smoke at that time. So, we were fairly confident when we got to White Hart Lane overground and out. We chased them on the High Street and nothing more to say, that was until the ground. They came at us from two sides, everyone stood outside our end though and I got a right crack, sidewinder. The OB didn't give a Friar Tuck at White Hart Lane, didn't like Leeds and apparently Liverpool, who I understand in their fixture there got absolutely smashed. We all got stuck in and Spurs couldn't believe it, they expected us to be off on our toes but it was a bigger, better firm than the year before.

A few more goes and then they let us in the ground, some Spurs came in with us and it went off inside. Leeds had too many lads for them but they at least did come in with us and have a go. One of them definitely had a blade in his inside coat pocket, he showed us it a couple of times so nobody got within a yard of him. Another bloke was giving it the Big Un with martial arts hand moves, until Alan P slotted him a beauty. In again with them, but a lad from Stockton, Russ, clouted the knifeman with a dustbin lid, the Old Bill separated us and lobbed them out. Knife man had a screw loose because he pulled the blade out, outside the ground and was shouting, 'Getting it, Leeds, all of you, no prisoners afterwards.' The OB swooped on him and day over for him. Absolute crank, big twat in a donkey jacket, I'll never forget him.

Match ended and it was same as the previous year – bedlam when the gates opened, tons of fighting but couldn't go right to Tottenham High Street and Seven Sisters. Sheer volume of numbers saw to that, the noise, the roar, the toe-to-toe time and time again, until the OB decided to hold everyone in for a while and clear the streets.

Same again, we did a left with the coaches and bang in the same spot near the flats they attacked us but this year, it was a firm out for revenge. More lads and some harder, gamer lads there, too. We had our fun but the reality kicked in as we got to the coach park. When the coaches were leaving it was just us that were left, about 150. Some of ours had jumped on a few coaches back to Leeds and up north. Never forget that till I die and I know who they were, too, so do they.

Two London coppers said, 'Right, lads, make your way to the station.' One of our best lads (RB, who's dead now) asked them, 'Which way?' Reply was, 'Back there to Northumberland Park or just straight up there to White Hart Lane overground.' We thought we'd take our chance to WHL overground, as we walked in, one of our lot said, 'Look up there, a massive firm of Tottenham.'

RB said, 'Fuck this, get anything you can get your hands on and walk, walk straight towards them.' Everyone's nerves were going but we walked towards them, nonetheless. They waited where they were, we walked and then a trot, then full pelt into them at a crossroads. Big shout, 'Come on, Leeds!' Nobody from any side moved. Bottles, bricks, bars, cones, everything into Spurs, toe-to-toe and then AP and RB held us all together, another big shout, 'Fuck this, we're Leeds,' then they cracked. They turned and we had them running, onto the High Street; this was it now they were off.

The OB came and were stunned, they let a dog off its lead and into us, not happy at all we had done Spurs at their ground. Some clouts and boots at our lot were random on the way back to WHL overground. We got there and a little firm tried having a go but no chance, smack, and back they went.

A few of us got cocky and walked over the road where the bridge was. They couldn't believe it, how game everyone was and genuinely up for it. We finally saw sense when the OB fucked us off back over to the station and it was getting a bit naughty for a handful, but that mob of ours was absolutely fantastic that day. Never been as proud of the lads. Many talk about it now as if it was yesterday and I'll be straight, it was very close to being a defeat but for two of our best.

There is a sad ending to this: a young Leeds fan from Bradford got killed at the ground that day, ambushed and set upon by Tottenham, and his killer got five years for the fatal punch. We didn't know this at the time, he died on the Monday.

The train journey home was full of high spirits, the night out back in Leeds fantastic, too. Being with a great bunch of lads at the match, overturning the odds together, not many things can give you that feeling but you know this was an excellent, honest, tough, game firm, and held in great respect by Leeds and not too dissimilar in their working-class backgrounds, social status.

Tottenham another year later was mental. FA Cup match, I got my nose broken and head split open with an iron bar. Many more times our paths crossed home and away over the years. It's a crazy adopted rivalry and I understand that they're not rated in London by other firms but that's our experiences with them. Don't know why they turn out for Leeds, unless it's a respect thing but I doubt it with them.

Ask a fan from another firm who they think our biggest rivalry is with or who they think/ know our biggest row is and you can guarantee a safe bet they will reply with Man United. Who am I to disappoint them with not starting with our biggest rivals and there's many reasons why they are 'THE BIG ONE'.

Every Leeds fan of a certain age can give you a reason why it's Man United. Some that have never experienced a Leeds v Man United game will have a reason why, too. Sadly, Covid-19 hampered our chances this season to renew old rivalries, especially off the pitch. The new young lads who have followed Leeds for the last few seasons and enjoyed the 'Ups and Downs' on our quest to return to the Promised Land, the Premier League (after 16 years away), will definitely get to experience that day.

I'll warn them now it's addictive and can be harmful on that day: the highs, the lows, the drama, the in-between, all of it takes over you. I've seen characters like Adrian Mole turn into Chuck Norris against Man United. The abuse I've seen thrown at them by us, by them to us, too, has been shocking. On that day it's been par for the course, an occupational hazard, goes with the territory. Fuck it, it the strongest survives and wins, it's just what happens with an us-against-them attitude.

A book about famous encounters – battles could be written on their own about this rivalry, by both firms and should probably be called *The Wars of the Roses*.

God, where do I start? There's been that many battles over the years and as I mentioned, it's the BIG ONE to many who follow both clubs, especially ourselves. Some Mancs will claim it's either Liverpool or City who are their biggest rivals but the honest truth is, I don't believe them.

Ask any Manc who they get the most excitement in playing, the vast majority say 'Leeds', who are the ones you all look for, and you will hear 'Leeds' from their main firm.

Some of their best lads have admitted to myself and my pals, too, that it's boring against 'The Mickeys and Citeh but never against you lot'. Yes, it's the BIG ONE. There are many more rivalries to be restored with other teams' firms, and they know who, but this is really it. It's bred into you from the earliest age, all those feelings and memories come flooding back to you.

I can't remember what I had for breakfast at times, but I can remember most of the encounters with Man United, what we were wearing, what they were wearing, the many victories, the defeats, too (off the pitch). The elation in seeing them turn and run, the disappointment in the times we haven't done it but always tried to hold a good account of ourselves because it's them. The injuries, the nickings, the Battle of Burnden Park, the City Ground semi (encounters from our older lads but nonetheless important and impressive to us coming through). Dirty Leeds v the Busby Babes, Jack v Bobby, Bremner v Stiles, Giles v Crerand, Hunter v the Lawman, Reaney v Best (who was probably the greatest full-back to squash Best's unbelievable talent at the time), Sniffer v Anybody, ha ha!, Champions (Leeds) v Relegation (Man United). Hillsborough, the return of the Scum from the Second Division. Jordan and McQueen's return, the hordes from hell, the Clarke victory at Old Traffold (a very small amount from Leeds in attendance), the Terry Connor draw and emergence of the Service Crew, the famous '3rd of May' (now that WAS our finest hour), Cockney Reds at the back of the South Stand, Euston Road and we're not even playing each other. The Mighty Flynn and a brief visit to heaven, bye-bye, Leeds, you're going down, 1990 return to the Promised Land and the Wheatsheaf, Old Trafford one way (1990), the Rumbelows semis, Lee Sharpe and mayhem. The Trilogy in ten days, the

Battle of Ringways (Pride and victory in defeat), one of the best ever, Cantona's departure and return. Just a day out, anyway, it's Yeboah's debut (FA Cup '95), Wilko's sacking (Henry's bar and the opening of the club shop), O'Neills bar and Piccadilly (absolute blinder).

The beauty of Boar Lane and Weatherall, we love you; Warrington drinks and May Day Madness at Oxford Road, Galatasaray v Munich chants (Old Traffold battle bus). Holbeck, Rio's return and the 30 million pieces of silver, the bravery of the Drysalters, we'll meet again and the Rocket.

Premier League Champions v League One hopefuls, Grayson's glory in the Cup, what a firm! Catch-up night out in the League Cup and the Templar, Australia Tour (I wasn't present) and we're going, anyway.

All of them important, exciting experiences and facts but some definitely stick out more than others.

HARK NOW HEAR UNITED SING, THE MAN U RAN AWAY, THERE WILL BE A MASSACRE UPON THE THIRD OF MAY

The 3rd of May 1980 was probably one of the busiest, most hectic, lawless, exciting, vicious, violent clashes against Man United, or anyone else, I've ever experienced. I'm certain fans from both sides will admit that, too. From 9am until midnight, the last match of the season a dwindling Leeds side playing for nothing but pride and giving their suffering fans some brief joy. Man United needed only a point at Elland Road that day to win the league over their other big rivals, Liverpool. We never thought about that statistic, we never even thought that the impossible could happen. We were just turning out against THAT LOT. We'd played Wolves away the week before and had a great day out.

We had taken a cracking, tight-knit firm on the train and more than held our own at Molineux, so confidence was running high for the BIG ONE. We had also (some of us) attended the semi-final replay between Everton v West Ham, enjoying fun at the ground with Everton and back in Leeds city centre against the Cockneys, celebrating their unexpected victory. The talk was building up towards the end of season about the 'last match'. We had viewed the clothes worn by the other firm's 'lads' and had 'run-ins' that year with everyone.

A lot of us were still young lads but had built a great bond with the older lads because everyone was game as hell. Prepared to stand anything and everything, regardless of the consequences, the older lads were hard lads, with hard backgrounds, tough jobs. They were very experienced in fighting for Leeds but respected the bravery shown by 'Our Lot' breaking through the ranks. We had had some tough days out – Tottenham, Arsenal, City, the Scousers, 'Boro, West Brom, Wolves, Coventry etc. – but had weathered the storms well.

The day had arrived and we met up early, 9am in a café in Leeds. There were some good faces out early. Not a lot at this point but some cracking lads, some who are sadly no longer with us but 'Our Lot' will know who they are. We were chatting, laughing, taking the piss out of each other, just trying to pass time and the shout went up: 'They're here, scum are here!'

That was it, the café emptied, they had come off Leeds station dead early and Boar Lane was a mess, a battleground. Shoppers running into BHS for cover, traffic stopped, the odd few Old Bill trying to get to grips with it and failing.

Fair play to Man United, coming in early to oblige us. The fighting then spilled into the City Square, which was a paved area north of the station, and the old Black Marias were zipping about to try to control it. A brick hit one of them and a big roar went up: 'Come on, Leeds!' Another little foray into them. They stood and it was toe-to-toe, punches swapped, boots going in, madness at its highest level. Nobody really giving way until one of the older lads shouted, 'Any one runs, I'll chin 'em!' Leeds was in again and some movement backwards for Man United spurred us on.

They turned and ran the short distance back to the Queens Hotel and the station. A few got caught, knocked down and kicked about. A tall blond fella, a black lad and a stocky dark-haired geezer made a stand and tried to help them but there were too many of us. They did manage to get a couple up and took some flak, before having to run into the hotel for safety. The Old Bill running in, truncheons not just drawn but waving them about like conductors at the Royal Albert Hall, probably didn't help them.

There was no politically correctness in those days by that mob (the Old Bill), everyone was fair game to them and they were brutal. I guess they had to be to some extent, Battlefield Britain every Saturday afternoon and Wednesday night. Don't think they didn't love it either, course they did, another chance for some to pit themselves against the reputations of the rising, disgruntled youth of Thatcher's Britain. Some of it just training for some of their hardliners against the experienced hard men in the cities and on the terraces that they had fought with for over a decade.

Back onto Boar Lane for us though, talking, laughing, ecstatic about the whole affair. Daft young lads caught up in a crazy situation but knew no better. That was the scene, the fashion, the 'norm', the only excitement for some to escape the tedious surroundings of work. Hard, tough, in some cases abusive family life, the political mess the country was in, the mediocre, biased news portrayed every night on the TV (still crap today, ha ha). They were making a go of it themselves, building relationships/ camaraderie with other like-minded lads and men, who had had enough of being put down. Told what to do, told you're no better than the last generation. They, too, were hooligans and mindless morons; this was it, this was our revolution, our time.

Meeting up, knocking off college and going shopping/ robbing to Liverpool or Manchester for our crazy fashion clothes. Getting sussed out, having a row to stop them robbing your gear. Going for a pint in one of their boozers, again having to sidestep a little band of thieves waiting for you at Lime Street or Victoria, getting a crack but laughing about it on the train back with your new wares. Ready to parade like peacocks (pardon the expression, Leeds) the next Saturday against another like-minded bunch of lads from whatever opposition, in our uniforms. With that confidence all Leeds lads have.

Into the pubs and it was going all day around the station, another train coming into Leeds, us 'out-of-towners' coming in had been warring with them, that were being held in the station and getting off of trains. Another firm would go up for another chance to pit themselves against the Red Army, we would blag it past the Old Bill and have a couple of minutes with them. Then get chased back out by either the Old Bill or Man United, loving it and laughing but just in a state of ecstasy (pre-rave/club days) with the adrenaline. The clock struck 1pm and they came, it felt like thousands of them, over the barriers, dogs barking and lunging at them, biting and ripping clothes. Coppers batoning, kicking and punching them, many getting past the Old Bill and down the ramp towards City Square. They waited, mobbed up together, and then came the almighty roar: 'Maaanchester na, na, na, Manchester na, na, na'. There's a different version around the country, which is more like 'Maaanchester wank, wank, wank', as we all know.

It was like a wave, a big Man United wave; tons of lad's faces filled with venom, hate, inspiration, spurred on by being together. Ready for revenge, no different to us at all, they had a lot and we fought like lions but the numbers pushed us back after a bit. A few casualties on both sides but Man United winning that one on points and numbers, just.

As we got down towards City Square the pubs had emptied, the Scarborough Taps, Black Lion, Prince and even some further into town like the 3 Legs and Piccadilly bar. Sadly, the Old Bill had closed off the entrance to the station and we couldn't get to them but could see them, they were gobbing about 'doing us'. Which wasn't the case; they'd backed us off a couple of times down the ramp, at best.

A few pint pots were hurled at Man United and the Old Bill were getting really sick of Leeds, their patience in monitoring the situation was wearing very thin. More and more vans were arriving to block the front entrance off, to move Leeds not so gracefully, ha ha. A load of 'mad Leeds' older than us were turning on the Old Bill and hurling the glasses at them. Skinheads, punks, ska boys, even a crazy rockabilly tried jumping past them to get at his enemy. Needless to say, he got battered, then nicked and taken into one of the waiting Black Marias. Absolutely bananas, he would probably get three years for that nowadays. That was it, 'CHAAAARGE!', just like the cover on the Clash album, the coppers running at Leeds, moving us on, splitting us up, dodging truncheons, shiny boots, punches and charge sheets. Back onto Boar Lane, away from a future court case at this point, sweat dripping off me like everyone around me.

We gathered our senses, and all the talk was about how good the day was; did you see those big old Manc bastards? They were hard-game lads. One of my pals from Wortley said to me, 'Sean, come with me, if we can get past. I'm sure Man United came out of the side exit of the station, when the Old Bill charged us.'

He's well known and still around now, not a big lad but extremely game, fearless. He's still great fun when we meet up on the odd occasion. That's the beauty of Leeds: you don't see anyone for ages if you don't go much now but it feels like last week when you meet up. A unique bond, though many are in their fifties, sixties, even seventies, the feeling is just the same and the enjoyment in each other's company because of what we have been through together.

He was right: they had got out and were going down Wellington Street. It was mission impossible getting near them, too well policed, but they didn't have many Old Bill with them looking from a distance. If we could just get near them with our firm it would be a blinder, it really would be anarchy. The tone was set for us to try at least. We were buzzing with all of this and had only had a taste of what was to come; everyone was the same, to be honest, and we had all forgotten there was a game still to be played.

One of their best lads told me that some of their firm were robbing handbags from women near the 1815 bar car park. Then some of these lowlives wanted to take it further: they all got round these two women and put their hands up their tops and tried to pull down one of their jeans. This was until one of the older, very well-known Salford lads stopped it and made sure the women were OK. Good lad, whoever you are. That would never occur with Leeds and we are disgusted on hearing/knowing this – I'm sure every firm in Britain is, too.

That was the madness of 3 May, with a mixture of the fixture, the heat, the intensity, the alcohol; two top firms going head-to-head. The hatred and respect sometimes rolled into one, their importance on winning the game and our intent on trying to stop them. Our pride and passion, common sense was just not prevailing and this was all pre-match, not even at the ground, which was still to come.

THE BATTLE OF ELLAND ROAD
(Little Big Horn)

We all walked to the ground as it was impossible to get one of the old P2 buses, you had more chance of winning the lottery. The traffic was bumper-to-bumper all the way from town to the ground. We walked and talked; the topic of conversation was what we had experienced that morning, about our lads, their lads, the Old Bill. Everything and anything as the heat became higher, probably frazzling our minds, too.

As we got near the ground after Holbeck Moor, it was jammed, everyone going one way, towards the battlefield, like gladiators towards the Coliseum. All of a sudden, the pace picked up; you couldn't do anything but go with the flow, forwards towards Valhalla. We couldn't work out why. Then it became obvious: a renegade Man United coach had come up the road to the ground. By the time we got there, it was demolished, mainly by our 'scarfies' but the scrap dealers couldn't have done a better job of smashing it up.

There were coppers surrounding it, very hard, nasty but efficient coppers, having none of it and no protocol like nowadays. There were casualties all over the place, Man United inside the coach and a few off it (fair play to them, having a go) and Leeds who tried attacking it (cut heads, bloody noses, par for the course). From the far side of the coach came a charge, a little volley of ammo and a massive roar; absolute madness.

One of our main lads from Farnley (God, I miss you my old pal) said, 'Come on, Sean, fuck this! Get to the ground now, it will be.' He was right. As the sun was boiling everyone's brains, he saw the chance to try to get to their firm, leave the madness to the 'scarfies' and lunatics. A wasted nicking and not our game anyway. He got a light little firm together on Lowfields Road (I'm sure a few firms know of it); it was guerrilla warfare, one group of Man United coming up under the tunnel, then another, then another. You have a pop, we'll have a pop, sheer bedlam, skirmishes everywhere, adrenaline flowing; the lust for battle rising every time another group of the enemy came under that tunnel. Their objective to defend their reputation, each other and their existence to be fair as Leeds had the taste now. They had some good goes, the Red Army in full force that day. We knew it was not even half-time, Jesus the game was nowhere even starting. We had to get into the ground and it was only about 2.30. As a few of us passed the Peacock pub on

Elland Road to go round to the fish shop and meet more of our firm, a massive surge and roar went up: 'They're here!' We tried getting back to the Lowfields Road, but the sheer volume of people made it impossible; we were gutted, too, their train firm had arrived.

Time and time again we tried to get them but the crush was horrendous, the heat; it was so near but so far in a way. We could see it, just a mass of arms thrown at each other from two sets of warring tribes. The noise was deafening, the Old Bill couldn't get to this that quick nor could the bunch I was with, to be fair. It went on for ages, then movement from Leeds forwards. We could see it: they had cracked, backed off to the wall and were getting it.

Again, I will give credit where it's due: well done, Man United. They, they came, they had a very good go and held their own in spells and took it in others. Some of their lot I know, who are in their sixties and have been everywhere, told me it was their best battle ever. Better than their Second Division days, Wembley finals and Europe, where they terrorised everybody at that period, unbelievable numbers. This had been coming since their promotion, to be honest. Some good ones at Elland Road previously, but they were going for the title on this day and we were there to stop them.

We walked around the back of the South Stand and, in a minute – BOOM! What the fuck was happening? Didn't have a clue, nobody did, but it became apparent very soon – with a bloody nose. A mob of Cockney Reds and Mancs (around 300) had come round the back and bang, straight into us! I was on those steps with some fantastic lads; nobody moved, you couldn't, and every one of us had received a facial injury. So, what we did, we held off that bunch until Leeds numbers became too much and they were pushed towards the Lowfields. We laugh about it now, over a pint on brief catch-ups, mainly big birthdays and sadly funerals.

Again, the Old Bill were none too happy or obliging with that Manc Cockney firm – you could see the truncheons going in as they were escorted past Leeds having a pop at them. Definitely wouldn't happen now, but it did and it gave us a great memory. I don't think there's one of our firm or theirs can't say they didn't experience anything that day.

We all went into our respected parts of the ground. I got into the top of the South Stand that day for nothing but most of the lads were in the Kop and Lowfields. Man United had the Lowfields, but we didn't realise how many they had – definitely the most anybody's ever brought to Elland Road.

The atmosphere in the ground was probably one of the best I've EVER been in: them, us, everyone singing. Hurling abuse at each other; nothing new there but the ferocity was different that day, it was just another game against the scum for us but it was definitely more of a meaning to them.

Faces contorted with hate, ridicule, young, old, even an old woman at their end was giving us the V-signs, swearing at us. She was older than my mam but was very passionate in her support for Man United, or was it her hatred of Leeds? Ha ha. It was fever pitch; the sun didn't help, although we were slightly covered in the South Stand top, United were in the bottom and were mocking us. One of the old lot threw a paper aeroplane he had made from the match programme, another moment of madness on the day the asylums in Lancashire and Yorkshire had been emptied. It was just sheer noise when the game kicked off and I couldn't tell you what was being sung. I've an idea but I have been to cup finals, Auld Firm games, many Scotland v England games (both grounds), even a Roma v Lazio derby and nothing could beat this atmosphere.

We were expected to get beat and the unthinkable happen – Man United Champions of England at Elland Road. Doesn't sound right, does it? Doesn't even seem believable, but there it was about to happen, in hard hitting-reality.

The fans and players of Leeds had other ideas. We had a very mediocre team at this point but that day the tenacity, desire and belief in ability was raised to a level beyond their own capabilities. I genuinely believe that the atmosphere and task in hand changed those players into world-beaters. Man United lift that title at Leeds, running around the pitch, gloating, celebrating, no chance. They probably saved every hospital in West Yorkshire tons of money in overtime that day. If scum had won it, unthinkable. They didn't, thank god, thanks to a performance of performances by those players and definitely a twelfth man.

We won 2–0, goals from Parlane and Zico Hird.

We had done it the unthinkable, against all odds and definitely underdogs that day, but are Leeds ever underdogs on THAT day? I couldn't believe the atmosphere could rise any more but it was absolutely deafening now. You couldn't think, then from below us they made a move: Man United tried to climb into our seats.

We were stamping on and whacking their hands, we had to or else it would definitely have gone wrong for us. A few made it but had to jump back down. Thank god they did, a few lunges towards us again and by our old lot trying to bang a head. As the Old Bill sorted it out, we made our way outside. We were laughing, joking, jubilant, respectful too of their valiant but crazy attempt to climb up into the South Stand, Elland Road.

Outside it was just a mass of bodies, all Leeds, everyone and every age singing, waiting for the gates to open for the final curtain. For that last chance to get at them. But this time annihilation, victory on the pitch had spurred us to want victory off it, more so. The Old Bill tried time and again to move us. No chance: 100 yards this way, 100 yards that way. They managed a couple of times and gates open, the amount of people and absolute desire pushed the Mancs back every time. Not that they didn't have a go, of course they did, they wanted it badly, too. Revenge for their failure on the pitch. To no avail, the hail of missiles was devastating for them but they were doing damage to us at the front, too. One of my pals copped a brick, split his head open; he still waded into the Mancs when the gates opened another time but game over for him.

The cavalry charged, the foot soldiers with the dogs came in, precision attack, bodies scattering everywhere, bodies getting trampled on, bodies being bit by the Alsatians. Injured fans being nicked to clear the way – wrong, but had to be done in the eyes of the guardians of peace. They managed to hold off a few more attacks and clear the lights, then as every Leeds fan ran onto 'the hill', the Law chased them. This gave around 200 of us (a cracking little 200) a slight chance to hold up and have another pop. We waited near CCL Alarms, now Revie Road (how fitting).

The gates opened, their coach lot to the left down towards the tunnel near the Kop, the train lot towards us. It seemed formidable. We looked around at each other and all smiled. It was a good 200, no passengers here. Definitely wary of what was approaching us, but this was it, our chance to 'have it' and we took it.

One of the Farnley lads said, 'Get in the industrial estate and keep quiet.' We did, and for two minutes – wait, it seemed more like twenty. One of the Seacroft was watching out, pretending to be at his car on his own, telling us every step they made. The Old Bill and front few got past the entrance. Immaculate timing, we went into them side on. Absolute surprise, toe-to- toe, everyone in – even if you couldn't fight, you were in – throwing punches, boots going in and dodging missiles and the odd truncheon.

All of a sudden, they broke and turned back towards the ground, the intensity and timing of the attack too much for them. Then the masses on the hill launched their bricks and ran down at them. The Old Bill cracked, too – it was like Rorke's Drift. Some serious casualties for the Red Army on this occasion, bodies strewn all over the road, Leeds kicking them in passing.

We were chasing them back to the ground and they made a stand. Again, our lot and the rest of Leeds into them full throttle. I'll never forget it going off (near where the Billy Bremner statue is now) and they were getting battered, a black lad and a red-haired geezer taking some punishing shots. This one older Manc (black-haired wedge, in a Fred Perry) steamed in to lessen the damage for them. He had huge arms throwing some big punches into us; they got forced back into the ground but what a stand he made. Respect to you, Mister, you definitely saved your mates that crazy, eventful day. He's probably nearing seventy nowadays or maybe gone up to the stadium in the sky; him and RB had a good punch-swapping session at that moment. RB will remember you and respect you, too – he always mentioned you when having a beer with him.

The thing that always shocked me with this row was that it was 6pm, an hour and a quarter after the game had ended, and everyone was still there at the ground. The helicopter, gunships and Imperial Guard would have moved you by 5–15pm in today's environment and incarcerated 2,000 of you.

There were many more skirmishes in town, at the train station mainly, but a good one on Infirmary Street. A band of Mancs had gone for a drink near the old Madison's. They had been spied on their way back to the station (not far); we managed to meet them from Jac's and have it out them. A steady one, everyone getting stuck in, both sides, a run, a stand, more fighting until I fell near City Square: he got it. To be fair, our lot let him up and get over the road to the station – we wanted the rest of them, too.

The pubs were full, we were celebrating all of our victories on and off of the pitch; everyone had had some 'fun/joy' that day. They had, too, but had had to take second prize but with much respect from us.

It kept going off until around 10pm, the Mancs and Cockneys came out of the City Arms rail bar for one last go. Up and down that ramp to the station again, time and time again, until the Transport Police moved them with much force and with the ever-hungry dogs who mustn't have eaten that day, looking at some of the leg injuries on show, both sides.

The season now over, what was an expected fizzle for Leeds ended in a crescendo, ended in victory. It also ended in a new dawn and high hopes, experiences for the coming season, a unity, solidarity. Old, hardened warriors from the Revie days and out of the '70s and into the '80s with hope and pride at what was to come. Our lot a new bunch of rag-tags being accepted and respected, learning every game in our lessons of football hooliganism. It was a marriage made in heaven – or would that be hell? – for the football world and the authorities.

SUMMARY

Nobody who experienced those times has ever whinged about them, about the charge sheets, the jail sentences, the injuries, the mockery from the media, the public, people who didn't experience them.

We never said it was right or wrong, it was part of society for those who wanted it or were caught up in it, their reasons being their own. Many of us across the country would have a pint together now and laugh about it, some of our firm and others have forged good relationships over the years. Some haven't.

We all have our memories and respect everyone else's or throw their side of it into a bin in our mind. There are firms out there who have blatantly lied: lads, deep down, you have to live with that lie. Just say it how it is, it's no great loss and we would probably respect you more for it. Fact is that law of percentages says you will have bad days along with good ones.

Every lad out there can relate to this, just remember it was part of growing up, it happened many years before us and has happened since. It can do on occasions in the future maybe but with definitely more serious consequences.

Some of the best guys I know were involved in the hooligan wars – decent, intelligent, hard-working, family men, who to this day would help a stranger out, show kindness and humanity but have a realistic, straightforward, direct outlook on life. Something that seems to be lacking. Remember, lads, they've not quelled the fire in you, you're just waiting patiently for the right moment to express your way of thinking, speaking and doing. Do it the way you know best and enjoy it.

There are tons of experiences left out understandably, this one experience of being with THE BEST, on our day, for over five decades, going into six now. There's been many a life situation that my experiences through football have stood me in good stead for coping with and giving a solution to. Making me the person I am today and with a confidence to try and overcome anything thrown at me in life.

YOUNG MUNICHS

'GOING MAN UNITED AND BEING IN THE FIRM'

HOTSHOT, MANCHESTER UNITED: Young Munichs was because everyone used to taunt and sing 'Munich' at United fans. So, we just thought we'll go into 'em, yeah. So that was us. Every time we went and piled into a fight, we were singing 'Munich' and it didn't matter what the fuck happened. We knew who we were and where we come from.

City, Everton, West Ham, Tottenham. It was just, the in-thing, wasn't it? The acid house scene, the lot. All the top boys were involved in it, you know what I mean. It was all on your estate. The Inter-City Jibbers, you already looked up to them, so that's the way it was, You wanted to be one of them, going Man United and being in the firm. We all regrouped after we got raided. All the raids collapsed, and we just regrouped; we were a major firm then. We went anywhere, we did the business everywhere.

I'd say there were about two firms on my side, there was the Young Munichs and the Men in Black. We just all started wearing black to the match. It came to our advantage: when the Old Bill come, no one knew who we were. We come from everywhere and no one knew who we were.

We were top there; after '92, we were going everywhere, we went round Europe and everything. Even Roma: they come to Old Trafford, they're swinging. I mean doing anything they wanted, but United just took 'em at the end. They were everywhere, all over the forecourt swinging chains, doing what they wanted to do. The Old Bill was doing nothing to them there, United just came from nowhere and blitzed 'em and came home with a fucking result at the end of the day. They just came from everywhere, just one of those things but there was just one top firm, one family, one top firm.

LIVERPOOL

'HAVE ALWAYS HAD A FIGHTING FIRM'

SCOUSE: I was eleven or twelve when I first started going to Liverpool, floodlight league game against Everton. We got beat by Everton. When we first started going, we would just go and stand behind the Kop end in the middle and everyone got to know each other because we used to stand in the same place then every game, week in and week out. I got to know everybody and at the away matches there'd be the same faces and I'd say hello. And that's how it went. I got to know everybody. Some good lads from Kirby, Halewood, Marsh Lane, Bootle, some good lads from all over the city. We just gelled – Liverpool have always had a fighting firm.

I don't know if the word casual was ever used but the first time I ever seen Lacoste was when we played Borussia Mönchengladbach in Rome 1977. And that's the first time we ever come across Lacoste because you used to go in the shops there in Paris and they let you try a pair on in the changing rooms. What we would do was put our own pair in the box and walk out in the new pair, and do the same with the tops – put them on and put back our old top. That's the first time I ever saw Lacoste. I know it sounds stupid. But we used to wear jeans, Lee Cooper, Wranglers. I never wore a donkey jacket. We used to wear jean jackets, Wrangler jean jackets. My favourite gear was jean jackets.

I remember West Ham here one year, one of the ICF fellas, was over there in the corner of the Annie Road and we were all right next to them. I go up to the toilet, I've got to come back. One of their lads shouted over, hey pretty boy, we'll have you later. I went, I'm going to fuck you for that, you little bastard, cheeky twat. The worst fashion was them multi-coloured fucking things – tank tops. They were fucking bad. We used to have a craze called – they actually were baker's kegs, they were white Levi and was baggy as fuck. We used to get them from the shops. And then we went to Sta-Prest, the white Sta-Prest, they looked smart in the early '70s.

MAN UNITED

Manchester United at Old Trafford. We all met in the wine lodge before the game, so we'd had a few wines – Aussie whites, which is quite potent. It's white wine, but it's falling-over gear.*

---

*A blend of Australian wines with grape brandy.

It's fucking good stuff. We often fuelled up on that – well-fuelled. And by the time we got there we were all well up for it. That was a regular routine for me. Football specials. Your own crowd, the same faces went away all the time. I don't think drink was a big influence. Obviously, before every game I think we all had a drink, but you were going there anyway.

We boarded a train going to Oxford Road and as we're going past Manchester station that's outside Manchester's ground a friend of mine pulled the communication cord and we all got off on the lines. Some of the lads walked to the station and some went the route at the back of the railway embankment. A train pulled in from Manchester carrying all Man U supporters and they got off at the railway station as we were walking towards the railway station. A big fight. Bricks and bottles. Anyway, we went to the station and the Man U supporters got behind and went towards the platform past the players' entrance. As we come out, they all started running back on us and we thought they were coming for us. We didn't know but they were trying to get past because they were running away from our other lads that went up the back route in. Obviously, when they run at us, they were trying to get past us. We didn't know that, did we? That was fucking mad, that.

Our other firm was coming behind them. Our little firm, we met. The police come and got us all in the tunnels. I'm afraid after that I can't say no more on that because I was arrested. That was one hell of a battle.

It's only a little tunnel. Where the players' entrance is, that's where the train station is, and along there it's very narrow so you can imagine, it was definitely toe-to-toe. This was '85. I think we drew 1–1. I remember coming out the police station and I was with some Manchester lads and was talking about whatever. I got the train home. Before I got the train home, I bought their pink football paper and it said on the front page the away supporters announced their arrival with a fuselage of bricks and bottles. I was unlucky; I was in the van, arrested. Two years' suspended sentence and a £250 fine. Thank you very much.

Man United, I fucking hate them. I think the reason is because the media say they're the best club in the world and we all know they're not. That they're the best sports club in Britain, which they probably are. The richest club, the richest this and that, the biggest fans, the best fans, the best this, the best that. Jealousy. There's no history but the rivalry is there, it's always there.

We all had a reunion. Everybody went from the seventies, the eighties. It was when we played Manchester United in the FA Cup tie in 1996. Everybody went, everybody. Because they give us 10,000 tickets. So, it was what was called payback time. But unfortunately for us it didn't happen because the police got wind of it. We got there and there were more police than us if you could look at it firm wise, and I mean that.

ROMA

Roma – they were out-and-out pricks, them. We had a run-in with Roma in the European Cup, but it wasn't a run-in with them. They were just throwing bottles from a big height. In Rome you've got a big platform where they walk across and they were just throwing bricks and bottles down, but I wouldn't put them as fighters more like crafty, just shithouses that like throwing bottles down. A lot of fans got stabbed. True, it's a different treatment once they know they're up against any English club. Exactly the same when we used to go anywhere abroad. We weren't treated unfairly, we were treated normal until more or less the day of the match or when the opposing fans started to come round where we were and then, as I've always said to everybody, you can't fight by yourself, if they're not there, you can't fight them. Now if they kick off on you, you kick off on them. But all the time I've been abroad with Liverpool I've always said this, the reason why the English are that bad is because we will fight any fucking, where some fuckers won't. They won't come over here and fight willy-nilly but we'll go over there and fight – we will fight them in their own backyard, if they want to. And then obviously, the police always jump on their side.

When I first went abroad, it was '72 for a tournament – I didn't realise that every country had riot police then. Now we didn't have riot police since the Toxteth Riots in Liverpool, that was '81. We had no riot police, but they did. So, they must have had trouble then, mustn't they? And that's my case there. And I always stick up for us. Every time I see police involved at games on television I say, look at them fucking bastards, look at them getting back at us again. It's only because we stand up for ourselves.

A mate of mine got banned from Liverpool games for two years. It was over in Russia, we were playing a Russian team. And he got lifted. There was trouble in a pub in Ukraine and they all got banned for two years. Now it's been stated that the Russians or whoever they were started the fight, so why should anyone get victimised? All we do is fight back. If I got punched in the face, I fight, and vice versa. You don't stand there like a fucking gobshite, do you? No. If you're caught fighting, you can't fight on your own, someone must have set you off and come over to you in the first place. Now I think our government are too critical of us, just because we go, because we take the most supporters in the world to another country, that makes us vulnerable. That the other crowds are getting into us – because we fight back, our country, our government go, well, you shouldn't be going. Well, why shouldn't we go?

CHELSEA

We were playing Chelsea in the FA Cup and we knew Chelsea were up for it, so we sent a couple of lads down with a little bag full of Stanley knives and put the bag in the locker at Euston station because when we used to board the specials at Liverpool, you used to get searched.

No bottles, no nothing. When we got to Euston, I think we had more armoury than the British Army. We'd send it down the week before. We left Euston station, our lad went over, got the equipment out and we went to Chelsea. In the FA Cup Fifth Round 1982, I think they beat us 2–0. We had a little bit of a ruck with them – nothing, really. When they come in first and realised we were tooled, I think they started to go, I think we'd better fucking stand-off here because we haven't got nothing. In fact, it was all over the papers because we were fighting inside the ground as well and we tried to go on the pitch. The police held our gate back. We tried to get on the pitch and they held the gate back. There used to be a little gate. A couple of thousand can't get past a little gate all in one go.

The worst ground I've been to without a shadow of a doubt is Heysel Stadium. That was a total joke. That was like playing in the middle of a park, it was a joke. The security was a joke, the walls surrounding the place were like an old corpus thing – you know, where they put them concrete slabs down. Well, that was the wall and that was a disgrace that, beyond a shadow of a doubt. That without any shadow of a doubt is the worst I've ever seen. And by the way, it wasn't a football ground, that was a running track. Luckily enough, I was outside and we were looking for tickets before we fucking realised what the ground was like. So, these fellas – two big fellas and one little fella that had all the tickets on them. So as soon as we saw them open their coats to do some business, we're in.

When we see the ground, how easy it was to get in, I actually give my ticket away to a kid, and it was a fucking joke. There were holes in the walls. Kick it like that, the whole fucking thing comes down. It'd come down on top of you. And the police were kicking holes in the wall to get through. A lot of pine cladding. And concrete. That was the wall. Now if you couldn't get through that, by the way it's only six foot high and there was no barbed wire on top. That's what I mean, that takes the biscuit. Meanwhile, the fella who had all these tickets tells the police So the police were after a black fella and the biggest, so we got arrested because my mate, he was a black fella and the biggest. The only black fella among us. And he's got a ski mask on, for fuck sake. I give up with him – I mean he's not soft, he could have a row but the fucking funniest man I've ever met.

RACISM

It's never affected me if a fan is a different colour or player either, anyone. I remember one game at Everton and they were lobbing bananas at John Barnes. Now a joke's a joke, but one lad I thought was beyond a joke but Barnes took it right on the chin, superb. A big bloke with a banana gives it to him and John Barnes passed it over. That's how it should be done. He took it off him. But I thought throwing bananas or whatever was out of order – Barnes took it on the chin.

I think in the early days there weren't in fact many

coloured lads that bothered to go, the only one who I knew was my big mate who went to Liverpool games. A couple of his mates started to go with us. I must admit that the coloureds never used to go to Liverpool. Why they never went, I don't know. I've never felt we was racist supporters. I never felt that people outside Liverpool were pointing the finger at us as a racist club. We always used to think, like Bradford and Leeds, they've got a big Asian community. London's got a big black community. Birmingham's got a big Asian community. And maybe other cities. But Liverpool haven't had a great deal. The majority of the football fans are predominantly white that go to the games. I didn't think we were a racist club. I will tell you this, how I got to know my friend. He was in the middle of the Kop and he was getting stick for his race. And I just said, fucking leave him alone, leave the fucking kid alone, watch Liverpool. Next minute, every fucking week he used to stand next to me all the time. That's how I got to know my mate.

In the '80s, we were involved in two major tragedies where the finger of blame was us fans. I think the media do try to overhype it because obviously they are the media, aren't they, and they want to sell papers. I think some of the violence at football grounds, where they say there's been violence and very violent, it's been like for argument's sake one guy on the other, they have a punch-up and then the police would become involved. But then they try to hype it, and say it's been murder here and there. I think it's just to sell papers.

The reason why we won't buy the *Sun* newspaper

up in Liverpool is because they stated that at Hillsborough, they were saying that we were robbing the dead bodies – and also, they turned round and said that some Liverpool lads, whoever they were, had wallets or different things on them, possessions. Now they might have been dippers, I don't know, or whatever; they could have mopped the floor and come across it, that's perfectly true, but I don't think they should be saying things like that. I mean when 95 people whoever they are, whether they're Germans, French, or whatever, they shouldn't say things like that, not at that time anyway. When it comes out a few years later, that's fair enough, but not when the people's just been killed. There was uproar at the time. We burnt the papers, the fans, the people of Liverpool, and no one buys the paper even today. But I think me personally, I think we should follow the editor around. The people who actually wrote the story, whoever he was whoever got the story, it's not the editor. These two people went to work for the *Daily Mirror*. And I think we should target the *Daily Mirror* because we should target the two people, wherever they go, we should ban that paper.

The paper's reaction was to apologise. They didn't do it at the time, it was only recently. Obviously at the end of the day, it's shown it's worked, hasn't it? So, we got them, and this is a classic example taken for the reporting coverage after the Hillsborough tragic disaster involving Liverpool fans when they played Forest at Hillsborough in the FA Cup semi of 1989 and even to this day, the effect of that can still be seen with Liverpool fans and Liverpool people themselves, where they still buy the *Daily Star* in protest to comments in the *Sun*.

Don't get much crowd trouble nowadays but I believe they still have a bit of a firm, they call themselves the Urchins. I believe they have a good little firm. I think there's a few coming through, as we said, the Urchins in Liverpool and all the Everton crowd. I don't think it would get on the scale of the early seventies or middle eighties, I don't think it will ever be on that scale where you had massive brawls on terraces. There's definitely a young element coming through in Liverpool. I don't think you'll ever see it like it was for us up there, major battles or war on the terraces.

I don't think football belongs to the fans any more, I think that's gone right out the window. The grounds are getting better, with the Health & Safety coming in. The other side of this is that I think the atmosphere has totally died. You were behind the goal getting crushed. I think it's right for them now because several years ago you were getting especially behind the Kop goal, I mean it were murder. There's 28,000 people and if the ball went down the left side or whatever, people tried to look and they all just come cascading down and if you got stuck on one of them barriers and you had 100–200 people behind you pushing you, you were in serious shit. And that was every game. Every game people used to pass out, over people's heads – that's how they got them out. But they started putting more push barriers in the Kop, like pens. It's really changed today. Well, the Liverpool fan base was the whole of the Liverpool area at one time. Since then, we've got a massive following in Scandinavian countries, also Germany and most recently from all over the country. And, basically, a lot of Asians started to go to the match now, which is obviously better for the football. There's a new fan base from the 2000s, it's changed without a shadow of a doubt. Most noticeable, yeah.

MIDLANDS

'WE HATE THEM, THEY HATE US'

BIRMINGHAM: ZULUS

'ALL YOU COULD HEAR WAS 'ZUUULUUUUU!!!'' '

MILLWALL

ONE-EYED BAZ (BARRINGTON PATTERSON), BIRMINGHAM CITY: There is only one firm that controls the city of Birmingham, that is Birmingham. Even in the city centre, Villa have no say in Birmingham. Blues rule the city centre, even if Villa are there and Blues turn up, Villa have to fuck off: we rule the town. Aston is only a small place in Birmingham and this is Zulu territory.

My name is Barrington Patterson, aka Zulu, One-eyed Baz. I don't carry tools, I can't speak for all people, I'm a fist and foot/boot man; I don't carry weapons, it's a last resort for me to use a weapon. We try to follow the originals, we're warriors, we don't fear nobody; you got all these teams especially those London teams, they think they rule the football scene around England. NO, we do. You get all those clubs coming down here, think they can control us on our manor. No, it ain't happening, with teams like Millwall, especially. There has always been a bit of history with Man City because that's where the name Zulus originated from. It was a reunion, people who ain't been football matches for years. Everyone turned up there, we even took their pub; lot of guys said they ain't seen a firm come and bring a firm like what we took to City.

I remember my first game, in the 1982/83 season, and thinking, there are no N*****s here! My first away games came a season later and then I was going to any big game after that; I can remember going to Leeds and being ambushed. I remember some games where I absolutely shat myself.

Leeds at home, Leeds away, West Ham at home, Millwall away twice – fucking hell, out of all the matches, that is the one that stands out more than any other!

All we heard about Millwall was that they were just like Leeds – a bunch of racists! We thought they were among the top dogs in London, but we always rated West Ham and Tottenham higher at the time. Everyone was geared up, but guys from the black and Asian communities were really geared up for Millwall.

I left work early that day and met up with the lads in town. 'We ain't buying a fucking train ticket! There's a couple of hundred of us going down there.' We went straight through the barriers and got on to the train. Some of the lads bought a McDonald's and others had cans of lager for the train, but there was a big police presence. We had a firm of 200-to-400-strong and everyone was up for the fucking row.

Everyone sat on the train chilling out, playing cards and cracking jokes. It took us about an hour and a half to get to Euston station. As soon as we got off the train, the police had their own fucking firm there! They were taking photos, asking our names and where we were from. Everyone had scarves over their faces, but they were telling us that anyone covering his face would be arrested.

I had a Burberry shirt and jacket, blue jeans and trainers and a scarf over my face. We were just about to break off from the police escort when they shouted, 'Come 'ere, lads! You're with this lot, ain't ya?'

We had a bit of a reputation at this time because we'd stood with a couple of top-rated English firms. So, we thought that not only would we be facing Millwall but that we'd also have to fight other London teams – probably West Ham and Spurs. The police put us on another train to the Millwall ground, but we managed to break off and meet up with a couple of guys from Birmingham, who now lived in London. Around twenty of us managed to get out of the pub and through a back door, then fucked off and left the rest with the police escort.

We stayed close by so we could see where the escort was and what was happening. Then the police put us on this train to Bermondsey. As we pulled up, all we could hear was boom – boom! The train was being fucking bricked! I'd never been to Millwall's ground but I could see it was near a fucking rough housing estate. Through every little corner you could see a firm. The police had their riot shields, but we were being bricked from every corner of the ground. They marched us into the ground, close to the pitch, then put us in an upper tier. We were behind the goal and some of us black lads took our shirts off. They were shouting, *'Fucking n*****s!'* and we were shouting, *'Sieg heil!'* A lot of Millwall were singing to Birmingham, 'You've got a town full of P*kis!' When Birmingham scored, we were singing, 'One-nil to Pakistan!'

Nothing could really go off in the ground, so we just stood there laughing. We were singing our songs about what was going to happen when we got outside, how we were going to have it out with 'em. We gave 'em the *'Sieg heil! Sieg heil!'* and you could see they just fucking hated it. The atmosphere inside that ground was electrifying. The police tried to lock us all in about fifteen minutes before the game's end, but I left with the final fifteen minutes to go. The police said they were going to keep the Blues behind after the game, but we started fighting them and breaking down doors. We just wanted to get out and get at fucking Millwall!

All of a sudden, the gates opened and it was like a battleground, like derelict buildings on a bombsite. There were bricks everywhere, cars turned over and a police horse had been fucking slashed and was lying on the ground! A big firm of us had to walk down to the train station, through a housing estate, and guys were popping up everywhere to try to brick us. They were throwing bricks, bottles, bangers – it was like a proper fucking warzone! This was on a whole different level. Some of the lads were glad the police were there, otherwise someone would have died. They were protecting us with their riot shields. We got on to the train and even that got smashed up – it was bricked from the outside and we smashed it up on the inside.

Even today, people still talk about that day at Millwall. It was one of the worst ever. It was football violence but there was no actual clash between us. And Millwall didn't like it because they couldn't get to us, so they smashed their manor up. We were shocked because there were bricks coming from all different angles, but I think the police were scared. Millwall didn't come out and fight us though. It's not as if they stood in front of us saying, 'Let's 'ave it!' And if they had, we'd have been a big enough, game enough firm that day.

TRANMERE

Another game that sticks with me was when we went to Tranmere, another cup game. I've never been called N*****, sunshine' in my life, before or since. We had a cup match away at Tranmere and a firm-and-a-half turned up for it. We travelled up by train and car. I was still living in Handsworth at the time and some of the guys, including Big Chest Leroy and Rupert, came round to mine. About five of us went in my car. We met up with others in town but everyone shot off at different times. We drove our cars up to a service station outside Liverpool – where we had a laugh and were chatting up the girls – and called taxis to take us into Tranmere.

I think we got there around 11am. People could tell

we were from out of town. From inside the car, we'd ask them where the football ground was, but they just didn't want to talk to us. People would walk off and ignore us, five black lads in a car, wondering, What the fucking hell is going on? We drove on and asked a group of lads where the ground was. 'There's no fuckin' d**kies up 'ere!' was their answer.

One of the lads tried to jump out of the car, totally furious, but they warned us, 'No! You can't do that around 'ere!' Just walking down the streets, you'd see a bunch of lads and it was, 'D**rkie! D**rkie! D**rkie over there!'

As soon as the police clocked us, they were round us like flies around shit. They locked us in a pub but some of us managed to get out. I got out before the start of the game and it was going off all over the place. We sent some guys over to have a row, so that the police went over to them while we were breaking into the fruit machines. In those days, it was expensive to go up there, so you had to make your money back. We took the machines off, bashed them and raided them.

We must have been in there a good hour-and-a-half before the police said we had to start making our way to the ground. Everyone started walking and just having a laugh in a firm of about 200 of us. All these Tranmere fans that we had to pass were giving it the wanker sign and more or less all you could hear was 'N******' etc. Even during the match, all you got off the Tranmere guys was 'd**kies' and 'c**ns'. There were a few skirmishes but everyone got into the ground, where the police started to get all agitated and lashed out at us with truncheons. It was clear to me that neither the fans nor the police had ever seen so many black lads at the football in their life and appeared to feel threatened by us.

Then we came out and it just went off! All you could hear was: 'The d**kies are over there!'

Later, we heard that Tranmere were up the road; we all rolled out of the pub and went to find them. They had a firm of around fifty; some of them were real dressers but some were like tramps from a local estate.

We were in some boozer without any character at all, near the train station. Someone walked in and said, 'They're over there' – across the road from the pub. We all piled out and had our bottles ready, lined up on some road on a council estate. It was really rough, with boarded-up windows and houses with no curtains. It was a really trampy area.

I think there were about seventy to eighty of us and about thirty to forty of them. Everyone brought their bottles out and started throwing them. When we ran out, we ran into them. I was getting bashed all over the place, but we chased and caught a few of them. We were stamping on their hands; we gave them a good hiding and headed back to the pub. Then the police turned up and it was like they had drafted in every available officer from all over Merseyside.

They came into the pub and started clattering some of the lads with their truncheons. Police and Blues were running everywhere. Fucking Tranmere were running everywhere! All you could hear was: 'You black

bastards!', 'You n******!' 'Get outside, get outside!'
Then they just left us there.

We got into our cars and headed back to Birmingham
city centre. After we got home, we went to a party at
Edward's Number 8 bar. We had a chat about it. There
were about sixty of us dressed in our Burberry and
Aquascutum. We all looked the part – know what I mean?

VILLA

I was brought up with Black Danny. I used to live in
Terrace Road and he lived on Villa Street, just around
the corner from me, and we've known each other since
we were six or seven years old. Black Danny was friends
with a guy called Lloydy, one of Villa's main lads at the
time, who is also my cousin. We've always been friends
and, as we're related, we've never clashed.

I remember going to a match and seeing Black
Danny, though we'd give each other a miss. We've had
it off with Villa loads of times and always had to go
looking for them. I remember a firm of us coming out
of their ground, walking all the way around and there
were no Villa in sight. We went down there looking
for them, they didn't turn up and they tried to claim a
fucking victory!

Villa were in the old First Division, now the
Premiership, and we were always in the lower leagues
during the mid-eighties, so we hadn't met for a long
time. We've had it with West Brom and Wolves, but Villa
are the main target. On one occasion that I remember,

me, Todd, Rupert and about fifteen of us met up in town and went to a pub in Broad Street. Half of us were in tracksuits. I always like to wear loose clothing so that I can punch, kick and run in it.

When we got to the boozer, the doorman said, 'Sorry, you can't come in wearing tracksuits.'

'You fucking what?'

'You can't come in wearing tracksuits.'

I pushed him out of the way and we walked into the pub.

Afterwards, we all got taxis down to Villa Park, but I missed all the fighting that went on down Rocky Lane. It was all organised and as it was going off, people were getting phone calls saying, 'Get down 'ere, get down 'ere!'

Rocky Lane is the street in Aston where everyone arranged to have it off. There's a pub nearby and when we got there it was unbelievable. You could hear battle cries:

'ZULU!'

'C-Crew!'

Villa had outnumbered the Blues but we stood there and gave it to them. It was the sort of fight where nobody would run off, just like when we played West Ham. Apparently, there were police stood there with their handheld cameras. They had it so easy that day – I wish I'd been there, I'd have been lamping the police with their bloody cameras!

I remember it was all in the news and the papers for about a week: 'The Blues came down Rocky Lane ... X amount of people were arrested ... X amount of police were injured'.

When the Blues played Villa at Birmingham one time, we were coming up from one of the boozers in Digbeth and we got a telephone call saying Villa were coming over the dual carriageway. So, we all ran up to the top, where the pub is. There were about 200 lads up by the dual carriageway; somehow, I made my way to the front of the firm. We were walking up and could see quite a few black lads coming down. All we heard was 'C-Crew, C-Crew!' Me, Brains, Rupert and Dougal all stood there. Up ahead I could see Black Danny, my cousin and another couple of lads I knew. We were heading away from Birmingham's ground, with Villa coming towards us. Everyone squared up, but then Villa took out baseball bats and knives. We just ran into them, though I bypassed Danny and my cousin.

Usually, when I see a tool being drawn, I back off – but I didn't want anyone to see me doing that. Dougal, who's a big fucker like me, was shouting, 'Come on! Come on!' There were now about thirty of us so we couldn't turn around and run, or we'd be running into ourselves. There were more of us, maybe two to one, but they were tooled up. I don't mind taking a beating off a bat but I don't want to get fucking stabbed!

As Lloyd and Danny ran past me, I kicked this geezer – then I backed off to the side. I did not want to get stabbed. All of a sudden, Dougal got banjo'd and I thought, Fuck this, man! Two minutes later, the police jumped in and it was: 'Thank fuck for that!'

When I saw Dougal, he was on the floor – completely spark-out. That's the point at which some fucking guy writes in Villa's book, 'The so-called famous Zulu cage fighter got knocked out.' I said to the guy who wrote it, 'If you think you KO'd me, come and have a square go at me then.' Black Danny knows it wasn't me who got knocked out.

Then the police turned up, so we picked up Dougal and went off to the match. I left the match with about fifteen minutes to go and that's when we saw Villa coming towards us. They were black lads so we shouted, 'ZULU!' That's our war cry. All you could hear was 'ZUUULUUUUU!!!'

Then they started shouting 'C-Crew!' It was all of the old lads. All you heard around town after that was that we got done. And yeah – we did get done.

There's always talk of revenge but there's bigger fish to fry now. The history is there though. Even if you don't go to a match for five years, you still turn out for Villa/Blues. Not just for the fighting – you have to be there for the games themselves.

The trouble with derby matches is that all the guys come out of the woodwork. Blues don't go to England matches because they'd end up fighting with their own rival firms – we're not England, we're just Birmingham. We want the glory to ourselves. We don't want to say we joined up with Man U or blah-blah to beat fucking Slovakia or whatever.

If I had to rate the top five firms, I'd say they were Cardiff, West Ham, Arsenal, Tottenham and

Portsmouth. But, as far as the top firms we've personally come across, I'd say Villa, Leeds, West Ham and Cardiff, plus we've had some unexpected battles with fans in places like Wigan, Tranmere and Stoke.

Our group would always contain a mix of races: we had black lads, white lads and Asian lads; we were a pretty multiracial bunch. When people go on about the Zulus being black, that's just something that outsiders instantly think or feel. Even the name 'Zulus' never came about until '82, when we played Man City and someone in our crowd shouted out, 'ZULU!' The name has stuck with us ever since.

With the Blues though, we do have a large black following and when you go to certain away games, you see the team's fans thinking, 'Look at them N****** down there, man!' They start shitting themselves and you think, fuck me, we've put the fear of God into 'em already!

ASTON VILLA:
C CREW

'BLACK DANNY, WANTED DEAD OR ALIVE!'

BLACK DANNY (DANNY BROWN), ASTON VILLA: If there was a more on-top place in the 1970s and '80s than Goodison Park and Anfield, especially if you were black, then I haven't heard of it. I can't separate them, I see them as the same firm. Imagine putting Villa and Blues together, that's the size of firm they could pull to awaiting away fans. If there was a big game at Liverpool and Everton hadn't got a game or were at a place they didn't fancy going, they would often form a welcoming committee at Lime Street station or on the infamous Stanley Park. If Liverpool didn't get you in the ground then, depending on your mode of transport, they made sure they got you outside the ground. You were in their city and you were either leaving with a Scouse souvenir from a Stanley blade or minus your money or clothes.

In 1977, I made my first trip to Merseyside and I went

on the football special train. It pulled into Lime Street and we were ferried by buses to Anfield, to be greeted by a mass of red and white. As we walked through the back streets, reality hit home; it was 'Welcome to Hell' for blacks. I would imagine it would be a bit like going to Galatasaray these days.

We went in the Anfield Road end and it was supposed to be segregated but as soon as we got in and tried to get up the winding stairs, all you could hear was a deafening chant of, 'We are the Annie Annie Road end' and, as soon as we saw them, they were onto us. They kicked us down the stairs and threw a cup of hot tea straight in my face. I laugh when I see the sign in the players' tunnel saying, 'This is Anfield'. People say it is a sign that intimidates opposing players – well, a scalding drink in the face and a kick in the bollocks is a lot worse, believe me.

The Old Bill managed to hold them off but I was sick with fear. Me and two other black lads, who I had met for the first time (one who later became frontline in the C Crew), were targeted and abused like we had never seen before. The Villa fans were further up the terrace and the Steamers were rowing with the Liverpool lot doing well. People tell me one of the Steamers bottled one of the Scousers and had managed to move them, which was good news for my three-man tag team.

The game didn't go to plan as we actually won 2–1 but the three of us couldn't celebrate, as we were not sure we could get out of this alive. Us winning had made the bastards even worse. The game ended and the

Scousers were in their element, giving three frightened black teenagers just out of school maximum abuse, threatening all sorts and pointing outside. The police were no better and were pushing me and the other two outside but I wasn't having any of it. That was when the police showed their true colours, as they began pushing us towards the Liverpool lads, who were blocking the huge terrace exit. They were all grinning and waiting for their prey to be thrown to the pack.

In seconds it started, whack after whack after whack. At first, I was doing OK in fending them off but then the pack mentality took over and I was stuck in the middle of what can only be described as wild animals. I was punched to the floor and kicked repeatedly. I felt I was drowning and had to get away from them or I was dead. I remember thinking, where the fuck was the Old Bill?

I somehow pushed through them and climbed over the fence and onto the pitch, collapsing onto the turf, where the St John Ambulance men took over. I was taken to Walton Hospital. The nurse there asked me who had done it. I said Liverpool fans, but she said, 'How do you know?' and muttered something like, 'They wouldn't do that.' I gave up when she asked me who won and I said, 'Villa, two-one,' and she said, 'No, that can't be true either as Liverpool always win at home!' My day of terror didn't end there, as even on the train home I was bullied by Liverpool fans going back to Crewe. They pinched my scarf, my first ever Villa scarf, and I was powerless to fight back.

I decided to go to Merseyside again that season only this time it was Everton. At the time, *Roots*, which featured a black slave called Chicken George, was a very popular TV drama. I got recognised coming out and that's when I heard, 'Here's Chicken George again.' I was a marked man and I wasn't involved in the violence then, I was just a fan but times were changing and they became an enemy of mine from that day.

Revenge was never going to happen overnight and I had a few more bad days on Merseyside before I managed to get even, but on 10 January 1981, Villa hosted Liverpool in what was being dubbed a championship decider. It was a massive game; this was the big one, even the Blues game didn't run it close. I had some scores to settle with this shower after taking the biggest beating of my life, a beating that had me pissing blood all week, made this game special. For me, it was about revenge, pure and simple. I wanted their boys – their hooligans.

The instructions were everybody should wait for the main firm of Scousers to turn up at New Street station and not fuck the whole operation up by attacking scarfers if they arrived before the scallies. They didn't come on the first two trains, they actually arrived on the 11.15am and there must have been 300 comfortably on it. Now as far as I was concerned this was their boys, the scallies in their hooded bubble coats, bouncing down the platform like they were at Lime Street, all wedge heads and strong accents. Our C-Crew firm were in the bar waiting and the police had spotted them and pushed them out the station as the Liverpool lot came through the ticket barriers. They were out and on the streets as my mate's trusty old Mini car pulled up with me hanging out the window. This Liverpool firm had separated and were unescorted but they didn't have a clue that Villa were amongst them. The Scousers now realised Villa were behind them and all turning around. They steamed into my mate Andy's little mob, making that shouting 'come onnnn' kind of noise that goes with a mob when they charge. As they were exchanging blows, my mate took his monkey wrench out of the back of his jeans and hit the first Scouser and they started to panic, because by now they could see the blades and knew we were tooled up.

I was out the car, running towards them, screaming insanely to the lads, 'Get into them.' I was in a frenzy of rage. I will never forget the looks on their faces when I shouted out, 'So say hello to your old mate, Chicken George, then.' Their faces dropped and the courage and strength drained from their bodies. Whack, whack. The first man went down. Out comes the Stanley blade and I'm into them like a madman, slashing and cutting at anything and everybody. The lads later said I was gone and my eyes were glazed, they used the words 'indiscriminate slashing' and it was right.

Liverpool realised it was just a handful who were at it with them and made a stand, but then the rest of the C-Crew by the Mayfair came running round the corner. Now the Scousers were cornered and stood there glued to the spot. They were in sheer panic and were trying to get away from us. They were dropping all around, the ones who got away ran into shops screaming for help. Lads followed them in to finish them off. There was no hiding place. One dived under a parked car, thinking he could hide. It was all happening in slow motion. I could feel the devil on my shoulder. I started to have flashbacks of what they did to me on Merseyside, so much anger and hate in my head. I pulled him by the leg from under the car. He was curled up in a ball, saying, 'Mister, I'm only here for the robbing, I'm only here for the robbing.'

'Fuck off.'

I kicked him about the head and body, yanked him off the floor and said, 'Look at me, you c**t, look at me. When I close my eyes and go to sleep, I have nightmares about Merseyside and what you fuckers did to me.' Then I hacked at him. Some now looked in a bad way and there was blood everywhere. I was covered in it from head to foot. It had got right out of hand and a lot of Scousers have been cut seriously. The Old Bill are looking to lift people. We had got rid of our tools and knew the Old Bill would be on our case, as well as a lot of pissed-off Scousers looking for revenge. Word had spread about the ambush and the amount of Liverpool fans who had been cut was rising by the minute. We knew by the police presence that some of their mates were in hospital, and some had given statements, and although I didn't know it at the time, the Old Bill were looking for me, this six-foot-four black lad, for a total of nine stabbings.

Liverpool were playing at Wolves a few weeks later and word had got round about the slashings and my involvement and they actually came to the Hole in the Wall pub to try to find me, which I will take as a compliment. It's a game where I made my name and I have been told that Spurs the season after I had been sent down were singing 'Danny gone down forever and where's your C Crew' so I suppose you could say I got my notoriety at a price. Also, I have been told before a Blues game at Man City they had a minute's silence in mock honour of me getting sent down but that's typical of how they felt about me. It was around this time that the Blues had printed business cards and leaflets with 'Black Danny, Wanted Dead or Alive!'

About a month later, I was at the dole office waiting to get my cheque when the bird behind the counter said, 'I am sorry, could you wait for a moment, there seems to be a problem.' I just thought the usual that it was some poxy mix-up, but after an hour or two, the Old Bill came in and said, 'Excuse me, Danny, could you step in here, please.' They took me into an office and nicked me. While I had been waiting they had gone to my house, searched it and easily found the Stanley knife I had used on the Scousers still in my bedroom. That arrogance was my downfall as I got sent down for two sets of three years, one for affray and one for wounding, and the sentences were to run concurrently. At the time, that kind of jail was almost unheard of in terms of football violence but because of the seriousness of the offence they wanted to send a clear message out to all and sundry that it would not be tolerated. I was in shock. I didn't realise concurrent meant to run side by side and I actually thought I had been given six years. I was the only one to be jailed for the attack, leaving plenty to carry on where I left off.

WOLVES: YAM YAM ARMY

'WE TURN UP FOR THE BLUES'

'The Subway Army', named such due to the fact that visitors by train had to walk through a long tunnel where they would be ambushed, and, also, the Bridge Boys, targeted by the police in the '80s with Operation Growth – 'Get Rid Of Wolverhampton's Troublesome Hooligans'. They're also known as the Yam Yam Army. And one man's name stood out among that pack: Gilly, a Top Boy and Category C hooligan.

GILLY SHAW, WOLVES: Bridge Boys, Yam Yam Army, we came along when we beat Blues 1–0 and Yam Yam is a term that comes from prison – it's just Black Country slang, due to the way we speak: 'yam, yam', as Brummies call us. Yes, West Brom is our local derby but Brum are the rivals firm wise, one-on-one it's Birmingham City because West Bromwich Albion are a pisspot firm. Blues are bigger better, more organised; not like West Brom, what they've done you can put on a postage stamp. Good days, Moseley Road, 2000, we had a good battle with them in the early '80s, we used to land on each other all the time. The phone calls start, the credit starts running out. We turn up for the Blues, they didn't know we was coming, they were amazed; they said yeah, you've got a result. Blues were up there but started to earn a bit of money and gradually come out of the scene so think we were a bit better than them nowadays.

I think in 2000, we were one of the most active firms in the country, we were like doing things. If we were playing in London we'd land on Birmingham, if up north, we'd land on people.

West Brom to me ain't got a firm to rate but they will turn out for us. West Brom in Blackpool, play on a Sunday so I got a coach purposely knowing they would be in Blackpool because they were playing Preston and they would all be in fancy dress, the idiots. Thousands of Albion all in Blackpool, land there half past ten, and we walk in the boozer, there's 20 of them. Good morning, girls, we're here.

Now we was there four hours, telling them we were here and we're in the Dunton Arms, they were in Yates pub and it took me to go down there and coax them up. They did come, all 250 of 'em. We absolutely torched them, we done 'em, got on the coaches and went back home, that's all we wanted to do. Next day at the game, we were laughing our heads off; there was all people unconscious and everything. You can only fight what's in front of yer and if they ain't coming for it, you go to them. We're here for one reason and it ain't to go on the funfair is it?

A lot of Telford follows Wolves and they have a good firm: you would look at them on par with Championship firms, put them on same par, yeah, for a non-league firm. They're good, as are Shrewsbury, another good firm for the size of town.

Wolves went in two busloads with Telford to Kettering 2008, smashing the life out of 'em, smashing the life out of the town; they got jail and bans. I think they are a breach of civil rights; I even had to travel to Scotland to get round the ban and as soon as we got back, they were waiting for me.

For 18 years I've been banned. Nothing to be proud of, you can't call it a badge of honour: you get prison, it ain't worth it, you think you got away with it but cameras don't lie. Couple of days later, CCTV. What can you do, what can you do? Permission to go abroad: got to sign on about six hours before the game, absolutely pathetic. They don't need to take your passport off yer, it's total abuse. The Old Bill have done their job; we're more banned as a firm, can't go into town, I can't go to Molineux, ban for life but there you go, I done what I had to do years ago.

Huddersfield done what they had to do with us once, fair play. It wasn't with our lot. more with locals, but fair play to them, they landed but it was at the wrong pub, two miles out of town. We were on the blower to them, we were in the town, and they come off the motorway landed at a boozer, seen some of the lads obviously going to the game. There's about fifteen to twenty Wolves lads, they've two coach loads of Huddersfield. Fair play to 'em, boom, they've done it.

We are no bully firm. I know Portsmouth's moaning on some websites 'cos they got done. If you've got a firm running at you, and you're running at them, and they back off, you can't help that. If backing off to the crowd, you are running into kids, you can't help that, you can only fight what's in front of yer. Personally, I ain't going to do that, women and kids, no lad is, it's only an excuse because they got done. We ain't got to prove nothing to nobody. We ain't bullies, we ain't got to prove ourselves.

DERBY LUNATIC FRINGE

'WE WERE ONE OF THE ORIGINAL FIRMS'

THOMMO (PAUL THOMPSON), DERBY COUNTY: I've led the mob for 25 years, the Derby Lunatic Fringe from the early '80s same period as the bad old days when the firms started replacing the gangs, with your Chelsea and your Millwall and your West Hams and everyone. We were one of the original firms, there used to only be about ten firms, even little Bradford had a firm. You had your Leicester Baby Squad, your Chelsea Headhunters, your Bradford Ointment. Firms are what people don't even associate with these days going to football but that come about 'cos in them bad old days in the '80s there were two massive riots at Derby in space of just two weeks. First was with Leeds then came Chelsea, they followed each other. Our chairman turned around and said we don't want this lunatic fringe in our ground any more. That's how we came by our name, The Derby Lunatic Fringe.

We've got a lot of history for a small-size club, both on and off the pitch: in the '70s, our enemies then were Man United and Chelsea, big time. Lots of fights with Man U, wrecking the train on the way to Derby. Lots of footage on the telly and in the papers when they boarded up the streets before the Red Army come. Always a riot there in the '70s, then it switched into the '80s, like a pass-over from the skinheads to the trendies we were called then. Not casuals, trendies. We were all in Pringle, Lyle & Scott, Forest Hills … the whole dress thing had changed. Some of the old lads, they used to be called the Popsiders even they started to dress different. We were younger, we were already all casuals, seeing them up in Liverpool and liking the way they dress and that and that was the changeover time. So, it's kind of all merged, so it went from their kind of violence in the '70s, where everyone just meets in the middle of the road and has a good punch-up to our kind of violence, where it was all organised. In them days we never had mobile phones, we used to do it on the telephone boxes, you know what I mean?! Phone up their local pub and tell them where we'd be, but it turned really organised in the early '80s, right early '80s.

LEEDS

Right through. I mean, I try to keep out of it a bit now but I've been going through the years now. I'd like to say it's all over for me but like we went to Leeds one year, 50 of us. Didn't want no trouble, thought it was over and done with. Like a scene from the '80s come out the ground and the police are standing there with their big cameras, 'cos they've all got cameras. We're thinking, there's about 400 Leeds outside, how! It's as if the police want it to go off. Leeds have attacked us, we've put our hands up; we don't want no trouble 'cos we don't want to get nicked with the cameras and it was like the police let the fight happen. The police then lose control so we've had to protect ourselves. Now, this is 50 of us and we're 50 years of age, us lot. We only went there for the beer but sometimes if you have to defend yourselves, you've got to, so we had no choice but to fight. The blokes we were fighting were all 45-year-olds and 50-year-olds, too, and I thought it had gone away but it still seemed to be there, thirty years later!

Banning orders! Well, we were the first ones in the whole country – 12 of us as a group got a banning order, a civil action against us to stop us going to England games. This is the year 2000, I think it was 2000/01. We were the first ones in the whole country, stopped us at home, was banned for three years, stopped us going to England games. Wouldn't be too bad if we'd been caught doing something, but it wasn't, it was a civil action and to us, that's cowardly. So, they threw that on us, threw it on 12 of us top lads, took us out of the equation completely. Disrupted the mob for a few years but it never really hurt us 'cos in that day and age, everyone was at acid house parties and that and a lot of the firms went away from the football and started going to raves and that and having e tabs and that. So, there was a lull anyway and by the time our banning orders was up, we hadn't really missed anything 'cos we were back.

Well, yeah, in Derby you've got the DLF, The Orphans and The Derby Youth. These Derby Youth are about fifteen years of age, fourteen and there's about 50 of them and really, they've got no work, they all live at home with their parents; they're not bothered if they get nicked. They've just seen what past generations do, they've seen it on the internet and that, and they think, we'll have some of this. If you know what I mean, it's something to do if they get nicked they're not even bothered. Even if they get banning orders they'll still turn up anyway. All they'll get is six months youth custody, they're not bothered about that. But it's always gonna be there, you can't stop it. It's not like having a puppy, you know, it's not just for Christmas, it's here for life 'cos there's one generation passing it down to the next generation, similar to this. My old man was the first black doorman in Derby, my older brother was a leader in the firm in the '70s. I also ended up a doorman and I ended up leading the mob. It just passes down the generations.

DERBY LEICESTER ALLIANCE

I mean, look at Derby and Forest. The hatred goes back to Clough/Taylor days. We hate them, they hate us. Sixteen miles up the road. We went there one time, we joined up with Leicester once, stupid thing to do. I think it was known as a super crew then when two firms joined together, it hadn't been done before. We joined up and thought, fuck this, we'll pick a team and we went to Nottingham. A hundred-plus of us we went there, about 400 Forest. Come at us from everywhere, a two-hour battle in the middle of summer, no police. Not expecting it, chaos. We all went to prison for it but that just shows an example of two crews joining up against another crew. These things happen. How did it come about? From a rave club. There was some Leicester that used to go raving and they knew some of our lot, started taking ecstasy tabs together, getting to know each ther. We're thinking, you're lads, we're lads. We put our rivalries to one side and we'll join up and have a go at Forest, like.

Very short-lived. It lasted about four months 'cos some of our older lads didn't really like it so every time Leicester come around, our older lads would attack 'em and if we went over to Leicester, they're older lads who would attack us so it was terminated!

EVERTON

Derby–Everton '97, was that serious? Well, away we went there to Everton, walked outside their ground and it was all terraced streets just like Cambridge Street was in Derby. Just before kick-off, we walked in the pub, 50 of us walked in their pub. Scouse turns around, these look like the DLF. I don't know how you look like the DLF, it must have been my lisp or something but do you know what I mean, they knew. When we walked in the pub, what did they do? Walked straight out the back doors. They come down the same year, down to Derby, Fucking hell, about 200 of them mob-handed, a big fight outside the train station. I believe a *Daily Mail* reporter was there, he wrote disgraceful scenes and he only went as a supporter! But generally, Everton we never really had nothing to do with them apart from that year, you see. It just shows you how things can suddenly blow up 'cos you've made one visit, it's a return trip!

FOREST EXECUTIVE CREW

'100 OF US ON BANS, THAT'S OUR FIRM'

Gary 'Boatsy' Clarke is one of the founder members of the Forest Executive Crew. When English football firms were at their peak, Nottingham Forest's Executive Crew were genuine players ... a touch of executive class. But when the authorities clamped down hard on football hooligans at the turn of the millennium, the Forest firm felt the pain of tough banning orders. Boatsy was the first person in Nottinghamshire to receive a 'civil banning order'. With the heat on high-profile firms like Forest, attention switched to non-league football violence instead. Firms from bigger clubs tried to dodge police attention by joining up with neighbouring non-league gangs.

BOATSY (GARY CLARKE), NOTTINGHAM FOREST: The buzz, adrenaline ... lads against lads, brilliant. It was like being in a family, all lads together, socialising. It was more comradely and drinking, more than the violence, it was a day out and male bonding. We used to sit in the executive stand next to the away fans and we used to attack the away fans at half-time down near the cafeteria. We used to be known as the Mad Squad but that name goes back to the '70s, so let's call ourselves the Forest Executive Crew. We got calling cards printed up, copied West Ham, everyone did.

Banning orders in 2000 ruined our firm. When they first came in, it wasn't too bad because they didn't give you restrictions, we still used to go away games and sit in the city centre without going to the match. Games like Cardiff, you could go a day before on a Friday night and still be up for the row but it's when they put on the new banning orders with all the restrictions, that's what done it for me. It ruined Forest's firm. Papers said a hundred of us on bans, that's our firm, it ruined us.

DERBY

Just before I'd packed up my job at the market we had a prearranged row with Derby in Nottingham. It was one of the Derby lads' birthdays, so we knew they was coming to us, but the rumour going around was that they were joining up with Leicester and were calling themselves the D.L.A., which stood for the Derby Leicester Alliance. By 6 o'clock on the night, we had a massive mob waiting for them in Yates's pub, the football season wasn't even on as it was June but we had a firm and half out waiting for them.

We sent some scouts down to the train station to

watch for their arrival. There were no coppers about, and as far as we knew, they knew nothing about it. The excitement and buzz around the place were unbelievable. A few of the older lads were going around every body trying to keep everyone calm. People were getting fidgety and wanted some action. Pubs on the other side of the square were jam-packed with lads, all up for it. At about 7 o'clock, the scouts came running back and we knew the opposition were here. About 120 of them came across the square towards us and it looked good. There were only two coppers strolling across the square on normal duties and they were unaware of what was seconds away from happening. It was still relatively early so there were no Saturday-evening revellers out yet. Right outside the pub there was roadworks going on so there was lots of weapons and ammo on offer, if needed.

They came bowling across the square looking as if they were up for it and we just stormed out towards them. They were surrounded as we came at them from every direction. It went toe-to-toe for a minute before they got swamped and overrun. Then it was time for them to run as we gave chase and then they split and ran in all directions. There were little pockets of fighting going on down side alleys and side roads but the majority of them fucked off back up the road towards Derby, but for an hour after the Old Bill had restored some orders there were still skirmishes going on in various parts of the city centre.

They got mullered by us but they still say they had a result against us. For the life of me, I can't see how.

Why did they join up with Leicester? Why not come on their own? It's like us joining up with Stoke City to go to Derby. We wouldn't do it. It seemed they were so scared of us that they needed the support of another club to take us on. Even to this day they deny the Derby Leicester Alliance and say they know nothing about it, which is total bollocks.

On the night, the police managed to put what was left of Derby and Leicester back onto trains and buses. There were a few bodies lying out cold on the floor and it took the Old Bill two hours to restore complete order. There was probably around ten arrests but a week later, 70 houses were raided.

I was interviewed and charged with threatening behaviour, but they never had any evidence. There must have been six to seven hundred people in that square; there was no CCTV and no photographic evidence. I was only nineteen, a young lad. In their eyes they saw me as guilty. In court, we had a three-week trial along with the Derby lads, who had also been dawn raided. Out of the 60 in court, 30 of us received prison sentences. I got 100 days in North Sea Youth Detention Centre.

The place I was off to was run on a military boot camp basis with the emphasis on the short, sharp, shock treatment. The experience in there gave me a kick up the arse and I learned a lot. How many of the other 400 kids doing time in there could say that, I don't know. The discipline was something I was missing in my everyday life and I didn't regret being sent there, not one bit. I've made some lifelong friends from being in there, even though some are Derby County fans, but then again, all Forest and Derby fans love to hate one another. They're geographically our nearest rivals but on the other hand, just up the road is Mansfield, but it's the complete opposite to Derby and we have no problem with Mansfield and despite a few minor differences between individuals we get on great with most of their boys. We go to some of their big games and they come over to some of ours. On their day they can pull in some serious numbers and have a game firm.

Ask any team in the lower leagues and they'll tell you about Mansfield. Mansfield's main rivals are Lincoln and the two teams have had some right rows over the years. Believe me, Lincoln can be a right dodgy place to go to of a night. Go there looking for a row and I guarantee you'll find it. The whole town will turn out, first sign of trouble. If I went over to Derby for a night out, there would be a good chance I would get some grief. You don't get many people from Derby following Forest and I don't know anyone from Nottingham that would wear a Derby shirt in Nottingham. They'd get told to take it off or get a slap.

STOKE

We had a bit of a thing with them in the early '80s and they cut a couple of our lads. Then we didn't play them for years and I got married around 1995. The FA Cup draw was live on *Match of the Day* and they pulled out Forest and Stoke. I went fucking mad and was jumping up and down like a nutter. My missus just sat there shaking her head and looking at me like I'd totally lost the plot. It was like a scene from *The Football Factory* when Frank Harper's character is watching Osgood and Hudson do the FA Cup draw and out comes Chelsea v Millwall. I couldn't sleep that night, as I was so excited.

A buzz went around Nottingham weeks before the game and on the day, we took a massive mob over there. It's only an hour from us so it was a bit of a derby game. Most of us went over by car and we plotted up in a pub. It's like going back in time with all the Victorian houses and factory chimneys. It's another tough area, which breeds tough men. Nearly everyone had a sheepskin coat or donkey jacket on. The Old Bill didn't have a clue. A few of their lads came to the pub we were in and I clumped this youth outside, and he went backwards into some roadworks and fell down an open manhole. They're fucking nuts, though.

At the end of the game, we all came out with five minutes to go and a mob of Stokes' youngsters steamed into us. We had four thousand fans in the top tier in the stand behind the goal. We ran them off to the right and ran them back into their section of the ground. We went back out onto the street and we were right up for it as the adrenaline was pumping. I looked around and felt good. We had a good mob here.

It was pitch-black and a mob of them appeared in front of us. A roar went up and we ran them everywhere. From behind us came a mob of their older lads so we turned to face them. A big c**t in a sheepskin stepped towards me and I threw a punch but missed him, but the force and power of it pulled my arm out of its socket. I was on the floor in agony and have never felt pain like it. I had tears in my eyes, I can tell you. The Old Bill got round me and couldn't work out what had happened. A few of our lads had stopped with me and the coppers were asking what had gone on and were gobbing off. 'That'll teach you to come to Stoke.'

They thought I'd been put on my arse with a punch. An ambulance arrived and I was helped into the back of it. Another one of our lads was already inside as he'd been knocked down and trodden on by a police horse. In the hospital was one of our old lads, who had been stabbed in the arm with a screwdriver. My arm was pushed back into its socket but I didn't feel a thing, as I was as high as a kite on drugs. Not mine, the ones the hospital gave me.

The next day, me and me mate caught a taxi back to Nottingham and we went straight down The Friar Tuck pub, where my missus was working behind the bar. She took one look at me all strapped up, shook her head and walked off to serve somebody else. Throwing that right-hander cost me dearly. I had no money coming in for nearly three months and I suppose it cost me my marriage because after that things were never the same between her and me. She used to moan about me sometimes going to football but I think this is the one of the many straws that broke the camel's back.

If I'd caught the bloke with that punch I'd thrown, I swear I would have landed on the other side of the moon. The boys said they had some right battles in and around that graveyard on the walk back to the station, and in the replay at our place they came looking for it, but our lot was over at The Meadows estate fighting with the Old Bill.

In the disturbance, a copper got a slab put over his head and ended up in hospital. Stoke have got a major mob who are game as fuck and two of their main lads who are brothers come from Nottingham, so things did calm down. Now there's a mutual respect and there's no longer any hatred between the firms, although we do have one important thing in common: they hate Derby County as much as we do.

BRIGHTON

We come unstuck at Brighton, didn't we? Had it, didn't we? Brighton away a good few years ago. There was about twenty-five of us during the day. It was that new ground, weren't it? We had a booze. We didn't see them all day, never seen them all day, and a Scottish geezer come in the pub about five o'clock and said, lads, if you want it, hang around till the Old Bill clear off home and we'll hang about for you. There was about twelve to fifteen stopping the whole night. So, we said, all right. Everyone was up for it. Some cleared off. Anyway, getting phone calls off him all night. They say come to this pub eight o'clock at night. Went down to the boozer. They're not even there. So, we went and had another drink. Next minute, 30 of them come over the road from that park, come piling over. I couldn't believe it. All out the pub we were, straight into them, the lot went.

There was too many of them. Forest got backed off. I went straight down on the flipping floor, got kicked all over the flipping pavement. The pub got smashed. They were a good firm, I tell you they were game, game as anything as well. I've heard a few stories about Brighton, that they leave it till night time and they get a little mob together and they pick people off. They kicked me all over the fucking pavement. The windows of the pub all got smashed to fucking bits. I couldn't believe it. I was in fucking agony for about a week after. Fair play to them, one of them picked me up, you know, and said, leave him, leave him. Because apparently one of them had a blade as well and they said, leave him, he's had enough. I couldn't get up. I had had enough, I just couldn't get up. I was just getting booted. Fair play to them, one of them said leave him and he picked me up.

LEICESTER BABY SQUAD

'FUCKING CHELSEA ARE HERE, THEY'RE HERE'

The Baby Squad have had a number of fights with the Headhunters who follow Chelsea. In August 2000, Leicester were listed as the second most violent football club in England. In November 2001, the Baby Squad fought with hooligans from Luton Town at Leicester railway station before police split up the two groups.

In February 2008, 11 men were arrested after up to 100 hooligans were involved in running battles between fans from Leicester City and Coventry City outside a pub in Coventry. Police confiscated knives and one man suffered minor head injuries.

The week before the incident with Coventry fans, 13 men were arrested after clashes between fans from Leicester and Norwich in which some men sustained minor injuries.

CHELSEA

COALVILLE DAZ (DARREN SMITH), LEICESTER CITY: Our main rivals are Coventry and Forest, but who we turned out for I'm going to have to say Chelsea. We have had some turnouts with them going back to the '70s but the game that always comes to my mind was at home in 1989. In fact, it was the same day as the Hillsborough disaster, so I remember it well really. They had a massive mob, Chelsea, to be fair, a proper mob. Because they were good in the days, weren't they? In fact, come Friday night, some of the lads had had it with some of our lads, so it started Friday night, really. So, word got round. It was before the mobile phones obviously so people were ringing each other up, fucking Chelsea are here, they're here. What, Chelsea are here now, you're joking.

So obviously, people got into town, had the row. All day long it was going off. I mean, Chelsea were fucking massive that day, they really were. I hold me hands up to them. There were seven or eight stabbed or slashed that day. It was really naughty, it was a naughty day it really was. I remember after the game, they were coming out the ground and there were fucking hundreds of them, there really was. And we'd be about 150–200-handed ourselves, we turned out a good mob that day. But we did in them days, as many of you will know. And we smashed this fence down and behind the fence was a pallet of brand-new bricks and we just threw the bricks at Chelsea, and they threw them back at us, and it was going on for 40 minutes, which is a long time without the Old Bill being there, it's a long time. And even when the Old Bill come, to be fair they couldn't control it. Chelsea had more numbers than us, but we held our own I'd like to think but to be fair, there were cars damaged and houses – it was just a riot, basically.

That's the one that sticks out in my mind more than any. It was actually on Filbert Street. It's certainly the most famous one I recall and most of the other lads would agree, I would think. We got home at night and this is how I remember it; it's not too good really because obviously before your mobile phones, my wife was at home and her mum had come round and said there's been some people killed at a football match. And my wife at the time – we weren't married actually – fiancée at the time, she heard all the talk before the Chelsea game. She naturally thought that it was the game I was at. So, when I walked in half-nine to 10 o'clock, she wasn't too impressed that I hadn't been in touch. But I didn't know anything about the Hillsbrough disaster, you see. I've walked in the door and she's very upset, obviously. She says, 'What's going on? What's going on?' I say, 'How do you know?' She says, 'It's on the telly, it's been on the tele. There's people been killed,' and I still didn't realise. We put the old telly on then, obviously, it became clear what had happened at Hillsborough and, obviously, it did put it into perspective. It was absolutely dreadful.

It was strange and I remember coming home and I shot off and had a shower after it and I felt so knackered. I was knackered, my legs, my arms, everything was aching. Got a few bumps and bruises, as well, obviously. And I got myself dry and lay on the bed and I were thinking, what's all this about? As soon as I walked through that door, when my missus said dead, I thought, what are you talking about? Obviously, I knew that people had been slashed and stabbed. But then it become clear what happened. And then when I see the pictures on the telly, well, we all felt the same no matter we rival fans I think, didn't we? But having gone through what I'd been through all that weekend, the Friday and the Saturday, it did bring it home to me a little bit. It did really bring it crashing home to me. I thought, what the hell? It's not worth it, it's not worth it. But, obviously, the following day, you get back in the boozer with the lads and you're talking about the next game. There's nothing will ever change that.

THE WAY FOOTBALL
VIOLENCE HAS CHANGED

Just as the Edwardian yobs in the towns of industrial Britain chose to represent their neighbourhoods by fighting rival gangs from other streets, Peaky Blinders-style, the growth of football during the twentieth century provided these young men with the ideal setting for their pursuits. Football clubs represented towns and cities, and young men could identify with, and attach themselves to these clubs. Pride and fighting prowess were at stake, and crowd trouble has intermittently flourished down the decades since.

But in 1985 came Luton and Heysel. By inflicting such savagery and death, football violence had reached its nadir. It had to be extinguished. The government called for rigorous measures. Numerous reports were followed by substantial increases in the policing of football with improved intelligence and security regulations. FBOs (football banning orders) under which offenders were shut off from their football world, were followed by the introduction of the Violent Crime Reduction Act (2006). This gave the police powers to remove people suspected of planning to commit an offence.

Similarly, blanket CCTV surveillance and enforced segregation became the norm. Government think-tanks and reports, as well as academic analysis and media coverage, all appeared to confirm that hooliganism was on the wane. There were sporadic clashes and flashpoints, when long- established enmities were occasionally renewed. Yet the British political, legal and media establishments came to the view that football violence, if not entirely a thing of the past, was semi-dormant and under control. Not so. Despite such claims, it has never really gone away.

For the past two decades television has saturated the Premiership, inflating the cost of players to the clubs, and therefore ticket prices to the supporters. The casual terrace thug has been priced out of the market or so it seemed but he has simply gone elsewhere. The emphasis has shifted. Like mercury oozing across an uneven surface, football hooligans have found the cracks.

Ironically, the success of banning orders has backfired on the football establishment. Hooligan firms denied access to their preferred stamping grounds are gravitating to the lower, non-league world. Today, a growing number of fans follow two teams – their league club, which is likely to be a Premiership or Championship side – as well as their local non-league club – for example, Leicester City's Baby Squad are also known to follow Histon, Nottingham Forest in numbers have gone with Mansfield, Wolves have gone to Telford games. The old-fashioned terracing of the non-league grounds bears witness to growing tensions among supporters. A return to '70s- and '80s-style of football violence is now being played out by the old-school hardcore hooligans and a new generation of aspiring thugs. FBOs have become badges of honour and CCTV has bred defiance. It is arguable that the measures taken to curtail hooliganism have given rise to a new form in a different setting – the super-hooligan in the lower leagues.

Inevitably their limited resources of this level of football club are insufficient to hire enough police or stewards to be able to cope with serious crowd trouble when it occurs.

Apart from unsegregated and non-seating areas in the grounds, there are other differences which effectively allow the hooligans to operate more freely. Alcohol rules are less restrictive and crowd security and pub policing are less stringent. Ticket costs are lower, and coach travel is often unsupervised. The standard of stewarding is erratic and non-league hooligans are less likely to be exposed by police intelligence or spotters. Town centres and train and coach stations are thinly policed by forces not geared to coping with widespread disturbances.

The improvement in communications via mobile phones and the internet has given the hooligans wider scope for planning their tactics, and they frequently record their exploits for the glory of YouTube. To reveal the game of electronic cat and mouse between the law and the miscreants to what is the traditional way of attending a football match (cheap, standing on the terraces, freedom to create mayhem) which is the major reason for the growing attraction of a hooligan element springing up evermore in non-league football. As this offers more opportunities for adventure than the repressive and expensive environment of the Football League, the emphasis has shifted. Like mercury oozing across an uneven surface, football hooligans have found the cracks.

CAMBRIDGE UNITED: MAIN FIRM

'FOOTBALL TODAY ISN'T THE SAME GAME'

THE GENERAL (LES MURANYI), CAMBRIDGE UNITED: We came together in schooldays at the Abbey and grew into a decent mob. West Ham created a massive impression on me with ICF in 1979. I'd heard about the madness of Millwall's F Troop, Treatment and Halfway Line on the 1977 *Panorama* documentary. I chose the name 'Main Firm' for our crew in 1979. It was a Chelsea schoolboy gave me the idea when he used the phrase to large himself and his mates up. It had a very authentic ring to it.

The most serious ruck we had was undoubtedly the February 1984 Chelsea home game when we turned them over before the match. It wasn't the best fight we've been in but the overall scenes were unprecedented. Over 40 Chelsea went to hospital, one a near fatality. There were loads of arrests both on the day and in the weeks following, with 36 of us answering for it at the Old Bailey 14 months later. It was a huge thing at the time. The first big public hooligan trial attempted by the authorities. I got five years just for being 'the General' and had my picture all over the papers. That really put us on the map. The papers printed all sorts of outrageous bollocks about me when I got sentenced at the Old Bailey. They made wild claims that were nothing to do with the evidence – I should have sued them.

Drink always plays a part. It loosens you up for the job. You have to bear in mind though that when guys set out in the morning for a meet they're usually fresh and know exactly what their intentions are.

I've been impressed by a few mobs. Chelsea and West Ham in particular were quite scary when they came to us, the Abbey being only a small ground and close to London. But I can honestly say that nothing has shocked me as much as some of our own lunatic escapades. The near-fatal stabbing of a Chelsea fan on Newmarket Road with a broken bottle was the worst thing I've seen. It was an appalling spectacle. Blood shooting out of his neck. You can't seriously intend to take it that far.

I don't think any firm that was about in the '80s is still going as they were then. Other people have come up in the ranks over the years at Cambridge. It's developed. The feeling's still as strong as ever but you have to adapt to the times. Now it's more selective but when the opposition warrants a turnout, our firm as it is today will perform to high standards. But from what I know about these things if two firms seriously want to get it on, it can be done. You'll never get it in and around the grounds like before but with a bit of leadership, planning and guile you can get a result away from the ground. You have to give these new lads the respect they deserve. They haven't the freedom we had back in the day but they're eager to keep the traditions alive and seem just as enthusiastic. Mind you the test comes when they start banging you away for it.

I'm totally inactive these days. The thing is about your police spotter he knows you almost intimately. He's almost part of the firm. Our chappy has been going to the Abbey for decades. He's a local boy. You just accept that he's got his ear to the ground and will be there waiting to greet you at the away fixture. In a way, this close scrutiny from the police helps keep the lid on the violence which would otherwise just get everyone locked up for life. I've been in prison – from 2001 to 2004 – and was still on licence long after that, so it's out of the question for me. If you ask me if I would still have been a thug and then a crook if not for football then probably not. I'm a quiet bloke really. Ask anyone. Football definitely led me into the direction my life has taken. I don't follow the Premiership and never will, and you shouldn't have to pay more than a tenner entrance for smaller grounds. A neighbour was complaining to me recently that she paid £55 to see West Ham on Saturday. Fuck me! Is that what it costs these days? Premiership wages are a joke, too. How can you respect a guy who gets paid so highly and then doesn't give 110 per cent commitment? When you see top players out abusing their bodies with alcohol and drugs it makes you question the integrity of the whole sport. They're treating it as a joke. This surely doesn't happen so much abroad. Football today isn't the same game I used to watch from the terraces. You hero-worshipped players in those days.

MANSFIELD SHADY EXPRESS

'THE '80S AND '90S WAS MENTAL'

Mansfield Town and neighbouring Chesterfield are sworn rivals. The antagonism between the two teams is considered by some to be among the fiercest in the lower leagues. Mansfield also enjoyed rivalries with Notts County, Lincoln City and Doncaster Rovers throughout the 1980s, as well as street battles against troublemakers from Grimsby, Birmingham City, Burnley and Shrewsbury.

In 2006, Shrewsbury Town fans were in Nottingham for their game with Notts County. Chairs and tables were hurled through the air as 50 men waged a pitched battle in the upstairs family area of Yates's Wine Lodge in Old Market Square, with one man left unconscious after the horrific brawl.

The fight was pre-arranged with known hooligans supporting Mansfield Town and Shrewsbury Town. A firm of Mansfield Town supporters went to the Cross Keys pub before going on to Yates's, where the Shrewsbury fans had already arrived just ahead of them. There had been a huge amount of mobile-phone activity between the two groups.

Mansfield Town were playing at home that day – a further indication that the gang must have come to Nottingham for a reason. The Shrewsbury Town fans, whose team were playing Notts County, were monitored and escorted out of the county on their coach two hours after the brawl but the brawl was captured on CCTV – homes in Mansfield were dawn raided to arrest suspects and bring them back to Nottingham for questioning.

JON PALMER, MANSFIELD TOWN: In Mansfield, there's quite a few around from the England lads. It's a mining community and the miners were victorious at drinking and fighting. My grandad used to fight for six hours then go back to the pub and have another fight. Loved it and that's why generations are coming through – Grandad's a miner, Dad's a miner, loves a scrap, too.

Chesterfield, that's our derby. It was on my birthday, to be fair, and they played us for the first time in ages. They came to the pub and basically had a good row.

Every time we go away to Manchester, it's always good, I think most teams in the lower league do get police presence because there's supporters who'll go down there and cause havoc. It's got worse, especially in my case: I've been banned for ever and ever in lower leagues, the League has got worse. Non-League football, it does happen but I don't think it's as bad as it is in the League. In the conference, Wrexham have a firm, Cambridge have got a few boys. Most of us hate Luton as they are like the top horses in the League – behind us, obviously! Luton are the ones to watch. Notts County, Doncaster, Lincoln's got a fine firm, of course. Mansfield Town, Luton, Chesterfield are quite good, to be fair, Grimsby, they've got a good little firm yeah.

I think the young lads coming through are more dangerous 'cos we had fistfights, but those lads will get the tools out and they will use them nowadays. I think they're young, they're not bothered, are they? When you get older, you worry more about stuff. It's lower key now 'cos the 1980s and '90s was mental, wasn't it? I think you look at all this Football Factory, Green Street movies and they want to be like that, don't they? The buzz is there, it's cool to be a football hooligan. When it starts happening, they get a buzz, they want to be part of that buzz, like I was. I loved it. I still love it!

But the Banning Order affects your daily routine 'cos on a Saturday you can't go within a mile or even a 10-mile radius of where your match is, you can't go into the city centre. It's just year on, year ban, year on, banned again. It does yer head in. You can't do this, can't do that, can't go to the pub.

If I was to do a hooligan table of non-League firms, I would put Mansfield top, Luton second, and that's it. The rest wouldn't come anywhere near it. I think non-League's attractive 'cos it's not well policed, there's still lads drinking booze watching their team who want to scrap in the town centres, like Manchester a few weeks ago, then it's Newport but in the League police are everywhere.

Over 35 years ago, in 1985, back then football violence was a widespread problem, tainting our national game. It was a social and political issue. There was an infamous riot by Millwall fans at Luton Town and the Heysel tragedy. Football's decision makers decreed enough was enough, the game had to change forever. The threat of hooliganism had to be eradicated. But was it?

In May 2010, 25 years on, Luton's Kenilworth Road stadium was in the news again. In the second leg of a play-off semi-final between Luton Town and York City, violence flared at the final whistle. York City players cowered in the back of a stand as they were pelted with missiles from rival Luton fans and fights broke out with police on the pitch. Shocking images were the lead story on Sky Sports News for 24 hours. But there was something else equally alarming about the events at Kenilworth Road, because this was hardcore hooliganism at a *non-League* football match.

LUTON: MIG CREW

This firm's iconic name established itself at the height of the football casual scene, given by a lad who joined the firm and later wrote a book about it under the pseudonym of Tommy Robinson.

The MiGs got going really because of two things. One was the West Ham programme that was put on the telly, [a hooligan documentary featuring the Inter-City Firm]. A lot of the guys who watched that were at school and went back to school absolutely dumbstruck by it. We'd been watching a load of drunks running round the town on a Saturday, running round, laying into each other and then you see something like this, it just wakes you up a little bit. And very quickly, we was buying Pringle jumpers at Scotch House on Marble Arch and walking round school in them. Fighting next door school like all lads do. They would all come out in their leather jackets, we'd have our Pringles on. We started getting our airs and graces then if you like. From there, it just walked from there really.

The name MiGs very quickly came about because when you watch the documentary you see the ICF – the Inter-City Firm – and then at the same time the other famous name really was Leeds Service Crew. You hear the name 'firm'. These were unique words at the time, we'd never heard nothing like it. So a couple of clever guys decide that we'd call ourselves the Pringle Boys, MiG Crew. It's a bit of a play on words, really. With crew is what you need, and there's a crew on an aircraft, for example, and MiGs is a Russian word for fighter. So you get MiG Crew. It's just a joke, but it very quickly became Men in Gear. The press got hold of it, the police got hold of it, other firms got hold of it. It's our joke, we simply have a laugh with that one. This would be early '80s – '83, it started.'

LUTON V MILLWALL

DENNIS EDWARDS, LUTON TOWN: In '85, I was working in the local tyre factory at the time and they sent us all home very early, saying there was a big riot in the town centre. Back in those days, you never had mobile phones or anything like that or internet. I live very close to the town centre and there would be several pubs where our lads would meet up to have a drink before the games and obviously in the town centre there would be drinking establishments in them days. The pubs would shut at 2.30pm 'cos of licensing laws and the bar doubled up as a pool bar. The lads went in there and from what I've been told they heard that Millwall was coming down. Obviously, we thought it was Millwall but since then we've found out that it was all of London, basically all of London came down 'cos Luton was going down to London, kicking off against QPR, Tottenham, Arsenal, West Ham, Chelsea, and I think a lot of the London lads didn't like it. They all go together, they all know each other because they live very close, it's only ten miles square, same size as Luton really, but if we go back in the day we'd get 150 lads in that bar but there was about 30 at that time. They weren't really there for football some of them, some of them were. Obviously, they saw a larger gang of Millwall lads about twice our numbers and they chased them up to a place called Cardiff Road, where the police station was. A lot of the Millwall lads that I've spoken to over the years say that there were no police in the town on that day and they thought happy days, but they'll admit it, they did get a bit of a surprise.

Well, on the pitch, that was obviously mindless Millwall London lads. I was there on that day same as most of my mates. My brother was there, he's a steward, and they said that it was going to be a bit of a race riot but as you see from the footages there's a lot of ethnic people there from London, they tried to take liberties with our lads, but we have got a strong little firm, we always have done. It goes back to the '60s and it's still strong today. The youth today are just as bad as us, they're not really organised but they're really, really bad. As you can see from the YouTube footage, it's been going on for the last five, six years. On the pitch that day we held our own up until the police came on. There's other footage where you can see this – the national news shown clips. Once the police cleared the pitch a bit, sure Millwall come on and they just smashed up the pitch and the terracing. Well, a lot of their lads obviously were coming down, jumping over the fence on the pitch, chasing the police but that's mainly the footage that I saw at about 11 o'clock when I got home but in the day it's completely different. We chased them through the town centre, they had loads of lads up there. Some of them was real old school lads, mainly London lads coming down, thinking they can turn over Luton. If you ask a lot of them, they did go back with a heavy surprise even the next day. You know, Millwall lads who got nicked, the next day when they came out of court they found firms of angry locals waiting. You can't come to Luton without getting a surprise. You know, it's a good little tight town, everyone gets on. We've got our issues, sometimes it's with our youth, but everyone does get on: it's a good little organisation there.

When I speak to people that were there 20 years on, they say, blimey, I heard about it, but to hear from Arsenal lads that were there, Tottenham lads that were there, West Ham lads that were there, it was all London. When all London meets up together they don't really know each other, the main lads know each other but a lot of them don't and they get reckless, you know. But with us, we know all our lads, we know where they are and that's why we've always held our own 'cos it's a tight little firm. Our number could be 110–115 max and we get that for every game. Arsenal could bring down 500, like they did one year, you know, and we still done the business, they all know it. Yeah, we have been run, it's written in several books and all that, but a lot of the books written about us say that we've held our own, they've all dedicated chapters to us. Well, that proves the fact and there's that video on *Panorama* of the game in '84, I wasn't there on the day. The lads that I know was there are like six or seven years younger than me, you know, they were well up for their little tear-ups. They went down there and they met QPR at St Pancras station due to a long-standing rivalry, as you can see from the black-and-white camera footage, QPR come at us, we didn't run back. We never run, I've never known us to run. We always held our own, you know, and I think a lot of firms will tell ya, we do turn up in numbers and we do hold our own and that's a good video for a lot of casuals, 'cos some people like those activities, the youth and all that.

You know, in '85, I was twenty-five and I'd been watching Luton since I was twelve years of age. We've always had a little firm, each estate in Luton – I'm a Lewsey Farm estate boy. You had hot wiring steamers who were about 30 hard lads, they joined up with Lewsey. They'd all come together under one umbrella as the boys of Luton Town. Then you had the Castle, that was the firm's bar, and these were lads who were my age, nice bunch of lads. The MiGs came along from a guy called Tommy. It was a good name, everyone likes that name.

It was all about designer gear 'cos back in the day we all earned good money, still do. We had nice things, nice little town, nice girls, we had good lads who played good music, good little DJ's and all that. We were a firm that dressed well, went out well, had good prospects. Most of our lads all earnt good, got our own houses and that. They go on about football-related crimes and all that being middle class or unemployed right-wing skinheads when it's completely different. I've never seen that down our way, especially with all the firms you see Millwall, West Ham, they've got black people in their firms but the name MiGs was a good name for our mixed firm.

They wanna have a pop 'cos they know how tasty we are. You know some of them now are just 10-handed, not even worth turning up for, but you know a lot of our youth then wanna come out and do what they wanna do, teams like Hayes and Yeading because they're very close to QPR and when we played them they brought all their old school QPR lads out. What was all that about? All our youth went down there on their own! I got a phone call saying it was all your age group there! I said, you've got to deal with it, it's nothing to do with me. I don't know what they're there for but at the end of the day, you know they had men against boys but they still didn't perform. That's what I mean, Luton had boys out there.

I would say it's always been active, too. We had Aldershot, they came to ours – they brought a good little firm, you see them all over the place. Teams like coming to Luton 'cos they know they're gonna get a little message from our lads and they do, they go back home thinking that was exciting! It's an extension of their week really, you know. You do need this sort of level of activity out there, there's nothing for these youth to do at the moment.

PLAY-OFF V YORK

Well, that day it wasn't about promotion at all. Obviously, we come second and second is not good enough for our supporters. The pitch invasion was as you can see from the TV, it came from the other end of the ground, from the family stand. It was a disappointment to me and to a lot of our lads 'cos there's no hooligan element at all. It was a shock to the club, it was a shock to the supporters. It was like, where are all these people coming from? They were angry, they were angry 'cos we didn't get promoted. Basically, it was them lot who took over. Yeah, like I say, it was mainly people just running on the pitch, quite excited about the end-of-season shenanigans, no one there who you know. Most teams will do that, come on, wave their flags, have a bit of banter, but you know they just got carried away, the scarfers, as I call them, and they let the club down on that particular day. You would expect that from the hooligan element. Sometimes the hooligan element is very well behaved, they're not interested in mums and dads and all that. From what you hear and what you see, they go for like-minded people so that particular day, you didn't have no one whatsoever who was a thug or who represented Luton on that pitch. It did take the club and the authorities by surprise 'cos there was a lot of unknown people there you could not recognise as our hooligan element. There wasn't no firm involved, sometimes you look at the footage and they'll edit it and show it as an organised thing. I've watched it several times and half of the people I didn't even know. I was like, I mean we've got a hardcore of 7,000 fans here, most of 'em know me from over the years. As I said, I've been watching them since I was twelve years of age, but that particular day, it took me by surprise and it took our lads by surprise 'cos it was just normal people who were just angry! That's what football does to ya, if you don't win, it's what happens.

There was huge publicity after the pitch invasion of our scarfers saying football hooliganism was back, and in my opinion, it's never gone away. I've been there up and down, I had a little break for a couple of years when the kids were small, bringing them up but they've all done well, all three of my kids – one's a teacher, ones a psychologist, they've all gone to university. Like I said, we're all well-to-do people in Luton, this is like an extension of our freedom. You like having it at a party, at clubs, going out being with one another, it's just something that boys do. I walk through the town centre, it's more than that. I've been brought up as a good Christian person, I used to run youth groups, I used to go into prisons, talk to the prisoners about this and that. You know, they all know that so it's not always bad people. Hopefully, this will help the youth when they see someone like me. You know, you can run a little gang, you don't need to go round with guns and knives, and you do need to look nice and smart because girls like nice and smart lads and it brings the good things out of ya. You could help a lot of the lads out – a lot of them are lost, their dads aren't there, they're probably from a single parent, you know. A lot of them do come up to me, 17-year-old, 18-year-old lads. I'm on the phone to several lads on a regular basis, you know, with problems at work with their employers, like. They do take liberties, these bosses, and these lads are like, what should we do? You've got to guide them in the right direction. If they haven't got a father figure there then some of them do come to the older ones like me and you can help 'em out, so it's good to have that and some of them, ten, fifteen years later, are coming up and they're doing well in business and they're saying it's because of you, you talked me out of doing something crazy. That's good and it's good. You know someone's now driving around in a nice car 'cos ya doing well and you've steered them through.

YORK NOMAD SOCIETY

'IT'S ABOUT STICKING TOGETHER'

MR Y, YORK CITY: The YNS? I was always told that they started off as the nutters of York and for some reason it had to change so the initials changed to York Nomads Society as they were going to open a bank account and going into the bank and saying we're the York Nutters Squad, it's not really the best of ideas! So, they wanted to keep the YNS initials so that's how the Nomads came about.

A group of people in '81 associated with York City Football Club, who prefer to travel on their own on coaches instead of travelling via the clubs' supporters' travel. A lot of beer drunk, more drinking of beer than actually being in the model of what we would see as a firm type group. That sort of evolved a bit more in the mid-1980s, when another load of lads had sort of latched onto it and became more aggressive in a certain sense, still the beer drinking but it's generally kept as a way of not looking for bother. It's a case of defending your honour and defending your own in a certain sense, really. Those from the '80s don't really travel with the younger lads these days and the younger lads have come through, have their own ideas and their own minds. There's nobody telling anybody what they're doing, they just get on with it and have a good time. Day out, that's pretty much how it started.

It's not specific to a non-league club, just generally there's never been so much oppression and laws; whatever you can think of the police have invented to oppress you in football and throughout all that there's these young lads coming through, basically going like they don't care. One way or another, whether it'll be getting their arse kicked or dishing it out, they'll have to deal with it. We're not a group of 300 who can go around taking the piss out of people, we're a band of probably 40, 100 at best on a big day and 40 if we wanna travel, young and old. It's about friends, it's about York City, some clubs won't go other places if they don't have 100-, 150-strong, we'll go everywhere with 30, 40, 50. It doesn't matter where it is, we'll go everywhere 'cos we're a good group of mates and we're proud of York and if someone wants to have a say about that, good luck to 'em!

There's a lot of teams in this league where you are getting crowds of less than 500 and you're getting teams like Luton, who are getting crowds of 7,000. It's very, very mixed between its non-league teams and league teams that have fallen on hard times and are fighting their way back up. I guess when you're playing so many crap teams week in, week out, you look towards when those fixture lists come out at the start of the season. You're looking for the big games so you know if it's gonna be Grimsby or Luton or Newport, there's a chance it'll go off and think yeah, that could be quite interesting. Forest Green away? It ain't going to happen. So, you know it's hit-and-miss, it's 50/50 at this level.

At York we have a massive police presence. I think within non-league, they have some games that are non-segregated, every single York game is segregated without fail; even when we were playing likes of Boston and not expecting any trouble, there were at least 50 police officers down there. York's only getting two and a half thousand at home at the moment. You don't need 50 officers down there to do that: they turn up on a Tuesday night, you're against Hayes and Yeading United. It's the police trying to show their muscle and say, look, we're doing something about this when nine times out of ten, there isn't anything to deal with but that's not saying there is no trouble. Part of the reason is the lads at the bigger clubs – a bad season for them might be getting relegated and then having to spend a season or two in the championship. In non-League, you're talking about League teams who've nearly gone to the wall, teams that have gone bust, just about to go bust, probably going to go bust. What happens off the pitch can be a sense of pride, that's all you've got really. Some teams don't know if they're ever going to be in the league again, some might be going bust in a couple of years, it's a real threat to them so the pride's gotta come from somewhere. It's not gonna come on the pitch for a lot of teams so you've got to make your own pride really.

I think the police, especially in and around the York area, have overdramatised for years the problems they have with us to the extent we played Exeter years ago and they sent 27 police cars to an incident where someone was waving out of a pub window, simply waving out of a pub window. Got the whole street shut down and there were 10 arrests on the street with people saying, 'Why are you arresting him?' Police responding with 'You're next, you're next,' and on and on and on. The police intelligence in York is very easy 'cos York is more like a village than any city, everybody knows everybody. We know lads that are Leeds fans, Newcastle, Man United, they're all over the place. We don't necessarily box each other's ears, but the police know who it is, and they love to find the funding for their police intelligence. They have four officers who have intelligence on everybody. We are all on a hit list and I think that whenever a name goes into the computer, a little signal comes up and from personal experience I'm proud to say that I've never had a football conviction ever in the 25 years I've been associated with the football club but there's a reason for that, the reason being they're not very intelligent!

I think they've had a changeover recently. We once had an officer who followed us for the best part of twenty years who retired and to be honest, at times he was to some of us a guardian angel. He would help us out in tight spots and basically tell us when to behave ourselves a bit more. He was a very fair-minded officer if you ever find one of them. He understood and respected the fact that you were a couple of lads going out for the day following the club and secondary, if we were going to go looking for somebody that doesn't feature a lot with us really. It's more of a case of if you mess around with a scorpion, he'll sting ya.

If there's a big media focus on a particular football incident and it's been all over the papers, this is happened, that's happened, then it all brings up the pressure to make arrests for it. They've got to be seen to be doing something about it and that's what the general public expects. They come from a similar angle to us. There's a lot less games for us to look at so naturally there's a lot less games for them to look at and they've got to make their money somehow. The guys that volunteer to be police intelligence officers, they want it as much as the rest of us. They don't want boring days wandering around town doing fuck-all, they want it to go off.

I've been told before by an officer when I was saying I've had enough of this, I'm going to pack it in, he said why? You've got one of the best firms out there why would you want to pack it in now? So there you go, that tells you everything.

I think we were all a close-knit bunch of lads who basically look after each other's backs. You can't compensate for everything that happens. Out of every group there's always a wild cannon and you've just got to let them get on with it. We'll go places you know damn well are not going to be an easy day out with fifteen to twenty and no one gives a shit 'cos when you get on the minibus in the morning, everyone is fully aware of what could happen on that day.

Incidents of Mansfield setting about two lads in the town centre and stuff where two lads will stand their ground against ten, they're not bothered, are common. So probably 'cos we've been a small unit for years and years there's probably been five hundred lads who have cycled through the system for years at least. They come and go, they have kids, get married, they do other things – some people would say they grow up! But there's still that hardcore of lads and when they do appear on match days, it's all about sticking together. That's all it is. Sticking together.

I'm not disrespecting that or belittling for one-minute clubs who have big firms of 200 or whatever they are, but the fact of the matter is naturally if things are going to occur then there's more chance of people in a 30/40 firm being called upon in that instant. You can't get 200 people fighting at once, it's just impossible.

There's been instances in the past where we've heard of the likes of Leeds United being infiltrated a lot and getting a lot of convictions based on organised violence, where as I say that's never our intention. If you organise it, you get caught; if you go out, enjoy yourself, it's no problem. The chances are if you turn up in a town at 11 o'clock in the morning on a Saturday and stick around until 6pm, there is a time frame in there when anything can happen. The police know that, and whoever you play know that, and in fact you know that something may happen, something may not. Maybe being old school, I would say I hate mobile phones, I hate people who phone other people up and say we're here, we're doing this, we're doing that because what you're doing is you're arranging it and you're asking for it. It gives a licence to any police officer to say, look, they're arranging it and that's something that I've never done and I don't encourage people to do.

It doesn't matter if it's 100/200. I've been in situation like that, I'd rather be laid out on the floor, end up in hospital than back down. It's as simple as that really. We're from York, we're York City supporters; we're proud to be from York. If anyone doesn't like that then that's up to them really, we're not going to back down from it, ever.

I think a lot of people expect us to be teaming up with Leeds just because they're a big team down the road and they've got a heavy reputation. Get that anywhere you go in the country and meet lads and just talk about football. I was up the Empire State Building three years ago and I walked in, get the photograph done there, bloke said, where you from? York. He said you must be Leeds then, are ya? Couldn't believe it. No, we're not. We're from York and we're proud of it! It is an annoying thing but the lads from York, they know who's York and who's Leeds, simple as that. They don't really bother us about it or rip us about how poor the football club's doing. You go to school and schools full of Leeds fans, you grow up drinking, the pubs are full of Leeds fans, it just makes you even more proud to be York. It's not necessarily hatred just fucking sick of hearing about Leeds!

It does hark back to the small band of us again, sticking close-knit and there's others out there that you'd class as scarfers who had have as much vitriol towards Leeds as we would. Generally, our paths don't really cross. They did in the '80s – they were like-minded as us and are a lot older now. They don't get up to it as much today – they've had long bans and are obviously under rule of thumb of wife, I think I would say.

There will be odd occasions when some people will go to Leeds and effectively request to come with us and that would be one or two at most ever. They would basically just temp for the day, there's no form for it ever ... well, one incident when Doncaster came several years ago, I think Leeds came with Doncaster, a fair few of them, and came off second best all day. Hopefully it's gone away but again we don't really care who comes into town, you can shout Leeds all you want but don't cry if you get a smack in the mouth because we wouldn't want to be doing that, going around Leeds and shouting York this and not expect a smack in the mouth.

That brings us back to the numbers issue. I was walking back into town that day and literally 150 Doncaster, Leeds came off the station. We were drinking in the pub later on and there was maybe 35 of us at the very most and we knew damn well there was 150 of them in town. Over the course of the day, York came out on top three or four times. It was a case of sticking together and whenever you came against them, just giving a good account of yourselves. So, we came out on top all day long and it was something to be proud of. They thought they could come here and take the piss out of little old York and it didn't happen.

It's one of the things that is forgotten about York. It's is a tourist town, you know, there are lads who go all over the place but the thing is we're inundated with stag do's and those here for the races. It's an affluent city but you don't have to come from a council estate from hell to actually stand your ground and say we ain't having that. There's plenty on a Friday night, Saturday night, they come here. I've had friends from Birmingham who've come up, 40 of 'em before, but they've come up with the right amount of respect around the city centre. We went out with them, the doormen tried to shut the town down – they wouldn't let us in anywhere but that soon changed after a quick chat. We just said we could do this all night, we could cause some problems or you could just let us through and they did.

Everyone sees York as this nice tourist town and it is a nice tourist town but within that there are some lads who are really, really proud of where they're from. Shrewsbury are well known across the lower leagues, you wouldn't call Shrewsbury a tough place but you always know it if you came across Shrewsbury. I think on this level as well the non-league clubs maybe do team up with other clubs and it's like a secondary firm, you know what I mean. You go to Mansfield or wherever and it's a lot of Forest lads going with 'em. It's not like that in York, I'm proud to say that York is York, through and through it's just York lads.

I'd much rather we went everywhere with 30 or 40 and got smashed the fuck out of every week then went somewhere and got a result with another club. What's the point? We're from York, we'll support York City Football Club. We be what you if you need something else to be it. That's basically what it boils down to.

The most notable that we've had that you could say of a club coming to York was probably Oxford. Oxford brought the best firm I've seen into York in years. I think that was the first season they were down, and we went down there.

We got a lot of respect. There's an estate in Oxford called the Blackburn Leys estate. Apparently, a lot of firms won't go down there, it's a tough place to go. We found ourselves there and what happened, happened. At the end of the day I don't think anyone gives a fuck about reputations, they're just people like you really: if they're ready to stab you then we'll just see what happens really.

LUTON AWAY

We had a play-off game, we'd not played them for a lot of years to my knowledge. I don't know about the other lads, but I'd not been there with anything more than a handful of mates: it's a play-off game, it's a sell-out game, you think you're going to have a pretty tough day out. There was about forty of us in the town centre and we all thought at any point now it's going to start getting interesting really, they've got a bit of a reputation so every now and then there'd be lads walking past the pubs, spotters I'd guess keeping an eye on us getting on the phones waiting for the inevitable really and it never came. We got bored of being in the same pub all day so we walked into town. We had a light police escort with us, we came to a town and it was full of Luton fans. We tried to get in the pub, but they wouldn't let us in the pub, some York fans got a bit carried away and were head-butting the windows, I got arrested and banned for head-butting the window. No Luton came out. There were 30 or 40 of us and none of them came out and the pub was absolutely rammed full, three or four coppers at the most with us, they didn't want to know.

Later on, towards the start of the game, a few York got something to eat. They were called out on their own by about 15 Luton in full view of about 50 people stood outside the pub. These three gave a good account of themselves against 15 Luton! The rest of us joined in as our friends were in trouble and that was that. And then what went off in the ground was well documented. Don't really need to say an awful lot about that other than it's a fact that a lot of those lads who went on the pitch throwing coins and Mars Bars were the same lads who were in the pub earlier in the day and they wouldn't come out and play but they were on the pitch behind a big line of stewards, bouncing around, throwing stuff. Anyone can do that behind a line of coppers and call it on and chuck stuff but when it comes to the crunch and they got fronted, they didn't want to know.

There was only about twenty of us inside the ground. They were throwing stuff at families, anyone really. Obviously, there was 1,400 York fans there, they're not all going to be young lads who can fight back. They didn't discriminate about who they were throwing stuff at and at the end of the day. I think there are certain rules of the game and from what I saw, they'd sort of broken all those rules. For me it was the sheer factor that these lads, like I said they were throwing stuff against anyone. Families, kids, old people, women, whatever you want to call them, they were throwing stuff at them and when you see people that can actually have it earlier on in the day, they didn't want to fucking know but they are happy to bounce around on the pitch, acting the big man but they weren't the big man two hours previously, that's what sticks in the throat a little bit. That's what's quite hard. I think quite a lot of York fans made a bit of money that day! I couldn't believe how wasteful people were with money and chocolate. We're from Yorkshire, we're quite tight with our money, we're quite happy to keep hold of what we've got and they were just throwing chocolate and money everywhere. It was a bit of a disgrace really.

For me it drew attention to Luton as some kind of super mob who were up for anything but a few hours , they were up for nothing. There were 1,400 away fans in there and at some point, the police had realised they were struggling. There were a few times they could have got in, but they did the usual holding back approach but if they had got through, there was at most twenty of us to do something about it. My main concern was that there was going to be some sort of crush when people headed for the exits – that's what made me angry. Like I said earlier, they had an opportunity to confront individuals who could have a say back. They chose not to 'cos later on in the day they chose to do what they did. It just didn't sit well at all.

BURY HOME

York had a game in the play-offs in which there was an incident outside their pub, The Pack Horse, where a York fan had a leg broken. It was a her, and I think Bury are rather upset but the fact is that it happened 'cos every time we've met them since they always want to refer to it as we always do.

A year after the original event, York fans went to a charity shop and dressed up as women! Went into their local pub, which was full of Bury chanting, 'You only beat up women!' At that point, the place erupted. To be fair, Bury did come out but they didn't last too long. I think the air bomb scared 'em and the roman candles. So, if anybody is ever looking for something and you see the York Bury fixture, you'll see plenty of police and plenty of people on the street. And it just sparked incident after incident since then, there's been several ambushes up the street to the station.

Another very nasty incident, one of the guys nearly lost a finger with a bottle. That was after they'd put the windows in on a local pub, hitting another woman on the head with a cue ball so again another attack on a woman. They did want to try to brave it out and actually came into the pub and put the windows in then were rushed off. It was like the O.K. Corral. The police looked as though they were struggling to control it because there were so many people fighting.

Police in York have laid most of the blame for the violence on a section of home supporters. Only a week earlier, they made 13 arrests before our home game against Hartlepool.

Chief Superintendent John Lacy said: 'If anybody thought that football hooliganism was declining, they need only look at York City in the last couple of matches, including against Bury, where 20 arrests have been made in streets outside the ground.'

The main thing they can't contend with is at the end of the day when we play Bury every York lad turns into five lads, stuff goes out the window, no one gives a shit – it's the sort of fixture you look for every single year. You just see red when you get it. It used to be Scarborough 'cos it was an easy day, there'd be up to a hundred sometimes but yeah, that's the game.

We used to have fun in Rochdale on the bowling green but it's just again we're not bullies, we're not big enough to be bullies and even when you come across clubs like Rochdale you can bully 'em but we don't and we think Bury do and that's why we don't like 'em pretty much!

What do you say about the youth?! They're fucking frightening! That's all you can say about them. You're talking about 14- or 15-year-old kids that don't care. They don't care, they're not frightened of anything, they're taking it to a whole new thing.

They won't even answer back to their parents but when it comes to football I don't know, they're not even much to look at, they speak politely, they're nice lads. If you were a lass, you'd take 'em home to your mum, that kind, but get them together, they're fucking terrifying. I'd rather come up against some six-foot, twenty-stone lads than some little five-foot-two 14-year-old, they don't give a shit, they're like feral animals. There's always been youths, we were youths at some point but this lot! There's never been so many banning orders, pick your number there's a section for it! About why you have to go home, why you can't drink beer, why you can't do this and yet there's still these kids saying shove it up your arse, it doesn't matter how many things you bring out.

I'm not a fan of it but I think it's books, videos, films, definitely when you see some of the stuff they're wearing. We older lads try to give them an education and say it's not about that, you may have to go to hospital, you may get arrested and if you're going to carry on like that you will go to hospital and you will get arrested.

There's always been like, especially with the bigger teams, there's always been the mob and the youth we've always been from necessity more than anything else because we're just not big enough but now we're still as one but it all comes down to where you come from. The older lads be in black, dark clothing, the younger lads will be in green, red Fila tops, Sergio Tachini tops any fucking colour you can think of, there's a definite distinction between the two.

I've never seen so many young lads steam into a pub in a certain place, absolutely tear it up when there was a load of lads in there, whilst the older lads are stood there looking at each other, thinking what's going on? They were wearing the brightest colours ever so anybody with CCTV could just go him, him, him, him.

At a FA Cup match in Rotherham and I don't mind talking about this, a simple situation being played out millions of times across the country, tram station banter going back and forth between both sets of fans. Tram pulls in full of the wrong fans, giving it York, you're all fucking wankers and all that, our lot straight across the tram tracks, there were loads of police there. Twenty, thirty police all around, these young lads straight over, straight into them, knocking seven shades of shit out of you, in front of everyone, they just don't give a fuck. Once the police had tried to cordon us back in all the older lads are like, I've had enough for today we'll leave it, the younger lads are there going fuck it, and they're there fighting the police, there's police sprawled out on the tram lines, you're thinking what's going on? These are 14-year-old lads brawling out supposed riot police on a fucking tram line. They don't give a shit!

It's the next generation of nomads, innit? They're coming through. We've been on a couple of trips this season and they've took a bus load of youth and we've thought, you know, what's going to happen here, they're only young lads and that? But fuck me, they've really proved themselves. They've come through. It's nice the fact that they are the new generation of nomads but without meaning to sound melodramatic, I think they are just the new generation of young lads really. I don't want to see streets full of, no one wants to see the idiots who'll go around glassing each other, glassing indiscriminately, fighting indiscriminately, causing problems indiscriminately. Now what's worse, that or just like-minded people who'll have a tear-up amongst their own? Who's the biggest problem really? Our lot have always been like that, really. They're not going to Leeds, they're not going anywhere else, they're staying at York.

BLUE ORDER

'THEY CAN'T ONCE SAY THAT WE NEVER TURN UP'

IAN BAILEY, HARTLEPOOL: Hartlepool going back in time was also known as 'Chicago' because it was that rough, there weren't many jobs there, people were tough and crime was basically a way of life.

It's only a little town and basically on a Saturday night you can guarantee there was more that goes on there than ever what goes on over football. As people have witnessed, the women are just as bad as the men in Hartlepool, it's the sort of place that if you come for trouble you get trouble, you know if you come for a pint you get a pint, if you go to football you go to football but if you come for trouble, you certainly get trouble. It's such a close-knit town that people will come out of pubs, people will stick together.

We look after our town and we don't let people come here and take liberties. As I said before, it's a tough little town. We've got the big clubs behind us, you know Sunderland, Newcastle and Middlesbrough, and we've got a lot of local people who support them clubs as well, who probably thought they are bigger and better than what they are. The thing is we will not let them clubs come with us, Hartlepool is Hartlepool and we are what we are and that's the way it stays. Anyone who thinks they can come with us will get sent on their way as we have proved before. They have tried that and as big as they are, we have given them more than what they bargained for.

It's a ship-building town, a fishing town, and we've got loads of villages around us that are pit villages, people are miners and stuff like that where there is very little employment and like I said, basically crime is a way of life.

We are very tough people with a tough legacy, it's a tough town and you have got to be tough to survive, that's why a lot of people from Hartlepool can look after themselves. It doesn't have to be football people, it's a tough town where a lot of people can handle themselves – you've got to or you will just get taken out.

Blue Order is Blue Order, we don't join forces with anybody, obviously. We won't allow it and why should we? Why do we need anyone else to fight our battles? If we can't do someone, we get done simple as that and we have been done. I'm not saying we're the best firm in the world 'cos we're not, we are what we are and we have been done in the past and I believe in my opinion there is no firm in this country who hasn't been done.

You find that there's not a lot of firms who will admit that and I don't believe that for one minute and I'm not ashamed to say we've been done because we have been done and I will admit that.

We are our own town and we stick together and we will let no outsiders take any liberties, we let no other outsiders come in. We've got Darlington down the road and they will team up with 'Boro. That's why there is a bit of rivalry between us and 'Boro, we don't want that and if you can't fight a battle on yer own then why bother? What's the point in having them sticking up for our own? We get it all the time, we take massive squads everywhere, at one point the smallest bus we'd have would be a 50-seater and we started turning over firms or doing them. They started saying, oh yeah, they must be with Sunderland, Newcastle or 'Boro and we have never been part of any other firm whatsoever, Hartlepool is Hartlepool. People can start making excuses but you can ask anybody from Sunderland, 'Boro or Newcastle whatever. We have never ever gone with anyone and never will. Go down the road and there's a place called Blackwell and Easington where everybody walks about with a Sunderland shirt or a Newcastle shirt on. I've always supported Hartlepool and it's always been part of me.

BLUE ORDER

We started in the mid-1990s because before then we used to have a nasty firm called the Moose Men. They were good at what they did but we hadn't had a firm for years and years because of the rave scene; it took them to one side and eventually phased them out.

How we started was we used to get on the terraces, then go home and away, a group of us, about fifteen of us we hire a minibus and went to Torquay away. There was no firm, no name as such. Then just before kick-off, we were only young lads and we got into a pub and the next thing you know, the door bursts open, twenty-five to thirty Torquay fans bursts in there. Next thing you know, they were the usual bollocks, C'mon, then, do you want it?' and we weren't interested in all that, we weren't even a firm, just a group of lads, some who could handle themselves and some who could seriously handle themselves so we thought, right, this is what you want, let's have it, and we took it outside and smashed them to pieces and chased them all down the street. I was running and capturing them with people coming behind me. It was kicking off in a doorway, one of my friends puts one of them through a newsagent's window, there was some serious disorder going on.

It was actually from then, we thought, hang on, we are quite good together, we can handle ourselves. Basically from then was when Blue Order started. None of us went to football to start a firm, it just sorted of happened from that bus, a group of lads who can handle themselves. From then, it just got bigger and bigger. So, we needed a name, we were gonna take over the Moose Men, keep the Moose Men name going, but as a new firm, new songs. We came up with the idea of Blue Moose 'cos the team play in blue.

Blue Army was another, then someone suggested Blue Order because there was a band called New Order, that's how we finally got our name.

Blue Order is anything between 50 lads and 150–200 lads, we took 250 to Hull – police weren't expecting it. We took two 50-seaters, four minibuses and cars. There was that many for the police to maintain that we shocked everybody even Hull themselves that they locked us in the car park, during the game, and after the game. We didn't even get into that game they put us in the car park and sealed it off and we sat there for about an hour and a half. They didn't dare let us off that bus, because there would have been like a scene out of the '80s, a large-scale disorder, especially with Hull having the reputation they have got and they were calling it on and we went. We weren't afraid to turn up. We caught a lot of teams by surprise, because we were such a small town, a pinprick on the map. Not a lot of people were expecting the firm we had, we impressed everybody. We went from no firm at all to a massive firm; we had a lot of people didn't even know where Hartlepool even was, fuckin' Hartlepool ... where the fuck is Hartlepool? That's why we have put Hartlepool on the map because the first thing they say is Blue Order ... These massive firms or clubs, to get recognised like that from nothing at all to a massive squad is unbelievable.

Blue Orders heyday, I would say, was in the late '90s. It's still there but not in the way it was before a lot of key members have got away from what has gone on before, got wiser, but if you come to Hartlepool you are going to come up against something definitely and that has been proven. Leeds were shocked at what we've got and what we were capable of – you know, we don't have to win the battle but we are there to turn up and we won't lie down for anybody.

I would say Darlington is definitely our main rivalry. We've got quite a few rivals, Carlisle and we did have York at one point obviously. Darlington is definitely the cream and the one we want – if we get drawn against them, that's it, there be parties. Hartlepool and Darlington has been going on for years and it ain't never going away. Obviously, they're not in the same league now so we don't play them any more but we still look forward to them, we still didn't want them to go out the League when they went bankrupt or anything like that, much as we hate them but it is certainly very eventful with them, the police have certainly got their work cut out.

I remember one time Hartlepool v Darlington we had a bigger police presence for that game than the next day when Middlesbrough were playing Man United. Because we became such a massive squad and we were voted very highly in the football violence league in the *Sun* and all the main papers, probably got this information off the police, we got the most banning orders in the League and the most arrests and it's because of that every game became classed as Category C – you know, the highest amount of officers to police a game, and every match we played was like that.

It was published a couple of times, say 2002, and we

were just an up-and-coming firm and everybody ain't heard of us then because we were just coming through the ranks. And I think we were about mid-table then – about 2005, I think – the *Sun* actually done an article about the worst yobs in the table and we become forth in that table. That is massive, you know, from a firm that didn't exist to that in the space of a couple of years.

We got massive attention off the police, who used to do a lot of Section 60s on a Saturday afternoon, where they can arrest you four hours before and four hours after the game. We have had many of them, letters off the police, lads been advised not to attend – if there is disorder they are going to be arrested and things like that.

When Blue Order started, we started with all the hi-technology, CCTV, mobile phones. The police didn't have all the powers back then and we're still doing it week in, week out. We were still there every day ... With the powers the police now had it got harder and harder. We still thought, fuck the powers, we're Hartlepool and it doesn't matter what the police said, we're going to stand up for our town. We would still be there, it's our town. <any years ago they didn't have the technology. We got away with murder really because obviously then they didn't have CCTV, the technology ... when a lot of things would happen because of the cause ... Now because of that CCTV, you don't need to be doing anything because all they have to do is catch you on that CCTV, go to the game with that person or group and that's it, they nail you. The intelligence officer does a booklet on yer, reports what game you've been to and it's

supported by the CCTV and that's it, you get a three-year banning order for doing nothing at all.

It was wiping out our firm massively, banning orders, restrictions and all the powers the police had was reducing it. It wasn't curing it but it was reducing it and eventually the police did have the upper hand but I think it's back on the rise but it's not publicised. You don't see it in the papers no more and I think why they're not publicising it no more is fear another rival firm will think they did that, we will want to do that and we want to do that better than them.

The Blue Order now I wouldn't say it's non-existent but a lot of them are still banned. We had one of the highest banning orders – we got 35–40 banning orders at one point.

First of all, when Blue Order started everybody wanted to be a member when they heard all about it, word was spreading and every hoolie wanted to be a part of it and that's how we became the numbers we did. After so long we started to be a menace to our town – people didn't like us because of what we were doing, they didn't approve of what we were doing, they didn't understand why we were doing it and they didn't like it. Local folk in our close-knit community thought we were scum, the scum of the earth or violent thugs. We're just hooligans but we didn't do it for that, we done it for the buzz and they couldn't understand it. Not only that, we were stopping people coming into town and smashing it up, because it has been smashed up a few times. We stopped that and put our own seal on it. Still, some people say we are violent scum and they don't like us. There been quite a few violent altercations with local lads against the Blue Order. I think they are a bit jealous because of what we have done, because some of ours couldn't fight but they still part of the firm and obviously they got a bit jealous of that because they have known a certain person for years. You know what's he doing with that firm, he ain't hard, I'm harder than him, and it's caused a bit of local rivalry. But you don't have to be particularly hard to be in a firm. Yes, you've got yer respected lads who can seriously handle themselves and everything but a lot of lads in our firm come from good jobs, respected jobs, and even have a fight on the terraces on a Saturday. You don't have to be scum or a thug, some of these people just want a quiet life but they were there, getting involved in it and they had very well-respected jobs.

We are an up-and-coming firm and when we got promoted,we thought, right, we'll be coming up against some of the big boys and we'll be fucked, that's the end of us, we're gonna be smashed to pieces each week but that didn't happen. We got bigger, better, stronger because everybody was looking forward to going to some of these clubs … Nottingham Forest, Leeds United, Sheffield Wednesday, Bristol City, you know Hull, stuff like that. These are big high-profile clubs to us, especially clubs like that … We're a small town, more or less a back street club, we're a pin-prick on the map and I think everyone got a buzz out of going to these teams. We actually doubled our numbers, I would say, and we also impressed them.

They thought they were going to come to Hartlepool. Some of them may have heard of the reputation we had and thought, we'll smash 'em to pieces. They certainly didn't do that and I'm not saying we have done every team we had but we have certainly impressed them and they have walked away shocked and surprised, definitely.

I've got to say Darlington is our main rival, Carlisle and Leeds United as well. They were massive when they came down, probably crème de la crème. They were what we wanted and we didn't hold no prisoners.

LEEDS

We've had a number of altercations with Leeds United. Obviously, the police prevent a lot of it but they've been fierce encounters. Some twelve to thirteen years ago, Leeds thought, we're Leeds United, we do what we like, we do what we want, but you don't come Hartlepool and do that. Obviously, we have only a small following and they are massive so what they thought they would do is buy tickets for our end, but you don't do that if you come to Hartlepool, it's bad enough but to go to Hartlepool into our end is just asking for trouble. So, they started singing Leeds, then that was it, it just kicked off. They got scattered in our end and some of them didn't make it out of our end, most of them running back into the Leeds United end obviously to get all their friends or to get out of there.

Hartlepool Blue Order chased them across that pitch, the police came on and there was massive disorder in the ground. The game was abandoned for fifteen minutes while they tried to sort this out, police dogs were drafted in, police horses and all that. The Leeds, they did not make it out of the stadium, they were in a right mess. It was a very eventful day.

DARLINGTON

The Darlington game, everybody heads to Church Street because there is only one route from the station and into the train ground, one way in one way out, so they've got to come in one way and come out that way. So, what we did is we sit there and waited just across the road from the train station, there be quite a lot of local pubs and we sit in these pubs. The pubs are always packed in Hartlepool ... Biggest game of the season, there's hundreds and hundreds of people. Not just Blue Order but locals who come out for this game as well, everybody comes out for this game, you don't have to be a hooligan. And we'd wait for them coming off the train and there are that much police, and helicopters going around. The police horses, people being rushed in side streets, there's police batons being drawn ... trying to push us back. There's police dogs attacking us, they're doing everything in their power, trying to push us back. They've got lads drafted in from other counties to deal with it and the same thing you got after the game. During the game you used to get your skirmishes and things like that. After the game the police would keep them in for 20 minutes, which was a mistake because that would give us time to regroup again. Get people on the phones, get them down there, get them in the side streets ready for them coming past. Half the time the police want it to happen to justify the arrests, they do it all the time to justify how the money was spent, 'cos they spend a lot of money on helicopters and things to police a low-level league football match.

And we'd wait for them coming back down the train station, there be thousands of them with the police beside them and hundreds of Hartlepool fans trying to get at them. Their only hope is if the police look after them. They never once tried to break that police cauldron because if they did, there probably would have been someone murdered. The police wouldn't be able to handle it for the amount of squad we had out for them ... they get escorted to the train station. Obviously we mill around ... in and around the stations ... there's people running in and out the streets, there's bottles being thrown ... large-scale disorder ... police couldn't handle it ... couldn't cope with it. There's helicopters above, trying to keep some sort of control. Sometimes the police did do a good job doing that ... the atmosphere down at Church Street was phenomenal. At the game is unbelievable, you couldn't buy it. When you're looking at it, I'm not going to sit here and slack them off them 'cos they're a good firm even though thay don't give us the same respect we give them.

We've had quite a few altercations with Darlington ... I remember one time we attacked their main pub, there was 60–70 of us mob-handed, we got through the police cauldron. They didn't detect us through the side streets, we were at the pub and they didn't expect it. Luckily for them, the police were outside it, there was probably more of them than what were inside the pub; they prevented us from going at them. There was a larger group of them down the road and we got there before they came up. We ran up there trying to get at them, the police charged us, batons drawn and pushed us away and off we went. At least we tried. They have never ever done that, never once, they always come in by escort. Many a time they said they are coming in and they never have and they have disappointed many times. At least we have travelled to them and they know that ... they can't once say that we never turn up because we are always there.

CARLISLE

We went to Carlisle, got the train. When we got there, it was straight to their main boozer, where they said they would be. I don't think they were ready for what we had for them, everybody was shocked at the size of the squad we had out for that day, 120 Blue Order. We hit them early and they weren't prepared for it ... arrived at that pub and the only thing they could do to fend us off was beer glasses, bottles and a massive plant pot which went straight through a car windscreen and as the bottles were being thrown, they were bouncing off the lampposts ... and the police also weren't ready for it, we totally took Carlisle by surprise.

This just shows them what we are capable of and this went all the way to the game and after the game. Give Carlisle their due respect, the game, obviously the phone calls. Look at the size of the firm they've brought, where do we go from here, what we got to do to sort this ut? They've got on the phones to all the local pubs and bars open at that time to make their way to the ground. There were metal gates or fencing parting between us and a steward during the game left the gate and left it unlocked. That was a big mistake and one of our lads run over and opened that gate and that was it. We clashed in the ground then the police came over but there was more disorder. Again, it gives them time to reform and I give Carlisle their due: they pressed us that day and showed us what they are capable of.

I don't think it was just their firm, I think everyone in that ground just backed them up that day because they had to. It was scary, quite scary, and they couldn't control it. We had that massive squad and we did that pub before the game. After it was a different kettle of fish – they had twice the numbers more than we had. There was a police presence, both at the front and at the back; also police vans at the front.

Now under heavy escort, we are walking up the road and we were like in a bubble with the police, either way we were stuck in that cauldron. We couldn't go anywhere – had to stand and fight, there was nowhere for you to go. You've got Carlisle attacking you from the side streets, bottles coming up. They were very impressive that day after the game because they come from side streets attacking the police cauldron ... police were attacked and they were trying to attack that escort all the way to the station. People were getting hit with batons, you had nowhere to go, and they had to stand and try and stick together. I would say for a 300–400 walk, it took about an hour to get there. There was dozens of police but they couldn't control it, there was that much going on. There was stuff going on behind them, stuff going on in front of them; they continued to come from various side streets.

As we got to the station, the pubs started coming at us. The police didn't seem to know what to do. I think the police were really caught off guard that day. There was now disorder in the train station and most of all, I don't know what happened but the train was cancelled ... the police, fuck what do we do now? If you see the look on the police faces when they see that train was cancelled and they got about 150 plus the supporters and Hartlepool's Blue Order on that train station surrounded by what was going on behind them ... Finally, they got a call from the train station, pushed everyone back ... then some two hours later, they had to put some coaches on to get us away from there.

I got away from that sort of thing. I don't really go to the games any more and not only that, you have got to come to a stop. You get older and wiser, you've got to come to a stop – comes with age.

WEDNESDAY

Sheffield Wednesday certainly got more than they bargained for. These are massive games for clubs like us who like a pinprick on the map. We're a low-division team, and what happened was there was no trouble before the game but after the game, because of the result, everyone was deeply upset because of it: 5–0. Wednesday, they're singing and chanting and they ribbing us because of the result and what happened was as they trooped off to the train stations, they saw the local pubs and people gathered in there ... They were escorted to the ground and some stragglers broke the police cauldron. Lads tried the local pubs to the train station, also the train was delayed, but the police went and left them in the train station. I can't understand it. Like I say, sometimes the police let these things happen and yer know ... and some of the away fans in the pub got rowdier with bit more drink in them and I think it upset some of the people in there. As they got to the train station they started to give it the big 'un c'mon, then, as they do, as they're walking away. Wasn't many of our lads in that pub at the time and there wasn't many of them either to be fair as most of them were in the train station.

What happened was they've run over one guy, who was seriously injured. He was just an ordinary fan, well known, well liked ... it was the people he was with. He didn't do anything, obviously he was caught in that crowd ... people don't know him and obviously they're going to think he was part of that crowd that was there. They've got into the train station. Obviously, some of the Hartlepool lads have chased after them. Two guys got caught up in it and were seriously hurt, had to be airlifted to hospital. One of them was in a coma and they didn't think he was going to make it through the night. His family was called in Sheffield on that night because they didn't think he was going to make it through and some four weeks later he has come out of a coma.

It's still there but it's not publicised – you don't see it in the papers – and it's little teams like ours is where all the action is, where it's happening week in week out, but you don't hear about it. It's like one of our players comes out of a pub drunk or drink driving or whatever it is just drink driving, but if you've got a Premiership player like Wayne Rooney, it's massive headlines. It's the same as the violence, you don't hear about most of it. I don't know why it's not publicised. If we were a Premiership team or a massive club, it would be making the news ... it's always going to be there.

BANNING ORDERS

It's different how it was all them years ago. I mean, it's changing the play, the police and judges think they've got it all sown up with their new powers and bans. You know, I would say to all them young kids coming up, don't do it. I would certainly say to my kids, don't do it, for you don't realise the dangers. When you go to the football and you're doing the things you do, you don't give a fuck, it's only later in life it sorts of hits you as you realise you can get hurt and hurt people's families too. You know people might not be coming home from football. You don't think about it back then.

Those banning orders certainly changed the game but football' is an addiction and they'll never kill it, and as much as they try to prevent it with all these powers, it's still there. They will just take it further afield and not only that, they are infringing your civil liberties, yer human rights – you know, giving you a map where you can or can't go. Back in the '80s, you got away with murder. You know, a massive kick-off and you'd be getting a fine, but now people will be putting you away. Basically, people are getting a three-year ban just through association, a massive fine and everything, like getting banned with an exclusion zone from their own town centre and I think that's a breach of their human rights, but the police seem to be getting away with it. Some of my friends who've been drinking with just on a Saturday have never been into football violence, not even interested in it whatsoever, but because they have been seen with a certain group of people they have been slapped with a three-year banning order. That's the way it is now, that's the way the police think they can handle it, but all it's doing is taking it further afield and taking it away from the town.

The police get away with it, you are never going to beat them. They've got the biggest firm, a well-funded firm, and whatever money you've got, you are never going to beat them. We have even tried to beat them in court ... you are never ever going to win against the police, no matter who you are or what you are, you are never ever going to beat them. It's all about the buzz really for us. I urge all these youngsters not to get involved really because they make yer life hell. Once they get their teeth into you and you are on their radar, that's it, you are not getting away from them. They will do everything in their power to make your life a misery.

The addiction is you know that you are never ever going to get a buzz like it and to walk away from that is hard. I know they're yer mates from the club, but you are more or less like a family, you know. You drink together, you do everything together, you look after each other, you are not just leaving the football you are leaving your friends behind as well and that's the most important thing, you know.

And if you don't leave your friends and get away from that element whatever you are getting slapped with another banning order through association. You don't have to be involved in the game or doing anything, just be in that pub on that Saturday afternoon with a group of friends or certain people then bang, they slap you with another banning order for nothing when years ago, you had to do something silly.

I made the choice to walk away from it – it was either walk away or get taken away, simple as that. Because of me past, I've had like three banning orders. I have actually served seven and half years out of nine, and I got another for good behaviour overturned, but as soon as I got a banning order lifted, they would give you another one. It comes part and parcel with the job: if you're going to get involved in this sort of thing you've got to be able to take it on the chin.

CONCLUSION

In 1958, as a baby, I was fostered and placed through Barnardo's with a white family in Slade Green, which was Greater London at the time, and life outside the home was very different then. There were no anti-racism laws or culture awareness and there was a lot of bullying. I felt I had to fight my corner from a very young age out of necessity due to my surroundings and those around me and all those I encountered when I left the sanctuary of my adopted home.

It was a next-door neighbour who first took me to a live football game as he was a season ticket supporter who followed West Ham. He was not a hooligan, and I was just eight years old. My foster parents couldn't afford to take me money-wise, and I saw it as a chance of a day out in 1966 when it seemed like the whole country went football crazy because England had won the World Cup.

I remember the feeling of that period, when I was of the ages twelve to fourteen and part of a school skinhead gang that had older lads that had left school and went to work, when you would all be part of a gang in the area or town you came from and then continue it on with the football team you followed. The excitement and first feeling of just being free to do what you want and go where you want was interesting times, and they were also happening times of going to football; call it adolescence or whatever. The black-and-white Pathé footage of Man United's Red Army fans rioting really captures it as for the next few years football hooliganism spread throughout the country. It had been the emergence of a new skinhead gang culture on the streets that spread to the football.

So what are the main reasons why they participated in football violence? The love for their team, a need to display their masculinity or maybe just an escape from life's problems, or to rebel, or simply because we just hate the idea of opposing teams and their fans getting one over on us and taking liberties, but it certainly wasn't any membership card arrangement. I would say the memory we identify most for when you first start hanging out on the terraces with the lads would be what the old skin Pat tells us – he could not have put it better, no matter who you supported:

I'm standing outside the ground and about 200 or 300 Southampton fans come up. I still didn't know the score and I see this lot and think, blimey, and then they're all giving it gob, but it's still very low-key, not how you would have felt in the seventies ... frightening. Then they go in the Fratton End and within ten minutes, Pompey had them off and they were burning their scarves on the terrace, and I said, 'This is wonderful.'

I'm fifteen, I'm terrified. Don't get me wrong, I'd been the first to move. You're just little kids and you're on the periphery of it, you're not right in the centre, and then you start recognising faces.

At the time, you never talk about being a hooligan to family members and if questions got asked you would deny you were involved. It was your own world of your own choosing that you felt pointless explaining as you knew if they were not a hooligan nobody would understand anyway, so what's the point? I hurt my family every time the police called or knocked on the door at home and the guilt was heavy, for I knew this but never wanted to stop enough at the time to truly walk away from it all. I lost my first girlfriend as her family moved to get her away from me because they were hearing stories, I was now getting a reputation and once that happens, you're marked.

During the ICF show trials of 1987, I will always remember I had to ask the court's permission to allow my bail conditions to be changed to go and attend the hospital after my son was born because I was in the dock for football charges. I lost my job every time I was imprisoned for football arrests, and even lost the chance to gain a City and Guilds advanced qualification grade on my trade in painting and decorating at the time when I was attending Erith Tech College. So, yes, both work and family, it affects you, but not your friends as you never lose your friends because it's the thrill, the excitement in going to football with your mates, and that buzz on the terraces for many was second-to-none. Most lads I knew had no thoughts of seeing violence or fighting and had gone there to see the game but would accept it would be part of the purpose of going to football.

The train pulls in and everyone piles out at once, singing and chanting. Your group is first out of the train-station doors, bouncing. What police there are might as well not exist because the home supporters – your rivals – are all waiting; it's not a nice sight when you have hundreds of rival hooligans wanting to hurt you. You'll be thinking, 'Do I turn and do a runner?' or 'What's the next move?' 'Well, I'll be damned if I'm going to let my mates down!' Then you hear that roar, the mighty roar coming from within your own group that would have the hairs standing up on the back of your neck – that would be the precise moment, the buzz kicks in right there. You see them running, with arms out wide, heading towards you. The adrenaline starts pumping, your old heart is going, and everything just goes crazy, and you wouldn't believe what can happen in just a few minutes when it's all kicking off. It always ends suddenly like the referee has just blown for full-time. It really is all over and done yet you can't bring yourself down because you are still high, in fact, you're ecstatic. The atmosphere around you is just electrifying, the lads are being totally boisterous and full of themselves as each person relives the moment, for they've just done in your rival's main firm and had them on their toes. You're just thinking, 'Fucking hell!' And you would be buzzing all week, right up until you meet again for the next game. You see all the lads walking around with these great big silly grins on. You can just get carried away at football but the friendships you make I still personally value today. Friends who've through it all and are still standing together … UNITED.

Many a friend you make at football you will form life bonds

with because they know what we shared and went through for our team's name and our own fans' reputation. Today, we have got older and settled so it's our only chance to meet up just like old times. Though they do it more to socialise today and only on the odd occasions, it's to mob up to show their fiercest rivals that they are still capable of being a force – admittedly, very much watched over by the police operations. The Millwall game of 2009 was such an example. When that happens, I stay right out of the way as I've no wish to return to old ways. I've nothing to prove to anyone and today in my eyes it is pointless.

So, after a culmination of events and a past violent lifestyle as a leading member of a notorious football gang that saw me being sent to prison for the first time by the age of twenty, it was at this time that I first really began to write. 'I decided to write down my version of events, about football hooliganism with the firm and my own life and times. That said, it was still a surprise and shock when, following the cinema release of the movie *Green Street*, I had my own life made into a film. Directed by Jon S. Baird, it was simply titled *Cass* and released in 2008. I'm forever grateful to Jon and the film's producer Stefan Haller for keeping it real and believing in my story and the project, which was not to make another football movie but a biopic about a man's life where the football acted as the background to the story.

POLITICS, RACISM AND FOOTBALL

Here in England, we pride ourselves that the supporters in the main keep their politics away from the football terraces, but there was this dark, short-lived period during the back end of the 1970s, when politics were creeping into football because of the right-wing policies of the British National Party (BNP) and National Front (NF). Maybe because of the political climate of that time they felt they could target certain fans. I was an active shop steward working as a painter for Islington Council so I started to question myself when looking around at what I was seeing over at Upton Park.

Around one to two hundred skinheads *sieg-heil*-ing in front of the club directors' stand and nothing was done to challenge any of it for a couple of seasons. The police did nothing to question this – you can work out for yourselves why they would do nothing – and not just the club but some of our own fans had questions to answer, too. We didn't really have many black fans, but those we did have I would say could look after themselves physically – they were tough lads and that's a question right there itself: were we welcome or even tolerated at West Ham because we simply had a use, or did it not matter? So many questions in my head and my single lone action before kick-off of walking into the middle of the unofficial far-right section of the Westside terrace of our ground was the best way of finding out many answers. What those answers were, amid the uproar and the attentions of those around me, which included a wall of police uniforms stood at the back of me threatening to arrest me, was the sight of a small group of ICF in the adjoining South Bank stand attempting to clamber onto the pitch in order to get across to me in support, a sight I witnessed that will forever stay with me.

I remember local boy John Charles being the first black player I ever saw play for West Ham. He never got any stick from the home fans as he was out of Canning Town in the days when the players would walk home from the ground with the fans. As I've said earlier, I lived and grew up in my childhood years in Slade Green, Kent. I used to collect the football stickers and do swaps in the school playground; John Charles was always an unwanted swap as was Albert Johanneson, who was another black player who played for Leeds. Manchester United had Georgie Best. We had at West Ham a black forward called Clyde Best and he was extremely popular with the West Ham fans but I still shudder at the racial abuse he got from a small section of our own fans. He was big and powerful when on fire but when struggling could look awkward, clumsy and lumbering so not a good look, but as a black fan on the terraces I could feel his pain, yet he could not feel mine as the comments fired in with pure unanswered venom off the terraces. Back then it was rare to ever see black supporters and even rarer a black footballer in the professional game.

Britain and its youth generation in the 1970s and '80s showed a very black and white divided place, depending on where you lived, with lots of subcultural stuff in the mix. There was football hooliganism, mass unemployment, punk rock, skinheads, scooter boys, soul boys and a fair bit of open racial hatred. I say 'open' because you could read it in foot-high letters sprayed on walls and even around the football stands. So, I value the interviews in this book with those who were there, who can look back and talk now about those times and reveal to us what they encountered and how they themselves saw it.

You must understand the time period when looking back to the '60s, '70s and those early '80s. It was a Britain before multiculturalism was established. It was Great Britain rather than the UK. And a white working-class culture is what I grew up around, both on the terraces and off. So, you had to learn fast certain ways to adapt in order to survive because the country was institutionally racist from school beginnings to the workplace. This was near-impossible to change at top level without the political will to do so, but down on the streets we could change even if it was a warzone of youth subcultures. I recall the late 1970s: in one summer we had six subcultures, from punks, skinheads, Mods, new romantics, soul boys, football casuals and even the Teddy Boys were still knocking about, only the hippies as a trend were dead. Being in the wrong place and wrongly dressed was just as risky as being the wrong colour.

It was also that period of the late '70s and early '80s when the nation was divided and broken with strikes, high unemployment and race wars when something clicked on the streets to change all that. The punks teamed up with the reggae boys and paved the way for 2-Tone music to bring both black and white together, if only in the clubs and concert halls. Bands like Sham 69 and The Clash supported the Rock Against Racism movement and on the football terraces the casuals ran any right-wing skins off and went from being white-only gangs to multicultural firms, like The Gooners, Leicester Baby Squad, MiG Crew and of course the infamous Zulus. Meanwhile, the public and the UK government, led by Prime Minister Margaret, had nothing worthwhile to say about its young generation unless they were dying in the Falklands. To many, we were out there on the streets causing mayhem and so we were, but in a strange way we were also uniting the youth, through football, fashion and music.

BLACK DANNY, VILLA: In 1977, I made my first trip to Merseyside, and I went on the football special train. It pulled into Lime Street, and we were ferried by buses to Anfield, to be greeted by a mass of red and white. As we walked through the back streets, reality hit home: it was 'Welcome to Hell' for blacks. I would imagine it would be a bit like going to [some foreign clubs] these days ... I decided to go to Merseyside again that season, only this time it was Everton. At the time *Roots*, which featured a black slave called Chicken George, was a very popular TV drama. I got recognised coming out and that's when I heard, 'Here's Chicken George again.' I was a marked man, and I wasn't involved in the violence then, I was just a fan, but times were changing, and they became an enemy of mine from that day.

SCOUSE, LIVERPOOL: I didn't think we were a racist club. I will tell you this, how I got to know my friend. He was in the middle of the Kop, and he was getting stick for his race. And I just said, fucking leave him alone, leave the fucking kid alone, watch Liverpool. Next minute, every fucking week he used to stand next to me all the time.

SAMMY, TOTTENHAM: Going back to this 'we are the Yids' business', we've never had any big Jewish support in the ranks. Personally, I can only remember this girl back in the '70s. It all started off to wind us up and at the beginning we were being wound up and if rival fans know you're getting wound up, they will keep winding you up. But once you accept it and say right, I'm a Yid, so what, you're taking it back away from them. And yes, we do march down a road chanting, 'Yids, Yids,' but that's because we are Tottenham. If you've a problem with that, then what about Birmingham fans chanting 'Zulus, Zulus'? It's just a football thing.

ONE-EYED BAZ, BIRMINGHAM: We were behind the goal and some of us black lads took our shirts off. They were shouting, 'Fucking N******!' We were shouting, *'Sieg heil!'* A lot of Millwall were singing to Birmingham, 'You've got a town full of P*kis!' When Birmingham scored, we were singing, 'One-nil to Pakistan!'

There has been a huge change in the mindset of many a football supporter since then, but today players of other skin colours and/or ethnicity are still being offended

It is what it is, every case is different. It's good today that black players speak up much more as in my day they said and did fuck-all, but I do worry which way it might backfire today, for we live in a world where everybody is offended by everything, and for me politics and football can never mix, race or otherwise. Today, we are moving towards religious hatred so you can lump the two together, since it is no longer just a black and white thing. Tottenham fans have long been embroiled in the controversy over their war chant, 'Yiddoes, Yiddoes', particularly if Chelsea or West Ham are the visitors. And the Leicester lad Khan makes an important contribution here with his own experiences of being an Asian football casual, which was so unusual to learn as there were very few Asian lads going to the game during those peak hooligan years.

KHAN, LEICESTER: I got abuse from opposing fans, sneers and offensive words like 'P*ki' or 'W*g', but I was used to it at school, so I became immune to it in and around the ground. Even some Leicester fans would comment, those who were still skinheads. However, the other lads I was with did not like what they were hearing and would always say something back. I found that there was a loyalty when you attended the matches if you were one of the crew and it would go beyond the boundaries of colour.

As a black football fan who grew up going to matches in the '70s and '80s, I know more than most about the beautiful game's troubles with racism. I can still recall my own club, West Ham United, being the first English Football League side to select and play three black players, Clive Charles, Ade Coker and Clyde Best, in their starting team on Easter Saturday, 1972.

Nowadays, racism in football is less obvious but it still exists – and needs to be called out. But I'm convinced that 'taking the knee' isn't the way to do it. Why? Because the more footballers insist on bending one knee on the ground before kick-off, even if fans boo them in response, the more trouble is likely to erupt inside football stadiums as a result. This gesture also allows those within football who could be doing far more to tackle racism to hide behind its own players while changing little to deal with racism, because it's not the players who make the decisions or rules. Even those who support players taking the knee must be able to see that it may have run its course and a newer response is now required.

And the more this divisive gesture is rammed down fans'

throats, the more problems it's going to cause. Is this really the best way to demonstrate that Black Lives Matter? I'm not convinced. After a season of being banned from football stadiums due to Covid-19 restrictions, the fans are keen to get back to just the football; indeed, many fans are angry. This group of fans who do boo those players taking the knee are mostly white, middle-aged, working-class blokes. And if their only means of voicing their displeasure at what they see as an unacceptable political gesture is to boo, then some will use it. Of course, many of the younger generation of fans don't agree with this view. They are more likely to support players taking the knee.

For me, our football clubs need to find a way to ensure these different groups of fans can come together. Whether some fans like it or not, players are genuine in wanting a way to speak out against racism. But to avoid alienating fans, they should adopt a gesture that isn't linked to Black Lives Matter, which is seen by many as a political movement whose critics grow with every flaw revealed about that organisation.

I'm a supporter of anti-racism both in the game and out, but I find it interesting that the lads who shared their experiences with this issue in this book have never been approached by football's anti-racism organisations, when we all know that here are names who are influential personalities on the terraces. It's clear that taking the knee is now more of a hindrance than a show of solidarity. By adopting this gesture, players risk alienating as many people as they persuade. I simply don't see any plans of where to go with it after the initial impact it made, so what's changed?

THE FIRMS

The ICF was rolling in big numbers on their way to the away matches and Green Street was a fortress during the home matches. We played 42 games a season and were fighting in half those games. I've maybe experienced a couple of decades of mayhem as firms come and go, but certain firms were consistently at the top end of the aggro league. The ICF was certainly better organised but not in the way the press and media make out, but our rivals knew how organised we were. Millwall you will always have to rate as pure evil, Chelsea was quite organised as they were disorganised with large numbers who had the whole package, we likened them to the Man U of the south, but Man U had always been a fucking huge travelling army and whenever we played them the atmosphere in the ground was like that of a London derby.

A fan rivalry is not always on a par with any natural club rivalry, our older heads always say the fan rivalry goes back to a famous Man U victory at Upton Park when they won 6–1 and clinched the title with weeks to spare. Mickey Smith's account in the early part of the book backs up the press headlines as to when the modern-day football hooliganism phenomenon began with over 100 arrests and the same number in reported injuries when West Ham played United and the same stats repeated when Celtic played Rangers on the same weekend. It's an unrecorded social history to living times and the scene in 1967 were repeated at different levels through and on to today. I don't know what the scenes was and looked like when the sociologists bang on about the Houlihans (a rowdy Irish family living in south London in the 1900s), it was not my history or anything like the terraces I encountered.

The Scouse were up for it in a fight, both Liverpool and Everton, but we always rated Everton more. They once gave Millwall a lesson they will never forget. Midland clubs were a-plenty, we just give it to Birmingham as the Midland number one hence we took a firm and half there in the Cup in '84 when we had the pitch invasion, but firms like Stoke and Forest also had their day as a mob and so did Villa, Wolves and Leicester, even Coventry at the time. Their problem was the Midlands clubs' fans never travelled en masse to the capital. The northeast region was tough to visit, even smaller clubs like Hartlepool and Darlington. Any of those northeast clubs had real hard men but we have never seen fans with such crazy passion as fans like Newcastle's Geordies, plain daft lads. Middlesbrough were respected as game fighters, and over in Yorkshire, Leeds was massive, too, but as West Ham, we had more epic encounters with Sheffield United in truth.

In the Southeast, Portsmouth was good, but we never really played them; over in Wales, Cardiff were tasty in the '90s, too, but London is where it's at, all with firms I've already mentioned, and you will have to add both Arsenal and Tottenham over certain periods of time – they are worthy of a top firm's history. For all the respect given here, we can only talk of experiences of West Ham going to them, few even tested us at Upton Park back in the day. Every firm with any history was the same in that they had developed and formed from the skinhead era of the late sixties, coming to height during the casual era of the early eighties. We were a football firm with both a history and reputation. Personally, I would go so far as saying what kept us apart from the other rival firms was our higher-than-average criminality background. The ICF contained this fact within the ranks, our hated rivals Millwall being very similar in background and makeup too.

The most memorable battles at away games I was involved in and can recall would be Millwall, Middlesbrough, Liverpool, Sheffield United, Stoke, Birming-ham, Man U and some Arsenal games too. These battles are not just moments, they are memories of the fighting going all through the match and outside, whole game, and all day; again, this was the '70s to '80s seasons. We had created modern-day football violence and as bad as it was for what is our national game, the lads still refer to this period as the good old days. It was what it was, and you can't reinvent the wheel, for today in England it is a low-key scene now and gone underground. The law has strengthened so much – when I last appeared in court for the infamous ICF football show trials they wanted to give me 10 years in prison until the case collapsed when we successfully challenged the integrity of the police evidence. Now with CCTV, football banning orders, civil courts, etc., it's never going to go back to those dark days. Football has moved on, and so have the fans unless we draw our most hated rivals in a cup game – then you discover the football hooligan still exists. The Hartlepool lad puts his views in this book that I know are noted by many:

IAN BAILEY, HARTLEPOOL: Those banning orders certainly changed the game but football is an addiction and they'll never kill it, and as much as they try to prevent it with all these powers, it's still there. They will just take it further afield and not only that, they are infringing your civil liberties, your human rights – you know, giving you a map where you can or can't go. Back in the '80s, you got away with murder. You know, a massive kick-off and you'd be getting a fine, but now people will be putting you away. Basically, people are getting a three-year ban just through association, a massive fine and everything, like getting banned with an exclusion zone from their own town centre and I think that's a breach of their human rights, but the police seem to be getting away with it. Some of my friends who've been drinking with just on a Saturday have never been into football violence, not even interested in it whatsoever, but because they have been seen with a certain group of people they have been slapped with a three-year banning order. That's the way it is now, that's the way the police think they can handle it, but all it's doing is taking it

GOING CASUAL

My first venture into following any sort of fashion was the original '60s skinhead subculture, Trojan records, working class and proud. The clothes were cool as a kid watching the older lads look the part and get the girls and have a fight. I was always going to get into that, and that hooked me into the interest of lads' fashion. The '80s casual-fashion interest was a whole new level and had the biggest influence on my wardrobe that cannot be topped for me. Khan, who was part of Leicester's Baby Squad, summed up the 'casual' era when it had spread nationwide:

We didn't care if you were poor or rich or if you were a different colour, we didn't care. It wasn't about that, it

was about going to the football together and watching each other's backs and you standing your ground, both home and away, that was all that mattered.

Every firm was the same in principle. It was part of this casuals' subculture that had developed and formed from the skinhead era of the late '60s, coming to its height during the casual era of the early mid-eighties. We were a football firm with both a history and a reputation. Anyone who was of an age and living those times understands this.

I still today favour the brand wear of Lacoste, Henry Lloyd, Ellesse, Peaceful Hooligan and today have my own brand launched and in production called Old School Football Clothing.

As we all now know, Liverpool fans claim that they have been the first ones to bring European casual brands like Tacchini and Fila to the terraces, and the Mancs also have equally strong claims to the beginning of this move towards the boys going to football wearing designer brands and labels. And you see that the change in the way football fans dress over the seasons did leave a genuine legacy, and today brands like '80s Casual Classics serve us well, keeping the casual spirit alive by securing retro brands to be re-issued under their own label. As for the scene, today it's not the same because the thrill of the chase and the exclusivity aspect has gone forever because you can click a button and with a credit card have your item delivered next-day. On my travels to Europe, I find it interesting that nowadays British labels are very popular, brands like Fred Perry well respected by Europe's ultras and beyond.

The football casuals' attention to detail and interest in their appearance fed into a broader revival of interest in men's fashion. While casual style in no way pushed the boundaries of fashion, simply focusing on styles and labels that were already available, it did have a significant influence in altering the status of sportswear and designer clothing within society. This look and style of the football casual lives on long after the golden age of when this subculture ended. Casuals paved the way for the wider success of brands like Stone Island in the 1990s and the widespread adoption of sportswear as acceptable fashionable dress.

Personally, I always thought the young Gooners firm, the Herd, were the best-dressed back in the day, while our own Under-Fives would be on my list, and, as an overall firm, the Portsmouth 6.57 Crew stood out, and I would add Sheffield United's Blades Business Crew, Leeds' Service Crew, Leicester's Baby Squad and north of the border Aberdeen Casuals were another tidily dressed firm back then for the period 1982–85. The late-'80s/early-'90s firms like Cardiff Soul Crew and Birmingham's Zulus took it to another level. I chuckle at the outrageous but very typical statement from those down south about the big northern clubs having all the right gear but no matter what they wore, they still looked scruffy.

Really important was the big debate about where it started, and we can acknowledge the late '70s was truly dominated by Scouse and Mancs, both convincingly turning around the London claims of being the first firms to influence casual culture. It was being orchestrated and driven by the northern lads themselves, or 'boys' as they referred to themselves in those early years.

As someone who had experienced nearly every British youth subculture through the 1960s, '70s, '80s and '90s, I thought it an interesting legacy that the football casual had outlasted them all and there had been no focus on this, all the films and documentaries focusing only on the violence, and for me that was not everything about going to football. I had broken down many barriers in my interviews with rival fans, even one-time sworn enemies, so I thought once again that Leicester's Riaz Khan and the 6.57 boys would be best placed to tell the story of the casuals as an understated youth subculture.

TODAY, LOOKING BACK

Almost everything I've mentioned above has changed. Music, football, even fashion. Everything today is safe and corporate. It seems like there is no new breed or new power emerging.

I always thought that the freedom of being young and making things happen was best expressed in music, fashion and football. For the working classes, this was our chance to make it big as a player and if just a fan or supporter, this was our chance to escape mundane daily life and expectations. Corporates and their money along with the PC brigade have tried to steal or buy what it is that belongs to us fans and do away with what means so much about being a fan. I can tell you that going to football was never about just 90 minutes of a match and fashion was never about the high street telling you what to wear. As for the clothes, I love the reissues of retro wear today that are popular with casuals.

I think the football casual hooligan was something that became a way of life for many. The reason being was the authorities didn't stamp it out when they should have so for that mistake the next generation, who were just kids watching it all, knew what they were going to do when they were that bit older to take over, and so you now had a violent cycle: they would take it beyond being just lads letting off steam at football, it all got serious and quite dangerous.

Personally, I think the football violence has all but ended for the clubs' firms that had the best reputations over the years. There's still a hooligan element that has evolved today out of the lockdown period but it's very small-scale. There is not a cause or any sense of adventure belonging to a football firm today. It had to go underground because the risks if caught are severe, which means it is very secretive, with little happening, and when something does happen it is so remote from the clubs or the involvement of most of the supporters that it appears to me that today they fight as hooligans on the simple basis that they *are* hooligans. This is something we never accepted; we hated being labelled as hooligans back in the days of real stuff going on. We honestly believed our cause was for the honour of the club's reputation and not just for ourselves. Today, it is evidently back and on the increase, but they fight for themselves, pure and simple. There is less chance of innocent fans being caught up in the violence because it is arranged by mobiles, and everyone knows this, so those involved all have two phones to avoid conspiracy charges. The fights are nothing spectacular and usually end up with trashing a rival's pub and claiming it as a result. Then they spend the rest of the time baiting their opponents and rewriting the battle on social media.

I will simply say this: among the cross section of lads making their contributions to this book, some of them are leaving a message to those believing they are in on what they had. Chaps, it's the wrong time to be a naughty boy today. My message would be it's not about your past, as what you learn and experience from your past shapes you as a person. What matters most is how you come out of your past, for we all make mistakes in life and hopefully move on, so anyone who wants to be jealous or pissed off with what I have achieved for myself and family today, then they should remember what it was to have had my life: I've been shot by gangsters, stabbed by rivals and fitted up by the police. My life was not a movie but as real as the street I walked on and as real as the people I crossed, and I have a huge respect for those fans who have treated me as one of their own when I have gone to the game with them, it's a real buzz that no longer exists in the English Premier League. Looking back, if it hadn't been for football, I don't think there was anything I would rather have my life wasted on. The difference today is that I have also chosen another path, one society can better accept, for none of us was born a hooligan.